# Race, Sport and Politics

## Theory, Culture & Society

*Theory, Culture & Society* caters for the resurgence of interest in culture within contemporary social science and the humanities. Building on the heritage of classical social theory, the book series examines ways in which this tradition has been reshaped by a new generation of theorists. It also publishes theoretically informed analyses of everyday life, popular culture and new intellectual movements.

EDITOR: Mike Featherstone, *Nottingham Trent University*

SERIES EDITORIAL BOARD
Roy Boyne, *University of Durham*
Nicholas Gane, *University of York*
Scott Lash, *Goldsmiths College, University of London*
Roland Robertson, *University of Aberdeen*
Couze Venn, *Nottingham Trent University*

THE TCS CENTRE
The *Theory, Culture & Society* book series, the journals *Theory, Culture & Society* and *Body & Society*, and related conference, seminar and postgraduate programmes operate from the TCS Centre at Nottingham Trent University. For further details of the TCS Centre's activities please contact:

The TCS Centre
School of Arts and Humanities
Nottingham Trent University
Clifton Lane, Nottingham, NG11 8NS, UK
e-mail: tcs@ntu.ac.uk
web: http://sagepub.net/tcs/

*Recent volumes include:*

Changing Bodies
*Chris Shilling*

The Body & Society
*Bryan Turner*

Peer to Peer and the Music Industry
*Matthew David*

Ordinary People in the Media
*Graeme Turner*

Globalization and Football: A Critical Sociology
*Richard Giulianotti & Roland Robertson*

# Race, Sport and Politics

## The Sporting Black Diaspora

Ben Carrington

Los Angeles | London | New Delhi
Singapore | Washington DC

First published 2010
Reprinted 2011

SAGE Publications Ltd
1 Oliver's Yard
55 City Road
London EC1Y 1SP

SAGE Publications Inc.
2455 Teller Road
Thousand Oaks, California 91320

SAGE Publications India Pvt Ltd
B 1/I 1 Mohan Cooperative Industrial Area
Mathura Road, Post Bag 7
New Delhi 110 044

SAGE Publications Asia-Pacific Pte Ltd
33 Pekin Street #02–01
Far East Square
Singapore 048763

Library of Congress Control Number: 2009937644

British Library Cataloguing in Publication data

A catalogue record for this book is available from
the British Library

ISBN 978-1-4129-0102-4
ISBN 978-1-4129-0103-1 (pbk)

Typeset by C&M Digitals (P) Ltd, Chennai, India
Printed in Great Britain by the MPG Books Group
Printed on paper from sustainable resources

For my mother, who made everything possible
Clare Anne Carrington (1955–2005)

# Contents

# Acknowledgments

I would like to thank all of those who have helped me over the years in what has been a somewhat strange and improbable intellectual journey from south London to Austin, Texas via the Midlands, the North and the south coast of England. Along the way many debts have piled up that I would like to recognize, if not quite fully repay, here.

I have had the privilege and good fortune to have studied and worked at some of Britain's leading institutions for the critical study of sport and with some of the best minds at those places. It was as an undergraduate at Loughborough University in the early 1990s that I was first introduced to the field of 'sports studies' and to the 'sociology of sport' in particular. As a failed professional footballer I found the perfect substitute to continue my sporting interests, albeit with a keyboard and library card rather than a pair of Mizuno's. Mike Collins, Tess Kay and Joe Maguire in particular helped to spark and develop my interest in sport and leisure studies. I owe a special debt of gratitude to Ian Henry whose expansive intellect, generosity of spirit and deeply humane approach to both scholarship and teaching is a model I try daily to follow. Without Ian's initial guidance I would never have started on this journey, and for that I am eternally grateful.

At Leeds Metropolitan University I was fortunate enough to find a community of scholars where some of the best work on race, gender and sport has been (and continues to be) produced. In particular I would like to thank Jonathan Long, Mick Totten and Ann Flintoff for their support and encouragement over the years. Special thanks to my fellow student cohort at Leeds Met, now all accomplished academics in their own right, who have pushed me to do better work, especially Kevin Hylton, Karl Spracklen and Beccy Watson. If I owe Ian Henry a debt for helping me onto the academic path, then Sheila Scraton and Peter Bramham have to take full responsibility for keeping me on that path when I should, by all accounts, have fallen off many a time. I simply could not have had a better supervisory team for my Ph.D., so thank you both. You will hopefully see the imprint of your words of advice throughout this book.

For their friendship as well as academic support I'd like to thank my former Chelsea School colleagues at the University of Brighton, especially John Sugden, Graham McFee, Udo Merkel, Gill Lines, Belinda Wheaton, Marc Keech, as well as my good friends Nigel Jarvis and Philippa Lyon. Special thanks must go to Alan Tomlinson from whom I learnt much over the years about both the importance of close reading and the craft of scholarship. Ian McDonald was then and remains today a close friend, collaborator and comrade. My work and thinking has developed over the years through the direct and frank exchanges we have had and for that alone I am deeply grateful.

Since moving to Austin, Texas in 2004 I have been supported by a wonderfully eclectic group of brilliant scholars, activists and intellectuals. For making me feel welcome and for always being around for advice on how to 'survive' the U.S., thank you to Bob Jensen, Lisa Moore, James Wilson, Jan Todd, John Hoberman, Werner Krauss, Christine Williams, Javier Auyero, Simone Browne, Sharmila Rudrappa, Gloria González-López, João Vargas, Jemima Pierre, Michael Ray Charles, Ted Gordon, Omi Osun Olomo, Juliet Hooker, Shirley Thompson, Cherise Smith, Jennifer Wilks, Stephen Marshall, Craig Watkins and Neville Hoad.

I have also found a supportive community of sports scholars across the globe whose own work I readily steal from on a daily basis in both my teaching and writings, as they'll no doubt find in these pages. With that in mind I would like to thank Anouk Bélanger, David L. Andrews, Peter Donnelly, Rick Gruneau, Brian Wilson, Michael Messner, Doug Hartmann, C.L. Cole, Alan Bairner, Garry Whannel, Jenny Hargreaves, David Rowe, Toby Miller and Jim McKay. Thanks are also due to a number of scholars whose critical work on race has informed my own thinking over the years and who have been supportive in ways both big and small at various moments in my career. In particular I'd like to thank Les Back, Manuela Bojadžijev, Jayne Ifekwunigwe, Eduardo Bonilla-Silva, John Solomos, Barnor Hesse, Paul Gilroy, Brett St Louis and Joe Feagin.

A few people (some already mentioned) took the time to read parts of the manuscript and some were kind enough to read through the whole damn thing. Thanks to Simone Browne, Dan Burdsey, Tony Collins, Rinaldo Walcott, Neville Hoad, Juliet Hooker and Stephen Marshall. I appreciate the time you gave in providing close readings of the text that helped me avoid some of the egregious errors I would otherwise have committed to print. Thank you all.

I've also benefitted from a small group of people who have provided advice and encouragement on matters personal, sporting, political and intellectual that has gone beyond the normal niceties found within academia. You can now stop feeling guilty for asking me 'how's it going?'... at least until the next book. A personal thanks to David L. Andrews, Max Farrar, Grant Farred, Barnor Hesse and Ian McDonald.

Finally, Sage have been wonderful throughout the process. And above all, patient. Particular thanks must go to Chris Rojek for having faith in this project from the beginning to end and to the wonderful Jai Seaman for her diligent professionalism and gentle prodding.

Some sections of this book modify and extend arguments that I have made before. Parts of Chapter 1 draw on Carrington, B., Andrews, D., Jackson, S. and Mazur, Z. (2001) 'The Global Jordanscape', in D. Andrews (ed.), *Michael Jordan, Inc.: Corporate Sport, Media Culture, and Late Modern America*, State University of New York Press. Parts of Chapter 2 and 3 draw on Carrington, B. (2001/2002) 'Fear of a Black Athlete: Masculinity, Politics and the Body', in *new formations*, 45 (Winter): 91–110. Parts of Chapter 4 draw on Carrington, B. (2008) 'Where's the White in the Union Jack? Race, Identity and the Sporting Multicultural', in M. Perryman (ed.) *Imagined Nation: England after Britain*, Lawrence & Wishart. I'd like to thank State University of New York Press and Lawrence & Wishart for permission to re-work these pieces here.

# List of Figures

# Introduction: Sport, the Black Athlete and the Remaking of Race

Sport is ambiguous. On the one hand, it can have an anti-barbaric and anti-sadistic effect by means of fair play, a spirit of chivalry, and consideration for the weak. On the other hand, in many of its varieties and practices it can promote aggression, brutality, and sadism, above all on people who do not expose themselves to the exertion and discipline required by sports but instead merely watch: that is, those who regularly shout from the sidelines. Such an ambiguity should be analyzed systematically. To the extent that education can exert an influence, the results should be applied to the life of sports. (Theodor Adorno)

A professor of political science publicly bewailed that a man of my known political interests should believe that cricket had ethical and social values. I had no wish to answer. I was just sorry for the guy. (C.L.R. James)

## The Invention of the Black Athlete and the Remaking of Race

The black athlete was created on 26 December 1908 in a boxing ring in Sydney, Australia. For the following hundred or so years, this new representation would provide one of the most important discursive boundaries through which blackness itself would come to be understood. This powerful fantasmatic figure – 'the black athlete' – had been a long while in the making. It was the product and perhaps the logical end point of European colonial racism, its constitutive parts forged from a combination of preexisting, centuries-old racial folklores, religious fables and the scientific tales of nineteenth century racial science. The recently institutionalized, putatively meritocratic arena of egalitarian (male) competitive sports, the emergence of a nascent global communications network and the development of cinema as spectacle, provided the social mechanisms for its conception.

Those present at the birth of the black athlete were unlikely to have been fully cognizant of the lasting and profound effect of this momentous event. That matters racial would never be quite the same again. However, as a 30-year-old boxer from Texas stood victorious over his defeated opponent, the spirited but outclassed white Canadian Tommy Burns, even the largely all-white audience on that warm Sydney morning would likely have realized that a disturbance of sorts had occurred within the heart of the white colonial frame. Burns went down in the fourteenth round of the fight under a barrage of punches. The police intervened, ordering the cameras to stop filming, and the bout was brought to a close. The big negro from Galveston, as the *New York Times* would describe him, was declared the winner. Jack Johnson, the son of slave-born parents, was the new heavyweight champion of the world.

While the very final moments of this revolutionary sporting moment would not be televised, the wider truth could not be contained nor denied by the averting white technological gaze. A black man held the title that only the bravest and strongest could lay claim to, the supposed pinnacle of heterosexual manhood, the very definition of patriarchal identity based upon violence, domination, courage and mastery: *heavyweight champion of the world*. Race as a productive category capable of explaining social relations and hierarchies, the limits and contours of whiteness, and even the nature of politics and subaltern freedom in the west, would all have to be rethought in the coming years and decades after this fight.

*Race, Sport and Politics* is an account of the political meanings and global impact of 'the black athlete' over the past century, the role of sport in the making and remaking of western ideas about racial difference, and the position of sport in the forging of gendered, national and racial identities within the broader African diaspora. I suggest that throughout the twentieth century and into the present there has been a continuous struggle over the meaning of 'the black athlete'. It has been contested from within and without. What the black athlete signifies has shifted and oscillated over the years: submissive and threatening, often obedient, occasionally rebellious, revolting and in revolt, political and compromised, a commodity and commodified. At various points in political struggles and during certain historical periods the black athlete has been despised and lionized, blamed for the woes of the black community and held up as its savior, seen as signaling a post-racial future and confirming the indisputable facts of racial alterity in the present.

What is most remarkable about 'the black athlete' is that it has been given many of these contradictory meanings *in the same moment*. Only rarely has the black athlete spoken, or been allowed to speak. It is normally spoken for. It is knowable in advance (before it speaks) and from without (by various others). It is defined by common folklore, sports discourse – most powerfully within the sports media – and by the advertising industries, by pseudo-scientific inquiries and the educational system, and by athletes themselves, fans, sports administrators and officials.

The black athlete is thus a political entity and a *global sporting racial project*. The invention of the black athlete was (and remains) an attempt to reduce blackness itself and black people in general into a semi-humanized category of radical otherness. The exceptionality of black athleticism thus moves through a double bind. It is on the one hand and at once *typical*; an *ideal type* that attempts to define the boundaries of blackness itself and therefore, by extension, the identities of all black people or rather, to be very specific, those racialized *into* the category of blackness. And yet this very *typicality* serves to render black people, as bodies, outside the category of the truly human as *exceptional*. *Typically exceptional* we might say. Black athletes – and therefore black people in general as the particular comes to *stand in for* the whole – become nearly human, almost human, and sometimes even super-human. Human-lite or human-plus. But very rarely, simply, *ordinarily* human. Thus the very boundaries and meanings that mark and therefore define 'the black athlete' come to be fought over and can be seen, I want to suggest, as a site of political struggle.

Finally, 'the black athlete' turns out not to be about blackness at all – although it has come to be seen that way. Historically, the black athlete developed out of and from a white masculinist colonial fear of loss and impotence, revealing the commingling of sex, class, race and power. The black athlete was created at a moment of impending imperial crisis; the concern that the assumed superiority of colonial whiteness over all Others could not, after all, be sustained. The colonial project was porous. It leaked. It could not contain the very aspects of difference that it helped to produce and claimed to both know and master. The loss of political power, and the concomitant fears of sexual impotency, finds its corollary in the rise of the black athlete. The invention of the black athlete, at the height of European colonial global governance, signaled not Europe's crowning moment of success but its impending decline. This colonial anxiety would require a rethinking of the very category of race and of what it meant (and means) to be 'white'.

More generally, *Race, Sport and Politics* addresses sport's historical and contemporary role in the shaping of racial discourse. It considers sport's place within black diasporic struggles for freedom and equality as well as the contested location of sport in relation to the politics of recognition within contemporary European multicultural societies. I argue that even within a putatively post-racial era, the institutional forms of commodified and hyper-commercialized sports[1] remain profoundly and deeply racialized. In part, this is a story of the continuing effects of ideas about race and racial difference within sport itself. But it is also, and perhaps more importantly, an argument that suggests that *sport reproduces race.* That is, sport has become an important if somewhat overlooked arena for the *making and remaking of race beyond its own boundaries.*

I use the term *the racial signification of sport* to indicate how sport, as a highly regulated and embodied cultural practice, has, from its manifestation as a modern social institution during the high-period of European imperialist expansionism, played a central role in popularizing notions of absolute biological difference while also providing an important arena for forms of cultural resistance against white racism. These 'acts of resistance' have ranged from the redemptive (sport as personal savior) to the transformative (sport as social change). In short, ideologies of race saturate the fabric of modern sports, sports help to reproduce race and, further, the discursive construct of 'the black athlete' becomes an important site for these various and varied struggles.

Two separate but interrelated general arguments also structure the book. The first, that precisely because sport is commonly viewed as apolitical it has had an important influence on not only black politics, formally understood, but more widely on how African diasporic peoples have viewed themselves *and* how these communities have come to be viewed. It is sport's assumed innocence as a space (in the imagination) and a place (as it physically manifests itself) that is removed from everyday concerns of power, inequality, struggle and ideology, that has, paradoxically, allowed it to be filled with a range of contradictory assumptions that have inevitably spilled back over and into wider society. It has offered a space for transcendence and utopian dreaming, often before other supposedly more important arenas of civic life were able to be changed. I suggest that taking this contradiction seriously – that is, *the political nature of the apolitical* – helps us towards a deeper and richer understanding of politics: what it means to act as well as the limits to human agency, what is at stake in the very claims for recognition and freedom, and how power itself is both manifest and challenged.

The second general argument rests on the claim that the deeply priapean nature of modern sports – and especially of competitive, hyper-commercialized sports – produces a homosocial space for the projection of white masculinist fantasies of domination, control and desire for the racialized Other. I suggest that this well-observed feminist and psychoanalytical reading helps us to understand sports as, in part, a stage for the white male imaginary to engage the latent (occasionally explicit) homosocial desires for and fears about the black male (sporting) body. Or what we might more succinctly and simply term *the fear of the black athlete*. Some of these popular sporting tropes of desire, yearning and ultimately of impotence are familiar, such as 'The Great White Hope' and 'White Men Can't Jump'. But we tend to skip past these commonplace utterances rather too quickly. I want to suggest that if we care to take them seriously we might find that they reveal something more fundamental about how the 'white colonial frame' continues to reproduce forms of white colonial desire and therefore of anti-black racism in the present.

The white colonial frame is my adaptation of what the sociologist Joe Feagin (2010) terms the *white racial frame*. Feagin defines the white racial frame as a centuries-old worldview that is based on whites' racially constructed reality of how the world works. This 'frame' then becomes the dominant way in which people come to 'see' race and provides a further function in enabling racism itself to be rationalized away while denying the historical forms of white supremacy that continue to structure contemporary social institutions, cultural processes (including language) and interpersonal relations. The white racial frame, Feagin suggests, is 'an emotion-laden construction process that shapes everyday relationships and institutions in fundamental and racialized ways' (Feagin 2010: ix).

The white *colonial* frame draws attention to how these racialized ways of seeing and framing the world derive not from some abstract and universal notion of whiteness (which, paradoxically, runs the risk of essentializing white racism) but from a specific set of European historical institutions (political, cultural and economic) that slowly begin to emerge in the sixteenth century and that structure much of the world in a very specific way, or what is commonly labeled European colonialism. In other words, the white colonial frame is a concept that seeks to highlight how both the lived experience of white supremacy (as a social and cultural phenomenon) and the systemic features of colonialism (as a political and economic institution) come together to produce forms of anti-black racism, both historically and contemporaneously, even after the formal dismantling of European colonial regimes. I explore this 'colonial model of the world' which underpins the white colonial frame in more detail in the following chapter.

I also read the dominant mode of competitive, hyper-commercialized professional sport within the west as a site for the ritualistic display and enactment of violence, both symbolic and literal. Sport remains one of the few spaces within modern liberal democracies for the sanction of acts of physical violence within and by non-state actors. Thus, sports have historically provided an opportunity for blacks throughout the African diaspora to gain recognition through *physical struggle* not just for their sporting achievements in the narrow and obvious sense but more significantly and fundamentally for their humanity in a context where the structures of the colonial state continue to shape the 'post/colonial' present. I argue that the (latent) sexualized and physical nature of the sporting encounter between black and white athletes becomes sublimated into a set of highly racialized discourses and representations about the black Other and that finds ultimate expression in forms of sporting ritual.

Throughout the text I use the *post/colonial* to mark the current period of racial formation. My use of the virgule is deliberate and meant to signal that the moment 'after' the colonial is itself caught in ambivalent tension between, on the one hand, the surpassing of formal colonial governance, and on the other, the continuance of neocolonial relations. The virgule can mean 'or' as in a divide between two different words. It can also be used to mean 'and' implying a strong association. It suggests a contextual choice of sorts as well, that even the meanings of the *neo*colonial (same/continue) and the *post*colonial (different/after) may themselves shift from one geographical and historical location to another, just as the post/colonial's formal linguistic usage implies that either side of the division can be chosen to complete the meaning of the sentence. To put it simply, different locations experience the post/colonial in different ways. I do not claim any deeper analytical insight beyond this attempt to unsettle the reader and to bring to the fore the political question of the colonial in the present by questioning the 'post' in the post/colonial. This does not, of course, resolve the problem that the post/colonial, as Ann McClintock notes, remains 'haunted by the very figure of linear development that it sets out to dismantle' (1995: 10).

In order to make sense of the shifts between human freedom and unfreedom, the politics of resistance and accommodation, longing and loathing, that mark the relationship between sport, race and politics, I attempt to produce a diachronic analysis. The time frame moves from the mid-nineteenth century to the early twenty-first century, with a particular focus on the past one hundred years. Key moments in the history of the racial signification of sport are used as a way to construct a historical narrative that can account for both change and stasis. An account, in other words, of the *intra*-relationship between discourses of race, the nature of embodied sporting performance, and the role of politics itself in the (re)making of 'the black athlete'.

### Improbable Articulated Objects: The Sociologist of Sport … Interested in Race

It has been more than two decades since the English translation of Pierre Bourdieu's essay 'Program for a Sociology of Sport' (Bourdieu 1988). In that short piece, Bourdieu warns of the dilemma – the double domination as he puts it – that the sociologist faces in trying to take sport seriously as an object of academic study. On the one hand, sports specialists – journalists, fans and players themselves – are often disinclined to think deeply about sport in anything other than an endogenous way, concerning themselves with discussions focused on results and great plays, and insular accounts of sporting history. On the other, many academics refrain from taking such a purportedly mundane, everyday pastime too seriously because the object itself is not considered fundamental to the inner-workings of society. Sport both hyper-accentuates and finds itself on the wrong side of a supposedly insurmountable (and deeply 'classed') dualism between useless physicality and purposeful intellectualism. 'Thus', Bourdieu suggests, 'there are, on the one hand, those who know sport very well on a practical level but do not know how to talk about it and, on the other hand, those who know sport very poorly on a practical level and who could talk about it, but disdain doing so, or do so without rhyme or reason' (1988: 153).

It would be comforting to report that in the intervening years such a denouncement of intellectual snobbery on the one hand and of willful intellectual refusal on the other has been overcome. Alas, it is not possible to do so. Sport remains a problematic intellectual object in a way that few other cultural forms are. Even when major social theorists do engage sport, it is often done in such a way as to reduce sport to a mere passing illustration of some other more fundamental point. The sociologist who takes sport as a *starting point* for sociological enquiry risks a certain professional disparagement.

Who, for instance, outside of the circles of the sport sociology community, knows that Anthony Giddens, arguably the most important and certainly most cited British sociologist of the past thirty years, studied the socio-historical formations of sport for his London School of Economics Masters thesis? Or that he is a huge fan of Tottenham Hotspur Football Club? Giddens's sporting intellectual antecedents are barely knowable from his extensive writings over the years that have explored in sophisticated theoretical detail just about every facet of society and culture, from macro socio-economic analyses of late modernity, globalization and the restructuring of the welfare state, to tracing the changing intimacies of everyday life, identity and emotion (Horne and Jary 2004). But not sport. A Giddens analysis of sport remains as rare as a major trophy in the White Hart Lane cabinet.

Even when such major figures do write on sport they often deny that they are in fact doing so. Hence Loïc Wacquant's stubborn refusal to concede that his widely praised study on the sport of boxing is a study of sport at all. Eric Dunning (2005: 171) – arguably the most prolific and distinguished sociologist to have come out of the sporting sociological closet – argues that Wacquant's (2004) *Body and Soul* is an important contribution to the sociologies of the body and sport, even though Wacquant fails to engage with the extensive sociology of sport literature on boxing, violence and embodiment (Dunning 2005: 175). Wacquant, responding to Dunning's review, flatly states that the focus of his study 'is not on the social organization and culture of athletic pursuits but on the twofold process of *incorporation of social structures*: the collective creation of proficient bodies and the ingenuous unfolding of the socially constituted powers they harbor' (2005: 454, emphasis in original). This sport is not a sport.

I have some sympathy with Wacquant's general position, which I understand to be an attempt to produce a radically reflexive contextualism on the one hand and a micro-sociological investigation of corporal reasoning on the other. The former position suggests that sociologists need to be wary of simply taking as the 'object of study' that which is presented to us within either popular discourse or public policy initiatives as a 'problem' in need of analysis. Or, as Bourdieu puts it, a large number of academic 'objects' that social science officially recognizes and related titles of study,

> are nothing other than social problems that have been smuggled into sociology – poverty, delinquency, youth, high school drop-outs, leisure, drunken driving, and so on – and which vary with the fluctuations of the social or scholarly consciousness of the time, as an analysis of the evolution over time of the main realist divisions of sociology would testify … For a sociologist more than any other thinker, to leave one's thought in a state of unthought (*impensé*) is to condemn oneself to be nothing more than the *instrument* of that which one claims to think. (Bourdieu and Wacquant 1992: 236–238, emphasis in original)

Indeed, many would argue that there is no such thing as a 'sport sociologist', only sociologists interested in studying sport. This shift – from adjective to noun – is important in helping to problematize 'sport' itself. That is, to avoid giving to sport an ontological coherence across time and space that it may lack while also enabling sociologists to avoid extracting sport out of its wider social moorings. Tracing the *historical* development of the meanings given to the human activities that come to be labeled 'sport' and the wider socio-economic forces that are bound up with sport's very production helps to avoid the dangers of unreflexive accounts of sport and its varied meanings. That said, and beyond these specific analytical cautions, there is still a certain academic resistance to being associated with 'sport' itself. In part, this is a desire of some to be seen as 'generalists', that is sociologists able to speak on any topic at any time, as though to have a 'specialty' is to reduce oneself to a redundant particularism and hence to marginality. When that specialism is sport the effect is deemed to constitute a double marginality.

It is not surprising then that Wacquant studiously resists the attempt to 'reduce' his work to something as parochial as 'the sociology of sport', having previously warned of the dubious credibility of such an intellectual pursuit. Toby Miller (one of the very few senior figures within cultural studies who *has* taken sport seriously in his work) has noted that Wacquant once surmised that he probably would have never studied boxing at all but for the cachet obtained from his co-authored work with Bourdieu. Such an association, Wacquant stated, saved him from 'disappearing into the oblivion of the sociology of sport' (cited in Miller 1997: 116). Miller goes on to reflect that:

> Wacquant ... demonstrates a cosmic personal ambivalence. At one point, he transcends social theory and careerism for a 'proper' understanding of sport based on allegedly pretheoretical experiential narration; at another, these very categories (themselves, of course, sociological and theoretical) are reinscribed as legitimate forms of argument. Here, sport does not necessarily refer to the fissures of the social, although it is assuredly informed by and informing of them. Rather sport is a mode of representation in which sportspeople are stars of the everyday, their performances conditioned by publicly available rules and dynamic intersubjective space (unlike in film) that can be imitated but never quite repeated. (1997: 117)

Similarly, the culture sections of newspapers, magazines and literary review journals, and the equivalent culture review programs of radio and television, remain enamored of a model of culture that has changed little since the days when Lord Reith's British Broadcasting Corporation decided to bring higher learning and Culture to the masses, or what might be termed the democratization of high culture (Henry 2001: 16–18). Despite the protestations of conservative (and occasionally liberal) commentators over the supposed postmodern collapse of cultural boundaries that drove the culture wars of the 1980s and 1990s, the canonical gatekeepers have managed to keep 'sport' safely locked inside its own bantustan and outside of the borders of 'culture'. Weekend broadsheets on both sides of the Atlantic, for example, rarely confuse their culture sections with the rapidly growing special supplements dedicated to the non-cultural: 'sport'. And the sports literati, found on the back pages, web pages, radio phone-ins and, increasingly, the dedicated cable and satellite televisual channels, have been happy with this cultural détente. Thus while it is true, for example, that discerning commentaries can occasionally be found in newspaper supplements such as the *Observer's Sports Monthly* in Britain and magazines such as *Sports Illustrated* in the United States, as well as in the perceptive writings of journalists such as Mike Marqusee and Dave Zirin, the gap between critical, sociologically informed work and the broader forms of mass media sports chatter,[2] itself often removed from 'serious' cultural analysis, remains significant. The promise that the arrival of extended sports television talk shows – such as ESPN's *SportsCenter* – would offer a mass-media space for critical, informed, if irreverent and idiosyncratic, commentary remains unfulfilled.[3]

In many ways the academic field reproduces such cultural distinctions. While a sociologist such as Richard Sennett can be admired for his cello-playing dexterity (Glenn 2003; Tonkin 2008), no such validation exists for the 'sporting sociologist'. Sennett's intellectual credentials are, if anything, *enhanced* by such bourgeois cultural associations, yet little if any cultural capital can be gained within academia by announcing that one is or was, say, an Olympic-level sprint hurdler or indeed a semi-professional footballer. The technical aspects of musical production and performance can be used as a way to rethink the physicality and creativity of 'craftsmanship' as a complex social practice and 'music worlds' can help inform a theory of the social mechanisms and collective activities that produce and redefine the very notion of the aesthetic (Becker 2008; Miller 2008; Sennett 2008), but 'sport' in and of itself is rarely accorded such elevated analytical status.[4]

Edwin Amenta's (2007a) *Professor Baseball*, an ethnographic memoir on his experiences playing for and captaining a New York softball team, is instructive here. Even the title of Amenta's book connotes a less-than-serious, somewhat jovial, association between the two operative words: 'professor' and 'baseball'. The title's 'hook' lies in the very, supposedly improbable, conjuncture of the avowedly academic with the irredeemably sporting. Indeed, Amenta reveals that the title stemmed from his fear that his soft-ball teammates would ultimately reject his attempts at using his (academic) analytical skills to produce better sporting results for the team: 'The last thing I need is for one of my teammates to ask, "Who do you think you are, 'Professor Baseball?'" The ridicule would be ruthless' (2007a: 59; see also 2007b: 41). Likewise, Amenta notes the spatial dislocation and unease that would result when he and his teammates would occasionally traipse across the New York University campus after a game, his baseball clothing signifying not just a sartorial breach of academic space but a deeper sense that no serious academic should be spending so much time on such an unserious activity as softball. Amenta confesses, 'My sporting and academic circles never overlap like this, and I worry about being seen' (2007a: 110; see also 2007c).[5]

Given this situation, it is important not simply to berate the cultural gatekeepers or the major sociological figures for not taking sport seriously. Such a response begins to sound like, and is invariably read as, sub-disciplinary griping that serves only to further reinforce the perception that the subject under discussion really is (and should remain) marginal to life's 'big questions'. In his prefatory note to Bourdieu's aforementioned essay, John MacAloon warns against 'the usual sterile lament' (1988: 150) of the sociologist or social scientist of sport, upset that, yet again, their subject matter has been overlooked, ignored or disparaged. Laments, sterile or otherwise, will not get us very far.

There is, of course, a danger in over-stating this 'marginalization' and further reifying a distinction between 'the academic mainstream' and 'the sporting rest' (stuck on the sidelines?) that may not be fully accurate nor helpful. For example, the sociology of sport is a vibrant area of study that since its formal institutionalization in the mid-1960s has grown and matured in ways that few other sub-disciplinary areas of sociology have in such a short period of time (Coakley and Dunning 2000). There are around half a dozen sport sociology journals alone and if a broader definition of 'sport studies' is used that includes history, psychology, economics, management, law and philosophy, there are in excess of twenty such peer-reviewed journals, many of very high quality published by leading academic presses. The International Sociology of Sport Association (ISSA) has helped to shape and develop the field in important ways, especially through its continuing and sizable presence at events such as the World Congress of Sociology conferences and through its own official journal, the *International Review for the Sociology of Sport*, which was first published in 1966.

Similarly, the North American Society for the Sociology of Sport (NASSS) continues to attract scholars from across the world for its annual conference and NASSS's official journal, the *Sociology of Sport Journal*, remains one of the preeminent peer-reviewed journals in its field. Indeed, this is where the English version of Bourdieu's essay 'Program for a Sociology of Sport' was first published. There are numerous sociology of sport textbooks servicing hundreds of dedicated undergraduate programs in numerous countries in addition to well-trained sociology of sport graduate students. Most major academic publishers now have specific series dedicated to sport. If the sociology of sport is indeed a space of intellectual oblivion which serious thinkers must avoid at all costs, it appears to be in a relatively happy state of effervescent oblivion.[6]

That all said, other indicators present a somewhat less optimistic picture. Given the huge amount of critical work on sport and its general importance to society – in terms of its economic import, cultural impact, political significance, centrality to the rhythm and structure of everyday life and discourse, and even, as James asserts in the chapter epigraph, the ethical insights produced therein – the number of sociologists whose research substantively (though not necessarily exclusively) engages with sport and who have found places to pursue such work *within sociology departments* is surprisingly small. Most critical sociological work on sport is in fact done by those located within departments of kinesiology (in North America) or physical education and sport management (in Britain) or other allied interdisciplinary fields.[7] In their review of the state of knowledge as regards sport and American sociology, Robert Washington and David Karen (2001: 187) conclude that, despite some progress, the vibrancy of the sub-field of sport sociology is actually a direct result of its historical institutional neglect by organizations such as the American Sociological Association and its attendant conferences and journals.

The key for those who do think that sport constitutes an actual object of study and an important one at that, is to think through *why* sport appears to be marginal to serious cultural critique and intellectual examination (without becoming overly defensive) while also demonstrating *what* sport adds to our broader understandings of diverse sociological issues – such as globalization, nationalism, identity and community (de)formation – while avoiding assuming the *de facto* centrality of sports to all issues at all times. It remains the case that much of the work within the sociology of sport rarely uses sport as *generative* of social theory and at best shows how concepts and ideas developed in other contexts can be *applied* to sport. This is not without merit and in truth is what many 'sub-fields' tend to do. But such an approach restricts the development of sophisticated ways to think about sport (and the related issues of performance, physicality and embodiment) and perhaps further impedes the attempt to think more deeply about sport and society more generally.[8]

I would suggest that the sociologist interested in taking sport *and* race seriously faces a further difficulty, a triple domination if you will. I make this point not to claim any particular academic 'victimization' status nor to engage in another 'sterile lament', but rather to situate the current study in order to reflexively consider *why* this situation has arisen and why an *interdisciplinary* approach therefore becomes necessary in trying to produce a cultural theory of race and sport. That is, to think about how the academic field itself produces certain thematic elisions so as to reveal the hidden normative assumptions about legitimate knowledge production that has made thinking about race and sport particularly difficult.

As has been argued, sport has occasionally figured within the conceptual apparatus of mainstream social theory even if it has rarely been central to such endeavors. Thus Bourdieu has shown how sport relates to class identities and the ways in which different dispositions to and discourses of the body – instrumental, muscular bodily contact of the 'vulgar' working classes versus the refined, aesthetic sporting body of the 'disinterested' bourgeoisie – can be seen not only in the *types* of sports played by different social classes (and also the competing fractions within classes) but also in *how* such sports are played. Thus sport becomes a key way of demonstrating how the embodied performance of social structure, or *habitus*, is made real in the production of class distinctions (Bourdieu 1978; see also Tomlinson 2004).

Similarly, although it would be an over-statement to claim that feminist theory in general has given sport a central position within its work, gender scholars have often used sport as a key illustration of important aspects of gender formation, R.W. Connell's (1987, 2005) hugely influential work on hegemonic masculinity perhaps being the clearest example of this. Jeff Hearn has pointed out that the term 'hegemonic masculinity' was first developed in a paper Connell gave in 1979 entitled 'Men's Bodies' that was subsequently published in 1983 in *Which Way Is Up?* (Connell 1983). Hearn goes on to note, in 'discussing the "physical sense of maleness", Connell marks out the social importance of sport as "the central experience of the school years for many boys" (1983: 18), emphasizing the practices and experiences of taking and occupying space, holding the body tense, and skill, as well as size, power, force, strength, physical development and sexuality' (Hearn 2004: 56). Sport has thus often figured prominently in the work of scholars of masculinity such as Michael Messner (1992, 2007) and Michael Kimmel (2006, 2008), among others.

But the same cannot be said for questions of race. As I discuss in more detail below, post/colonial theorists and critical race theorists have rarely centered sport within their analyses. When popular culture has figured in discussions of black politics it has tended to be forms such as dance, film, television and, above all, music, that have dominated the ensuing debates (for example, see Dent 1992). Sport remains a problematic object for sociologists, while it largely disappears from the theoretical compass for scholars of black cultural politics. Against this academic amnesia, I want to suggest that a reading of the race and sport conjuncture can produce important insights into both the (changing) meaning and structure of 'race' as well as the importance and place of sport within western societies.

It is often overlooked, for example, that Bourdieu starts 'Program for a Sociology of Sport' by referencing the experience of 'the great black athletes' – by which he presumably means black students on sports scholarships – on the campuses of elite American universities. Bourdieu recounts being told by Aaron Cicourel how such students 'live in a sort of golden ghetto, because right-wing people do not talk very willingly with blacks while left-wing people do not talk very willingly with athletes' (1988: 153). Bourdieu treats this discovery as a 'parable' (1988: 153) from which to develop his schematic program for a sociology of sport: 'one might find in it [the experience of the black "student-athlete"] the principle of the special difficulties that the sociology of sport encounters: scorned by sociologists, it is despised by sportspersons' (p. 153).

Bourdieu fails to develop any deeper reflections on this moment that might have opened up questions of racial formation in the context of sport. The 'black athlete' simply serves as a somewhat curious object with which to illustrate a broader, more important conceptual point. Neither the specificity of race nor the sets of classed and gendered structures within which the black 'student-athlete' are located are discussed. The conjuncture of race and sport is duly noted but left under-theorized in the rush to reflect upon the state of the sociology of sport. But what if we took the situation and lives of those young students seriously? What if, rather than merely using the experience of African American (so-called) 'student-athletes' as an illustrative anecdote from which to build an argument that at once denies the foundational and constitutive particularities of race, we instead paused to think about these difficult articulations? What are the sets of historical forces that produce the possibility of 'the black student-athlete' in the first place? What might those students on those campuses have to say themselves? Are they forever destined to be talked about – and over – as Bourdieu implies? *Can the black athlete speak?*

Leaving aside, for the moment, the problematic suggestion that we might infer from Cicourel's revelatory story, namely that 'right-wing people' and blackness are mutually exclusive (and maybe also that those anti-sport 'left-wing people' are by definition white), we might use this parable in another way: to illustrate how the sociology of sport has been negligent in failing to take the racial signification of sport seriously. That is to say, its failure in not thinking through the formation of sport in conjunction with colonialism, while producing accounts of sport that have underplayed the constitutive importance of racism, even when presented with a story that speaks to these very issues. As I explore in more detail in the following chapter, the class-centric framing of radical approaches to sport (something that has bedeviled rather mechanistic applications of Bourdieuan approaches in general) that simply disavow any analytic space for questions of race continues to be a problem.[9]

To think race *and* sport sociologically has, until relatively recently, meant to occupy an intellectual niche of such supposed specificity as to invoke outright incredulity of the type that C.L.R. James experienced many decades ago. Rather than feeling sorry for those who doubt that sport has social, political or ethical values worth considering, I explore in this book some of the reasons for the existing gaps in the literature in order to highlight what types of enquiries might usefully be pursued to rectify this situation and to open up a series of questions for critical scholars of race to address. How might we theorize the role of sport as an agent of and space for forms of resistance and change in the very forging of racial identities? What type of rethinking of established narratives within the sociology and history of sport is needed in order to open up and bring into conversation debates in fields such as the sociology of culture and critical discussions within African diaspora studies with those of sport? And what role has the black athlete played in the very making and remaking of race?

### On Method: Using Charcoal to Disappoint the Botanists and Pollsters

Given these over-ambitious goals, *Race, Sport and Politics* will inevitably disappoint and fall short. It will likely disappoint historians who will demand more by way of empirical substantiation and evidence for some of my grander claims about the changing meanings of sport and race, especially during the early twentieth century. While much time has been spent in various archives and libraries, and as I draw heavily on the historical scholarship of others far more accomplished than I in these matters, I do not claim to have exhausted every possible data source that would meet with the scholarly bar that professional historians might expect. But I do not claim this to be a work of history alone.

Sociologists too, at least those driven by the goal of wanting the discipline to become even more positivistic in mode and method than it already is, will definitely be disappointed. Instead, I necessarily rely on discourse analysis, textual readings, social theory (as opposed, simply, to sociological theory) and a somewhat eclectic interpretive and historical framework, a framework that extends far beyond the comfortable and predictable boundaries that many traditional sociologists, bound to hypothesis testing and statistical verification, would recognize as legitimate, in order to make sense of modern manifestations of race. My methodological approach, while sociological in intent, unashamedly reveals my intellectual debt to what is now commonly referred to as 'cultural studies'.[10] I similarly and willfully fail to follow the now seemingly *de rigueur* (American) sociological requirement to relegate the 'normative analysis' to a small separate section at the end of the book, presupposing that the rest of the argument somehow emerges from some apolitical vacuum of disengaged scholarship from on high. Especially when dealing with what Cornel West has called the Great Catastrophe concerning the racial violence that birthed 'the west', it becomes impossible to be non-normative on a moving train[11] except by accepting the ideological sleight of hand that reduces racial hatred, oppression and genocide to something sociology benignly calls 'race relations' (Feagin 2006; Steinberg 2007; Vargas 2008).

I will concede at the outset that my use of 'sport' is given a lot of conceptual work to do. Perhaps too much. Although I clarify my key terms and concepts in the following chapters, the theoretical framework and connections that I make across time, between social objects, and individuals, remains suggestive and provisional. The grand theoretical synthesis that attempts to produce, in the last instance, analytical closure is beyond the scope of this book and this author. These disclaimers aside, and less defensively, my goal is to provide a deliberately generalized account and theoretical map within which we can begin to make better sense of the critical conjunctures *between* race and sport within the wider black diaspora and the political effects of those moments of (dis)articulation within the west. To think, in short, of race and sport in a new way and to use sport as the site for the *generation* and not merely *application* of social theory. That is, to analyze the specificity (or unity) of race and sport while locating (delimiting) that very discussion within the broader ideological context and social fields of race, history and power. This, to adapt Althusser (2005: 66–70), is my *problematic*.

As this outline demonstrates, such an approach necessitates a certain abstraction and generalization, to read particular moments and episodes in relation to the wider set of historical forces operating at that time. To paraphrase Richard Gruneau (1983/1999: 62), I have sought to develop a plausible account through a theoretically directed narrative that emphasizes broad patterns, tendencies and critical moments in the struggle over the meanings of race and sport within which other researchers might be able to develop, improve, critique and challenge the reading of race and sport provided. But, hopefully, this is done without getting lost within either the types of careless extrapolations that descend into meta-theoreticism nor by producing an account that becomes so fixated on reading the particular that the analysis becomes sealed off from the broader flows of history and wider social structures that produced the event(s) in the first place. Thus my approach owes something to the spirit of Pierre Bourdieu's 'general principle of method':

Rather than being content with knowing in depth a small sector of reality of which one ignores, for want of asking it, how it is situated in the space from which it was abstracted and what its functioning might owe to this position, one must proceed in the manner of the academic architects who presented a charcoal sketch of the entire building in which the part elaborated in detail was situated. One thus must try – at the risk of running counter to the positivist expectations which everything, by the way, seems to vindicate ('better to make a small, modest, and precise contribution than to build grand, superficial constructions') – to construct a summary description of the totality of the space under construction. (1988: 156)

I have also consciously avoided discussing in detail the rather obvious markers that the reader might have expected to encounter through which to make my argument, such as the life and times of Muhammad Ali (Early 1998), the failed boycott of and political protests staged at the Mexico 1968 Olympic Games (Edwards 1969) and, of course, the writings of C.L.R. James (1963/1994) on cricket in the Caribbean from the 1940s to the 1960s. These moments, athletes and intellectuals have recently been subject to excellent critical histories and analyses that I draw on, directly and indirectly, throughout the book (see for instance Bass 2002; Farred 1996, 2003; Hartmann 2003; Lemert 2003; Marqusee 2005; St Louis 2007; Witherspoon 2008). However, *Race, Sport and Politics* has a different but related agenda: namely to provide a broader socio-historical and theoretical account that helps to make sense of these important episodes; to think through other moments that while less 'obvious' nonetheless remain pivotal in shaping the political inter-relationship of race and sport. Indeed, as I argue in the following chapter, the constant invocation of C.L.R. James in particular has served to *close down* rather than open up critical thinking on these issues. Or, to put it more provocatively, do we have the imagination to think race and sport beyond *Beyond a Boundary*?[12]

Another way to phrase this is to say that my method and approach, while located within a broadly sociological standpoint, is inter- and in some ways trans-disciplinary. Although invoking the importance and necessity of thinking across disciplines is now a *de rigueur* claim within the academy, few outside of cultural studies (broadly defined) actually attempt to do such work. And when they do, the disciplinary gatekeepers are quick to level accusations of poor scholarship (self-defined by the relevant discipline's most professionalized advocates) and cries that such work, even if it could be 'judged', does not belong within the said discipline's boundaries because the way of approaching the question does not fit with the established protocols of proper research. In contrast and in order to successfully construct a new cultural theory of race and sport, we might think of such 'border crossing', both in the disciplinary and epistemological sense, as *necessary intellectual work*. That is, to recognize the need to think outside of the established intellectual boundaries, beyond the sociological boundary if you will, in order to *reframe the question of race and sport diasporically* so as to get away from an overly nation state-centric approach to questions of race and culture. David Theo Goldberg nicely captures this move – which, of course, is deeply resented and resisted by those who have the most to lose by the challenge to disciplinary orthodoxy – when he argues for the necessity of an *epistemological hybridity*:

> disciplines are to the academy, to intellectual pursuit, as borders are more broadly to nation-states ... The transgressive threats possible in multi- and trans-disciplinarity seem as unsettling to some locally as migration and transnationalism seem to the relatively privileged more globally, and for related sorts of reasons. Settled ideas, practices, and institutions are challenged as a result, sometimes at considerable existential cost. The threat is not just that some or other discipline might transform, but that it might turn out to be redundant and disappear completely, that the power and privilege it has secured may be lost. Hence the investment in a conserving resistance. Relatedly, epistemological hybridity suggests new forms of thinking, new categories of knowing rather than resting (in)secure in settled ways of seeing and comprehending the world. (2002: 29–30)

My motivations for writing this book stem, in large part, from *my own* multiple disappointments of engaging with radical intellectual works that nevertheless constantly and consistently fail to address the centrality of sport in the making of race and of race in the structuring of sport; in reading otherwise excellent accounts of racial formation that pay too little attention to the productive force of popular culture and that focus almost exclusively on the institutions of State, the Market or the obvious actors within Civil Society. Of accounts on black popular culture, often and paradoxically indebted to the work of C.L.R. James, that develop sophisticated and significant theorizations concerning black identity and culture all the while ignoring (with at best a brief reference, line or footnote, normally on O.J. Simpson or Michael Jordan) what is arguably *the* most significant and public of popular cultural forms, namely sport. And finally, of accounts within sport sociology and sport studies that either ignore race altogether or treat it in such an epiphenomenal way as to relegate the racialization of western societies to some incidental, minor, passing episode. This has meant that, until relatively recently, the critical study of race and sport remained in a somewhat depauperate state.

However, since the mid- to late 1990s a number of important and sociologically informed case studies (as opposed to sensational journalistic accounts or descriptive statistical analyses) have been published on the politics of race and sport, particularly as regards the black experience. For example, in addition to the historical studies on the 1968 Mexico Olympics and the now iconic black-gloved salute of sprinters Tommie Smith and John Carlos, and the cultural analyses of Muhammad Ali and the politics of the 1960s previously mentioned, we now have detailed and insightful ethnographies of contemporary basketball in the United States, of football cultures in Britain and of boxing gyms in both the US and Britain (see Back et al., 2001; Brooks 2009; Burdsey 2007a; Garland and Rowe 2001; King 2004;

May 2008; Wacquant 2004; Woodward 2007). Beyond these familiar sites the contemporary student has access to important studies on sport in Africa, and of race and sport in former white settler colonies such as Canada (see Abdel-Shehid 2005; Armstrong and Giulianotti 2004; Booth 1998; Darby 2002).[13]

Such studies, while often descriptively rich and theoretically nuanced, have tended to be limited in both historical scope and in terms of their engagement with questions of diaspora and transnationalism. *Race, Sport and Politics* attempts to contextualize these currently disparate discussions so that we might be able, productively, to see how such accounts speak to one another and in the process deepen our understandings of racial identity, political mobilization and social change in the context of popular culture and everyday life.

## Prolegomenon

In Chapter 1, Sporting Resistance: Thinking Race and Sport Diasporically, I attempt to adumbrate my general theoretical argument. I survey how sport has been defined and understood within critical sociological approaches that have developed important theories of play and sport in relation to questions of freedom, constraint, resistance, and hegemonic struggle. I argue that while such contributions have significantly advanced the study of sport they have come at the expense of a deeper understanding of the relationship between sport and race and particularly the ways in which European colonialism profoundly shaped not only western liberal democracies and industrial capitalism but also sport itself. I further argue that Eurocentric tropes of the civilized/primitive and the rational/irrational have been incorporated into the conceptual frameworks of sports studies, especially as the field has narrated the historical 'diffusion' of modern sports from 'the west' to 'the rest'. I suggest that an engagement with post/colonial theory (despite that area's own neglect of sport) and diaspora theory alongside the familiar discussions on globalization, offers a corrective to the Myth of Modern Sport and a way forward for the critical study of race, sport and politics in the context of what I term the sporting black Atlantic.

Chapter 2, Sporting Redemption: Violence, Desire and the Politics of Freedom, examines why and how racial discourse shifted during the first few decades of the twentieth century and the role of sport in producing this change. It is suggested that at the beginning of the twentieth century, white supremacist logic posited the intellectual, aesthetic *and* physical superiority of whites over all the other races of Man. By the 1930s this logic had been significantly challenged, such that by the middle of the twentieth century, blacks were generally viewed as physically *superior* to whites. It is argued that the boxer Jack Johnson played a pivotal role in altering racial discourse. Johnson's victories were a clear refutation of the alleged physical inferiority of blacks that had become one of the foundational pillars of white supremacy and that underpinned the entire imperial project. For black people throughout the African diaspora, Johnson embodied a *figuration of freedom* (Hartman 1997: 11) that simply had not existed in such a robust and confident form prior to his arrival, thus situating sport itself as an important redemptive space for the production of black politics. Johnson reconfigured the political arena not so much for what he said regarding the racial politics of the day but more fundamentally and powerfully by *expanding the boundary of possibilities for black selfhood* via his very actions inside and outside of the ring. He helped, in other words, to reframe the nature of 'politics' itself, inserting sport into the heart of the debates over freedom, citizenship, power and agency, thus recasting the terrain that had previously attempted to separate sport and popular culture from the world of politics proper.

If whites were not in fact physically superior, and if the widespread early twentieth century belief in eugenics and social Darwinism was true, then the prospect of a reversal of the racial hierarchy suddenly became a distinct possibility. Were Johnson's victories allowed to continue then the likelihood of black revolt and therefore political emancipation became greater, and with it the even more frightening prospect of black dominance and a black future. If it is the case, as Robert Young (2001: 17) suggests, that European imperialism, despite the diversity of different colonial regimes, 'constituted a global political system' that was underpinned by the belief in white supremacy, then any fundamental challenge to the white colonial frame had potential ramifications for the entire system of imperialism. What social scientists would later call 'globalization' is prefigured here with the emergence of sport's global network that allowed for Johnson's diasporic politicization as an anti white supremacist figure. The chapter also argues that Johnson signifies both the threat of white racial suicide and helps to usher in a new racial subject within the west: *the black athlete*. This in turn begins to transform wider understandings of race and racial difference, that result in the construction of new sexualized stereotypes (and the origins of racial sport science) in which the black body becomes a commodified object of desire, thus rendering the radical political possibilities of black sporting physicality in the pursuit of freedom partial and incomplete.

In Chapter 3, Sporting Negritude: Commodity Blackness and the Liberation of Failure, I examine the ways in which 'the black athlete' as sign and the black athletic body as commodity get taken up during the later part of the twentieth century as highly visible and profitable markers of racial difference. Key here are the ways in which various colonial narratives – the perceived instability of black people and their alleged predisposition to madness, the notion of black people as savage and primitive, and the sexualization of the black body as both threat and libidinal release – get reproduced within the post/colonial present.

Using Ralph Ellison's powerful depiction of a battle royal in *Invisible Man* as a point of departure to think about the violence embedded within certain forms of black performance for white pleasure, I trace the question of black masculinity as a *subordinated masculinity* through the parallel and sometimes interconnected careers and lives of the boxers Frank Bruno and Mike Tyson. The chapter concludes by suggesting that both Bruno and Tyson have slowly and belatedly come to terms with their complex racial and masculine selves, but only after they have embraced the notion of 'failure' and acknowledged the limitations of forms of patriarchal masculinity, thereby renouncing the identity of 'the black athlete'. Somewhat tentatively, I suggest that both men may in fact offer a more 'positive' representation of black masculinity that refuses to play the game of hyper-masculine excess. Instead such 'progressive' black masculinities may provide a way to re-humanize the dehumanizing logic of the commodified black athlete.

Chapter 4, Sporting Multiculturalism: Nationalism, Belonging and Identity, examines the role of sport in producing and signifying cultural change within western European societies such as Britain. Particularly since the bombings in central London on July 2005 that left 56 people dead and scores more maimed for life, sport's supposed integrative function has been invoked as a way to deal with the 'problem' of racial and ethnic diversity. Debates about belonging and citizenship have thus shifted from an overtly racialized notion of biological difference and degeneracy that marked the colonial period towards a culturalist discourse framed by questions of 'integration' and 'assimilation'. The failure of the Parekh Report (2000) into the Future of Multi-ethnic Britain to shift the terms of the debate around identity and belonging in Britain is read, symptomatically, as signaling the end of Britain's brief engagement with state multiculturalism.

Using the examples of the Formula One racing driver Lewis Hamilton and the cricketer Monty Panesar, I explore how both athletes offer a new and more expansive model of Englishness that negates the easy tropes of assimilation and integration by providing a more meaningful form of everyday multiculture in which racial difference within the nation becomes accepted and unexceptional. Yet the failure of such athletes to articulate a political consciousness beyond the general platitudes of corporate multiculturalism and liberal 'tolerance' suggests that any advances in terms of expanding the possibilities of belonging to the nation will likely remain limited in scope and effect, unless linked to a more fundamental rethinking of British nationalism in general and English identity in particular.

In the last chapter, Conclusion: Race, Sport and the Post/colonial, I return to the themes that have structured the book's core arguments, reflecting on the complex ways in which sport today, in the moment of the post/colonial, serves to both reproduce and challenge dominant ideologies of race. In the Age of Obama, where the notion of a post-racial settlement has become a mantra for commentators from both the liberal left and conservative right, we urgently need more sophisticated ways to think about race and sport. This is required in order to avoid, on the one hand, the overly simplistic if provocative notion that trans-Atlantic slavery and the plantation system provide a useful frame of reference for comprehending the workings of racism today and, on the other, the myopic suggestion that racism has somehow magically disappeared from the

United States and the west more generally, simply because of the election of the first African American President of the United States.

Through the prism of sport, *Race, Sport and Politics* attempts to write a more complex history of how colonial relations and the white colonial frame impact and imprint the post/colonial present. The argument is not so much concerned with simply trying to narrate the history of sporting relations between blacks and whites since Johnson dispatched Burns to the canvas in Sydney just over one hundred years ago, but to show how the very categories of 'blackness', 'whiteness', and even of 'race' and 'sport' have changed over time and *changed as a result of their co-articulations with each other*. This is the deeper question the work attempts to address in producing a cultural theory of race and sport. There are no races, only ways in which we see race. And sport continues to play an important role in the making and remaking of these ways of seeing.

## Notes

1   Although it does not exhaust the possibilities of what sport is and can be, and mindful of the totalizing logic in reading developments (dominant or otherwise) within elite, professional sports 'downwards' into all forms of sporting activity regardless of the level of play and the locally determined ethical boundaries, David Andrews (2009) has made a powerful case, following Frederic Jameson, that we are now in a *hyper-commercialized period of late sporting capital*. The nature of commodity spectacle, that was always a part of professional sports, has shifted substantively into a new form of hyper-commercial sports culture that is dominated by profit-driven corporatization, to the virtual exclusion of other values and non-market ethics. While Andrews's somewhat pessimistic reading unnecessarily negates the possibility for alternative logics within sporting spaces, his general argument captures something important about contemporary sporting cultures: 'In seeking to follow the corporate sport hegemon (through developing a highly regulated, controlled, and predictable mass entertainment product, designed to generate maximum profit across numerous revenue streams), administrators and executives routinely adopt the following, seemingly *de rigueur*, commercial strategies: the cultural management of the sport entity as a network of merchandizable brands and embodied sub-brands; the differentiation of sport-related revenue streams and consumption opportunities; profit-driven executive control and management hierarchies; cartelized ownership and franchized organizational structures; rational (re)location of teams and venues; the entertainment-driven mass mediation of sporting spectacles; the reconfiguring of sport spectacles and spaces as sponsorship vehicles for advancing corporate visibility; and the advancement of marketing and promotional strategies aimed at both consolidating core and expanding new sport consumer constituencies. Indeed, while there may be alternatives (premeditated or otherwise) to this corporate sport modality, these are few and far between, and do not challenge its global hegemony. Thus, currently there would appear to be no sustainable, viable, or indeed, even imaginable alternatives to the late capitalist, corporatist, iteration of sport' (2009: 222–223).

2  Garry Whannel (2009: 76–77) defines 'sports chatter' as 'a form of exchange, largely between men and tending to exclude women, in which analysis of events and of tactics, of players and of performances blends with anecdote, banter and reminiscence. It serves to underpin the separateness of sport (a world of its own), to promote the circulation of an alternative masculine cultural capital, to reinforce and bind the coherence of those within this masculinist and heterosexist culture, while excluding and distancing those outside it … The combination of chat and statistic, which we could dub "waffle 'n' info", while appearing ephemeral, provides the structure of a core alternative virtual world – planet sport. Planet sport severs its links from the everyday – from the world of work, from the domestic sphere, from politics and even from sexuality. It is a space with its own values, rituals and symbols. Stars, action, gossip, anecdote and banter are all profoundly inward looking and self-referential'.

3  Grant Farred's earlier optimistic reading of ESPN is worth recounting: 'With its penchant for hipness, *SportsCenter* has crafted a distinctive sports discourse, an entirely new way of talking about sport. The ESPN show is that rare venue in which sports presenters borrow intelligently and innovatively from literature, politics and, most important, popular culture, with a special predilection toward the world of hip-hop … Linguistically agile, the vernacular range of [the] presenters … is such that on many occasions the 11:00 o'clock edition of *SportsCenter* offers the viewer an intoxicating intellectual rollercoaster ride' (2000: 100). Farred has subsequently recanted from that position, more recently stating that 'at the moment I wrote the paper, I believed it raised the IQ, but by now it is responsible for the deterioration of all sports talk' (cited in Bérubé 2009: 240). Michael Kimmel suggests that 'sports talk' among men can act as a form of racial healing, allowing conversations to take place that would not otherwise be possible, a form of cross-racial male bonding: 'Sports talk enables conversations across race and class, even if it sometimes offers a false sense of racial healing. It enables men to bond in a pure homosocial world, a world free of the taint of women's presence. It offers the solace of masculine purity, and the cement of those bonds. Sports – and talking about them – is a way for guys to feel close to each other and still feel like real men, feel closer to their fathers and, perhaps, further separated from their mothers. Sports provide a way for men to have their emotions without feeling like wimps. Sometimes, sports serve as the only way for men to talk, to connect, or the only way they can express their emotions at all' (2008: 142–143).

4  See Robert Washington and David Karen when they note: 'We end this review [of sociological literature on sport] with a call to sociologists to make sports more central to our analysis of society … Sociologists, most of whom, we suspect, did not play starring roles on their high school sports teams, have ignored this object of mass attention. While the upper classes have made attendance at other cultural events and institutions (theater, opera, museums, etc.) a component of elite status – and an object of sociologists' attention (!), sport seems to have escaped such appreciation. An institutional and reflexive analysis of sociology would suggest that, in ignoring sport, we have been following the scripts set by the powerful forces both in our discipline and in the larger society. It is time to give sport its due' (2001: 206–207).

5  As a point of comparison, we might note the elevated status that can be achieved even within the domain of popular music. For example, the sociologist Simon Frith is now the Donald Tovey Professor of Music at the University of

Edinburgh (Frith 2007). Frith has thus managed to successfully traverse the field of rock music journalism as well as chairing one of Britain's leading pop music awards (the Mercury Prize), all the while holding an endowed Russell Group Chair. Given the assumed gap between academia and popular sports discourse, it is difficult even to imagine Eric Dunning similarly chairing and presenting the BBC Sports Personality of the Year Award or Michael Messner the ESPY Awards.

6　For a critical survey of the development of the sociology of sport in the US see Ingham and Donnelly (1997) and for Australia see Rowe et al. (1997).

7　My own intellectual journey – though not my present destination – is indicative of many sociologists who study sport. Although I currently work in a 'mainstream' sociology department (which, as I've argued, is not typical), my sociological 'training' is far from traditional, having gained my undergraduate BSc in Recreation Management (an inter-disciplinary degree program that combined sociological, historical, philosophical, economic and management theory approaches to studying sport, leisure and recreation) from Loughborough University, and then a PhD in Sociology from a department of sport, leisure and education at Leeds Metropolitan University. My first job was also within a similar department, the Chelsea School, at the University of Brighton. These were all exceptionally critical and rewarding intellectual spaces, and offered one of the few ways in which it was possible to study (and teach) sport sociology in a serious and sustained way. Yet, within the status-hierarchy of academia, such intellectual routes, departments and institutions are often given short shrift, *regardless* of the quality of the work produced therein.

8　While it is true that sport is often *mentioned* by many major social theorists, sport is rarely used as a primary case study or object through which to develop broader theoretical arguments. In addition to Bourdieu, an exception here might be Norbert Elias, with whom, interestingly, Giddens came into contact during their time at Leicester. It is worth noting, though perhaps this is no more than a coincidence, that the one major sociological theorist who did take sport seriously enough to dedicate more than a passing paragraph or short essay on the topic, is himself a somewhat marginal figure within contemporary sociology. Outside of figurationalist circles it is still the case that Elias's work, despite its flaws, is not given the credit that it perhaps deserves. References to and engagement with his work as a major social theorist alongside the usual suspects, particularly within North American sociology, remain few and far between.

9　MacAloon's (1988) introductory preface fails to mention race at all, nor that Bourdieu starts his argument with an account of black athleticism. Washington and Karen's (2001) otherwise comprehensive overview of sport sociology starts with Bourdieu's essay but neglects to note the racialized example upon which Bourdieu makes his arguments for the double domination of sport sociology/ sociologists. Alan Tomlinson (2004), in his useful critical review of Bourdieu, follows in similar fashion. In contrast, and for a largely successful attempt at re-reading Bourdieu's insights on sport through the prism of black Marxism in order to produce a critical theory of race, class and sport, see St Louis (2009). Similarly, Douglass Hartmann (2002) uses Bourdieu's essay as a way to think through race and sport in his chapter 'Sport as Contested Terrain'.

10　It might be tempting here to quote C.L.R. James's anti-positivistic observation in defending his own part-biographical interpretive approach in *Beyond a Boundary*, 'A sample poll! A sample poll can investigate only what pollsters know, and it cannot do even that properly' (1963/1994: 154). Or Frantz Fanon's even more strident declaration in *Black Skin, White Masks*, that 'It is considered appropriate to preface a work on psychology with a methodology. We shall break with tradition. We leave methods to the botanists and the mathematicians. There is a point where methods are resorbed' (1952/2008: xvi). But I won't. On the severe limitations of using survey methods and opinion polls as the primary way to measure and understand racism, Brown et al. note: 'Because most surveys tap only surface commitment or verbal adherence to ideals, polling data may reveal more about correlation between self-presentation and socioeconomic class than about the persistence of racism ... The gap between what people tell survey researchers and what they actually do or believe is wide, and a very different picture emerges when one moves from political abstractions to routine behavior' (2003: 41).

11 With apologies to the late Howard Zinn.

12 To be clear, James remains invaluable for any critical account of race, sport and politics, as my various epigraphs and general 'Jamesian' method demonstrates. My point, rather, concerns the way in which James is often invoked and with that the thinking on race and sport ends.

13 Other geographical locations are slowly being explored, such as the role of sport within the Middle East (Sorek 2007) and South and East Asia (Hong 2006; Mills 2005). There is also work on race and sport that extends beyond the familiar black/white binary in the United States looking at, for example, aspects of Hispanic identity (Iber and Regalado 2007), Asian Americans (Yep 2009), and Native American peoples (King 2008), as well as work (de)centering whiteness (Kusz 2007). These and other studies are slowly helping to disrupt the deeply Eurocentric foundations of sport sociology, especially as it has come to be practiced and institutionalized within the Anglo-phone western academy. I would like to hope that this book, despite certain omissions, contributes to this ongoing multi-faceted dialogue.

# 1

## Sporting Resistance: Thinking Race and Sport Diasporically

The idea of diaspora offers a ready alternative to the stern discipline of primordial kinship and rooted belonging. It rejects the popular image of natural nations spontaneously endowed with self-consciousness, tidily composed of uniform families: those interchangeable collections of ordered bodies that express and reproduce absolutely distinctive cultures as well as perfectly formed hetero-sexual pairings ... It disrupts the fundamental power of territory to determine identity by breaking the simple sequence of explanatory links between place, location, and consciousness. It destroys the naïve invocation of common mem-ory as the basis of particularity in a similar fashion by drawing attention to the contingent political dynamics of commemoration. (Paul Gilroy)

Sport is a key site of pleasure and domination, via a complex dialectic that does not always produce a clear synthesis from the clash of opposing camps. It involves both the imposition of authority from above, and the joy of autonomy from below. It exemplifies the exploitation of the labor process, even as it delivers autotelic pleasures. (Toby Miller)

I believe and hope to prove that cricket and football were the greatest cultural influences in nineteenth-century Britain, leaving far behind Tennyson's poems, Beardsley's drawings and concerts of the Philharmonic Society. These filled space in print but not in minds. (C.L.R. James)

### Sporting Resistance: Gramsci and Sport

In order to produce a cultural theory of race and sport it is first necessary to map the theoretical terrain in order to judge what of the existing frameworks can usefully be retained, what needs to be revised and what should be jettisoned. Therefore this chapter delineates the core *conceptual problems* of this study and provides a general theoretical framework that seeks to show how the key con-cepts introduced in the previous chapter and developed throughout the book, namely the 'white colonial frame', 'sporting racial projects', 'the sporting black Atlantic' and 'the black athlete', are interrelated and help us towards a more complex way of thinking about race and sport both across time and space.

The chapter proceeds by assessing the ideas of key sport sociologists and historians, in particular the work of hegemony theorists of sport and the definitional framing of sport and modernity provided by the historian Allen

Guttmann. Despite the importance and widespread influence of these ways of viewing sport, it is suggested that a fundamental rethinking is required in order to take into account the significance of race in relation to both theories of social development within the west and the emergence of modern sport. It is argued that a profoundly Eurocentric model of sport's global 'diffusion' continues to haunt mainstream accounts of modern sport's development, producing what I term the Myth of Modern Sport. Seeking to develop an alternative post/colonial theory of sport, the chapter concludes by arguing for a diasporic reading of race and sport that might help to make better sense of the symbolic significance, social impact and political importance of sporting black Atlantic stars and their potential roles as agents of resistance to the logic and practices of white supremacy.

Within the sociology of sport it has now become something of a canonical orthodoxy to date the development of the critical, broadly Gramscian, moment in sports studies to the early to mid-1980s (Carrington and McDonald 2009). In particular, John Hargreaves's (1986) *Sport, Power and Culture*, a socio-historical account of sport, class formation and politics in Britain, and Richard Gruneau's (1983/1999) *Class, Sports and Social Development*, a similar analysis of the social transformations affecting Canadian sport, are often cited as two of the most important monographs produced during this period.[1] This 'turn to hegemony theory' enabled critical scholars to avoid both the latent conservatism of earlier accounts of sport that posited the inherently integrative functionality of sports and the economic determinism of Marxist approaches that tended to read sport solely through the prism of athletic bodily alienation, false class consciousness on the part of working-class fans, and sport's general capitulation to the ideologies of capital. Chas Critcher (1986: 335) noted at the time that for such theorists, 'the way out of the dichotomy between liberal idealism and vulgar Marxism lies in a model of sport as a relatively autonomous cultural practice within more general hegemonic class relations'.[2] Sport, in short, was viewed within such accounts as a contested site wherein the play of power could be found, a cultural site of class domination 'from above' as well as the location for forms of symbolic and material resistance 'from below'.

John Hargreaves (1986: 6–7) clarifies this central analytical point by arguing that 'sport was significantly implicated in the process whereby the growing economic and political power of the bourgeoisie in nineteenth-century Britain was eventually transformed into that class's hegemony in the later part of the century'. In other words, as Hargreaves's book title plainly states, sport has to be located as a central, contested facet of culture, that is itself immersed within the broader circuits of (predominantly although not exclusively) classed power relations. For Hargreaves, in what has now become a somewhat classic formulation of hegemony theory:

> Power resides more in the ability of the hegemonic group to win consent to, and support for, its leadership, and on its ability to pre-empt and disorganize opposition, so that the major forces in society are unified behind the hegemonic group and

forceful, coercive measures against opposition to the pattern of hegemony acquire legitimacy as well. Hegemony is achieved through a continuous process of work: potential resistance is anticipated, organized opposition is overcome and disarmed by broadening and deepening the base of support. Thus alliances with subaltern and subordinate groups are brought off, concessions to and compromises with potential as well as actual opponents are made. (1986: 7)

If the analytical concerns for Hargreaves center around class, sport and British industrialism, then for Gruneau, working through a remarkably similar set of issues from the location of Canada, the interrelationship of sport and class needs to be situated in the context of the study of social development itself. 'Put most simply,' Gruneau (1983/1999: xxix) states, 'I argue that any examination of the changing nature of human possibilities in social development must be drawn ineluctably to a very old sociological problem: the problem of class inequality and domination. It was this problem that defined many of the personal troubles and public issues of citizens in the earliest stages of liberal democracy'. Gruneau (p. 1) centers his study in the context of what he terms the two core problems of sociological theory, namely the problem of human agency and the problem of class inequality and structural change.

Tracing the dialectical relationship between freedom and autonomous play on the one hand and domination and cultural constraint on the other, Gruneau theorizes sport itself as a potentially liberatory space for self-actualization. Gruneau (p. 3) brings to the fore the 'fundamental paradox' of play, namely that it appears as both an *independent and spontaneous* as well as a *dependent and regulated* aspect of human agency. By extension, sport is viewed as a relatively autonomous institutionalized form that embodies play's central paradox: it is a space of freedom, creativity and human expression that can only come into being in the context of formalized rules that govern and delimit its boundaries, ethically, spatially and temporally.

In trying to avoid an overly voluntarist and metaphysical notion of play, as found within the writings of John Huizinga, Gruneau posits a more materialist account of sport, understood as a collective social experience that is actively made and remade by the participants themselves. An account of sport, in other words, that is 'sensitive to the dialectical relationships between socially structured possibilities and human agency' (p. 27). This requires an understanding and analysis of the historical conditions within which these dialectical relationships have taken place in order to map, in precise detail, the nature and consequences of these moments of freedom and limitation. Thus, as with Hargreaves, Gruneau utilizes hegemony as a way to think through the play of power within sport: 'the concept of hegemony allows for the idea of reflexive human agency in a manner not shared by functionalist models of inculcation or socialization' (p. 60).

## 'Additional Considerations': The Limits to Orthodox Hegemony Theory

In these insightful propositions we see both the promise of and limits to what a critical sociology of sport might offer for a cultural theory of race and sport. Hargreaves, Gruneau and other orthodox hegemony theorists, open up a space to think through sports as a modality for freedom and human actualization. Sport is read as a contested terrain wherein competing ideologies of domination and resistance can be traced. Nothing is guaranteed in terms of political outcomes. Sport is neither understood as a freely chosen leisure pursuit somehow divorced from the material conditions of its existence nor is it reducible to those very same economic determinants that would otherwise, and in the last instance, collapse all forms of culture making back into the logic of capital accumulation. Coercion as well as consent is ever present and sports and their participants are viewed as agents in the production of the very social relations from which they derive. Following this line of argument, Gruneau suggests that sports are 'active constitutive features of human experience' (p. 17) that should be analyzed in the context of the struggles over the limits and possibilities of the rules and resources through which they are themselves defined. Thus, depending 'on their association with divergent material interests, the meanings of sports, like all cultural creations, have the capacity to be either reproductive or oppositional, repressive or liberating' (p. 17).

But there are problems with how even these erudite theorists define the nature of political struggle and which forms of human experience are seen as central and which, by default, get cast as marginal. At first glance, these approaches appear to open up the possibility to think through racial formation (as well as questions of gender and sexuality) in the context of broader cultural battles over access to and ownership of sports, the meanings produced therein, and the effects of these contestations on social development more generally. However, such accounts' explanatory powers are rendered partial by their failure to engage in any substantive way with questions of race as well as their limited analysis of the structuring effects of European colonialism *on* class formation and on 'the west' itself.

*Class, Sports and Social Development*, for example, addresses the development of sport in the age of colonialism yet the theory of colonialism presented is significantly underdeveloped and there is a near total absence of any discussion of racism itself.[3] Thus, invoking C. Wright Mills, Gruneau's earlier remark concerning the 'personal troubles and public issues of citizens in the earliest stages of liberal democracy' (p. xxix) fails to acknowledge that for many blacks in North America and elsewhere the 'early stages of liberal democracy' were predicated upon their informal and formal exclusion from the very category of 'the citizen' and thus their reduced capacity to access and formally shape the public sphere. This begs the question, exactly which 'citizens' are being imagined here?

The 1857 *Dred Scott v. John F.A. Sandford* US Supreme Court decision vividly demonstrated that for black people the supposedly inalienable rights that derived from citizenship within liberal democratic societies were always conditional. Liberal concepts of citizenship were, from their very inception, explicitly racialized. In the American context, for example, Melissa Nobles (2000) has shown how the supposedly universal ideals of the Enlightenment and the claims of egalitarianism and liberty that were produced by the American Revolution were born in contradiction with the actual practices of a profoundly racialized American civic society. Nobles observes that racial identity mattered precisely because citizenship and access to the polity were dependent upon it:

> To be free and white and to be free and black were distinct political experiences. Free whites were presumptively citizens. In the early years of the republic, in the absence of federal statutory definition, they became citizens by choosing to support the republican cause and, by the early nineteenth century, by birthright. As citizens, they enjoyed the full benefits of political membership (including the franchise). The citizenship status of free blacks remained unclear throughout the antebellum period. (2000: 28)[4]

These significant elisions flow from how Gruneau (narrowly) defines the founding concerns of sociological analysis. It is not so much that Gruneau fails to 'add' race to his analysis but more fundamentally that his theoretical framework is itself structured in such a way as to preclude any serious consideration of the multiplicity of ideological determinations and inequalities that constitute the social field in the first place. Put simply, Gruneau's class-centric framing of the epistemic foundations of modern liberal democracies derives from his reliance on the 'classic sociological tradition' meaning there is little analytical room for theorizing domination, freedom and play (and hence sport) through anything other than a reified class lens. The weaknesses (as well as strengths) of the classical sociological tradition are then reproduced *in toto* by Gruneau himself.

The 'foundational' problems that Gruneau identifies concern *human agency* and the problem of *class inequality and structural change*. But the concept of 'the human' is left unproblematized. The opportunity to think through the (prior) category of the human, that is who was included and who excluded from this putatively universal nomenclature, is missed. Similarly it is not *social inequality* and the problem of structural change and social development that underpins the analysis but simply *class inequality* that is asserted to be the defining social division. Thus the analysis of the patterns of 'inequality, domination, and subordination in capitalist societies' (1983/1999: 48) starts and ends with social class 'and the particular organization of rules and resources that define class systems' (p. 48). From this premise Gruneau seeks to develop a general theory of industrial society and sport (p. 48) but, again, this 'industrial society' is one that is dislocated from the context of the colonial forms of exploitation and slave economics that made western industrialization possible in the first place (Blaut 1993; Williams 1944/1994).

There is, of course, much debate among economic historians and others as to the precise role of colonialism, the slave trade and the exploitation of slave labor itself in providing the economic stimulus and wealth necessary for the early formation of European and particularly British capitalism, and the extent to which capitalism then relied upon and thus sustained 'New World' slavery. While the dry calculation as to the actual level of profit extracted from the 'costs of investment' remain open to debate, it is undoubtedly the case, as Robin Blackburn (1997) has shown, that the super-exploitation of slaves enabled the development of capitalist industrialization to proceed on a level and scale that would not otherwise have been possible. This is not to argue that trans-Atlantic slavery necessarily 'produced' capitalism, in any simple economic or even political sense, but rather:

> that exchanges with the slave plantations helped British capitalism to make a breakthrough to industrialism and global hegemony ahead of its rivals. It also shows that industrial capitalism boosted slavery. The advances of capitalism and industrialism nourished, in fateful combination, the demand for exotic produce and the capacity to meet this large-scale demand through the deployment of slave labor. The slave systems of the late-eighteenth- and early nineteenth-century New World had far outstripped those of the earlier mercantilist epoch. (Blackburn 1997: 572)[5]

Thus having disavowed race and gender as *constitutive of inequality* in the west, Gruneau's analysis proceeds with such issues safely relegated to epiphenomenal features, allowing the inter-play between capital, slavery and colonialism to disappear as core conceptual problematics.[6] That is not to say that questions of race and gender are completely disregarded. Gruneau is too sophisticated a thinker to simply ignore them and he is clearly aware of the analytical problems that race and gender present for his class-centric framework. But these concerns end up shunted to the conceptual sidelines via the obligatory, unsatisfactory, use of the apologetic endnote. At the start of his second chapter, which is titled 'Problems of Class Inequality and Structural Change in Play, Games, and Sports', Gruneau adds the following endnote:

> I recognize, of course, that there are a great range of social relations beyond class relations which might influence people's collective powers to 'structure' play, games and sports and 'finish off' the range of meanings commonly associated with them. Gender, ethnicity, and religion, for example, all might be identified as influencing resources that can be brought to bear on the structuring of sport ... Yet, I think it important that this issue be understood in the context of the *ensemble of social relations* that define different ways of living in modern societies. In this study I have emphasized the role of class as a central consideration in understanding this totality. It is clear, however, that far more needs to be taken into account and I hope to do this in future work on the intersections of class and patriarchy. (1983/1999: 137, emphasis in original)

Non-class subjectivities are duly acknowledged as important and as 'influencing resources' *on* sport though it is unclear whether these social relations play an *a priori constitutive* role in the making of sport itself. Gender (although not race, which is presumably what the inclusion of 'ethnicity' above refers to) is deemed to be of some importance, but is left out of the current analysis to be included at some later stage. Chas Critcher (1986) argues that such omissions bring into question the degree to which the interventions of Hargreaves and Gruneau in particular offer a truly radical break with previous theories of sport and society. For Critcher the problem is that gender (although, again, notably not race) is central to any critical analysis of sport:

> The principled and theoretical point is that we cannot and must not produce a supposedly radical theory of sport that is as gender-blind (and in some cases, more so) as the conventional wisdom we seek to supplant ... It may be a commonplace observation, though it cannot then be taken for granted, that sport is a predominately male sphere of activity. The theoretical implication of this empirical fact is that sport is one of the most powerful representations of gender relations in contemporary society. The very absence and marginalization of women gives expression to their subordination. (1986: 338–339)

Whether a color-blind approach is equally unproblematic is left unsaid here, although later Critcher does add, in rather tokenistic fashion, that the 'social divisions represented in and through sport are not exhausted by the categories of class and gender; race and age require *additional consideration*' (p. 339, emphasis added). Critcher thus criticizes the failure of hegemony theorists to center gender within the analysis *but does so at the expense of a critical engagement with race*. Race simply becomes another social division, which, we are presumably to infer, has no more significance to the structuring of western societies (and by extension to sport) than 'ageism'. The inability to think race, gender and class concurrently and to explore their points of intersectionality and mutual construction beyond reducing non-class identities to 'additional considerations' has proven to be a serious intellectual obstacle for Gramscian accounts of sport.

In fairness, Gruneau does recognize the importance of colonialism as a central facet of his theory of social development in what he calls the 'unique pattern of Canada's colonial development' (1983/1999: 63). Indeed, he uses the facts of colonialism as a way to rebut overly teleological accounts that rely upon an endogenous theory of social change from the supposedly premodern rural through to the industrial modern nation state. For example, Gruneau acknowledges that Canada 'has a colonial past, and its class structure and cultural formations cannot be understood without some reference to the *dependency relations* it has maintained with colonial metropoles and to its own *internal* relations of dependency and development' (p. 58).

Thus on the one hand colonialism is situated historically as the 'colonial past'. Canada is read as a geo-politically subordinate space to the metropoles (i.e. Britain and France), hence the invocation of dependency theory as a way to think through relations between the 'core' and 'periphery'. But the closest we get to any discussion of the explicitly *racialized* nature of Canada as a *white* settler space is the suggestive but underdeveloped observation that this colonial past somehow has contemporary effects in structuring internal relations of dependency and development. What this actually means is unclear other than the ambiguous sense that forms of social domination from the colonial past influence the post/colonial present. Gruneau suggests at one point that the 'early forms of colonial games and recreation were local, unorganized, and often based on oral traditions that were indigenous to Canada's native peoples or, more commonly, imported from France and Britain and adapted to the Canadian situation' (p. 65). However, we are offered no account as to what these indigenous forms looked like and no discussion as to how these were displaced by the colonial Europeans in the forging of Canadian identity, nor of the violence of white colonialists towards native peoples during this historical moment.

It is apparent then that such an account of colonialism is limited. There is little sense of the *type* of (settler) colonial state Canada was and no discussion of the forms of racial privilege that could be obtained by white working-class European immigrants over the previously settled racialized others. The opportunity to theorize how race acted as an important mediator in the formation of white working-class identities (Roediger 2005) is lost. Colonial relations are locked into the past, negating the ways in which the Canadian state (and the production of Canadian citizenship itself) continues to engage in internal neocolonial practices of dispossession, disenfranchisement and dislocation long after the formal period of external colonial dependency came to an end.

Critical race scholars and post/colonial theorists have demonstrated how discourses of race have served to exclude certain Canadians from the category of national subject. Sunera Thobani, for example, maps the complex processes whereby Aboriginal peoples were compelled to concede land ownership claims in exchange for nominal rights of citizenship that were predicated on destroying notions of collectivism and instituting instead civil institutions based upon private property rights, wage labor and the development of a money-based market economy. Thobani states:

> Citizenship, as the quintessential hallmark of liberal democracy, was thus racialized from its very importation into the country; Aboriginal peoples were granted no democratic space or extension of rights and entitlements within the national political institutions that came to govern their lives. Indigenous forms of sociopolitical system, their organization of rights, entitlements, obligations, and responsibilities which bound the members of these communities together, were simply deemed non-existent and irrelevant by the state ... The subordination of Aboriginal systems of rights by the colonial state was coterminous with, and necessary to, the development of citizenship rights for nationals. Canadian

citizenship, therefore, represented an assault on Native peoples, a drive towards their cultural and political elimination; it articulated relations not only between citizens and their state but also between citizens and Aboriginal peoples as Indians and, hence, as non-citizens. (2007: 82)

For a state that was (and continues to be) fractured by competing Anglophone and Francophone conceptions of nationhood and where the very question of civic rights, group recognition, multiculturalism and belonging have dominated national discussions – 'a land troubled by questions of race and space' as Rinaldo Walcott (2003: 44) puts it – Gruneau's failure to push the analysis into a deeper consideration of how race frames these debates is surprising. The fact that colonial states were, by definition, charged with managing 'difference' and heterogeneity via regulation and repression (Goldberg 2002) does not surface within Gruneau's account.

In this respect R.W. Connell (1999) is correct when he notes in the Foreword to the 1999 reissue of *Class, Sports and Social Development* that despite its undoubted merits, Gruneau's reliance on the Marxism of E.P. Thompson and Raymond Williams was problematic as these authors had little to say about colonialism *per se*. Gruneau himself acknowledges that in addition to being in dialogue with a new generation of Canadian social scientists and political theorists, his analysis was 'greatly influenced by some important work coming out of Britain in the field of "cultural studies"' (1983/1999: xxx). Significantly, in the supporting endnote that lists the key works that influenced his analysis, Stuart Hall's (1978) co-authored volume *Policing the Crisis* is *not* included (Gruneau 1983/1999: 131). While the work of Raymond Williams, Paul Willis, and Hall and Jefferson's *Resistance through Rituals* are all name-checked, the omission of *Policing the Crisis* is significant as this text marks the moment of Hall's intervention against the disavowal of race and the inability to theorize racism on the part of Williams, Thompson and the New Left in general (Farred 2003). *Policing the Crisis* opened an analytical space for the interrogation and reworking of class and class politics to account for imperialism, colonialism and racism that would later be more fully developed by leading black British intellectuals such as Paul Gilroy, Hazel Carby and Kobena Mercer, among others (Carrington 2010).

Connell continues that while colonialism is discussed as an empirical fact, it does not register as a core conceptual issue: '*Class, Sport and Development* has little sense of imperialism as a system, nor of sport as part of a world structure of hegemony in social relations' (1999: viii). Thus apart from occasional remarks, Native peoples are largely written out of the account of Canada's social development and Canada's policies of displacement, disenfranchisement and underdevelopment as a colonial settler state (Bannerji 2000; Mackey 2002) are generally ignored.

In part, as previously suggested, this is due to the failure of class-centric hegemony theorists to theorize the capitalist state – be it marked as a colonial settler state or otherwise – as inherently racialized. David Theo Goldberg (2002) has convincingly argued that the modern nation state, as conceived in the west, was from its very inception racialized and racializing: 'As much as the modern state has been about anything – about increasing bureaucratization and rationalization, about increasingly sophisticated forms of democratization and social control, about the rule of law and the control of capital – it has been about increasingly sophisticated forms and techniques of racial formation, power, and exclusion' (2002: 49; see also Omi and Winant 1994: 77–91).[7]

Similarly, if the treatment and place of Native Canadians is given tokenistic acknowledgment then the position of black Canadians is equally problematic. It is not until the last page of *Class, Sports and Social Development* that the presence of black Canadians is acknowledged. Gruneau's analysis unintentionally propagates what Katherine McKittrick has termed the 'surprise' of discovering blackness in the Canadian context wherein the nation's dominant myths and narratives have served to silence and eradicate black Canada, creating a cartographic erasure of race, or what she labels Canada's 'systemic blacklessness' (2006: 92–97). Towards the very end of the book, Gruneau (1983/1999: 112) acknowledges the significance of the 'noncompetitive games movement of the early 1970s' and the 'important challenges posed by the struggle to equalize opportunities for women or blacks', but goes on to suggest that such interventions 'do not appear to have had much transformative consequence. I believe part of the problem for this has been the inability of these emergent and oppositional movements to offer anything more than mildly reformist strategies' (p. 112).

While acknowledging that the struggles of women and blacks in and around sport have been 'important', these interventions are then dismissed as merely 'reformist'. This is done on the basis that such 'oppositional movements' are both too particular (as opposed, presumably, to the universalist politics of class struggle) and concerned with inclusion *into* rather than transformation *of* capitalist hegemony. Gruneau further argues that such non-class social movements have failed to be transformative because they have lacked a broader vision and theory of freedom. Such reformist politics 'have never really been incorporated into the kinds of oppositional forces (e.g., political parties, unions, etc.) necessary to coordinate various pressures against dominant conceptions of capitalist life and channel them into the construction of *alternative structures*' (1983/1999: 112). For hegemony theorists, the only 'radical' space of contestation is class politics which is eventually read as redundant due to the eventual 'winning out' of bourgeois values over those of the working class. Critcher himself, while critical of Hargreaves and Gruneau on this point, proceeds to duly close down the possibility that sport can any longer offer alternative modes of political struggle, resistance or change. The contestations through which sport marked its formation during the latter part of the nineteenth century and into the twentieth, are, Critcher asserts, largely at an end. Capitalism has proved proficient at incorporating most forms of protest while the State has successfully promoted the notion of 'self-health care' such that sport has become little more than a self-disciplining mechanism supported by various fun-runs, jogging crazes and (internalized) desires for 'regular exercise'.

Thus, just at the historical moment when women and people of color have entered into certain sports in unprecedented numbers, and have challenged the white masculinist ethos of many sports cultures, sport is now read as having reached the end of its hegemonic cycle. The fits of contestation/ resistance that marked sport's development have largely been displaced. All we are now left with is an essentially conservative, and hence ideologically reproductive, culture of modern sport. 'Put in more theoretical terms,' Critcher announces, 'the conservatism of sport is an example of the near-total imposition of capitalist values on a popular culture activity. *The dynamic Process of hegemony has become a fixed state*' (1986: 340, emphasis added).[8]

Now that Critcher, and others, have decided that sport can no longer contribute anything meaningful towards the long revolution of social change, all that is left, we are informed, is to call off the cultural studies search for moments of disequilibrium and resistance: 'if a central part of cultural analysis is the identification of potential sources of contestation, then sport may not deserve a central place. If there is to remain a focus on sport in contemporary society, its validation may be as a study of a set of social practices that converse and do not challenge the existing social order' (1986: 341).

Why hegemony of all concepts has now suddenly and somewhat bizarrely, given its earlier definition, become a *fixed* state within the domain of sports is left unexplained. Quite how we would make sense of the anti-colonial struggles around cricket in the 1950s, the political protests around civil, sporting and human rights that marked the late 1960s, the global anti-apartheid sporting campaigns of the 1970s, through to the debates over gender equality and sexuality of the 1970s and 1980s, and the current struggles over inclusion, belonging and identity that have marked contemporary western sports cultures in the context of multiculturalism, is all left unsaid. The direct implication, however, is that such forms of protest that have challenged hegemonic forces *within* sport do not really count as, in the final analysis, they fail (allegedly) to connect with and to broaden questions of political economy *outside* of sport.

Gruneau (1983/1999: 112) suggests that the struggles 'against bureaucratization, sexual and racial oppression, and the constraints imposed on social life by the hierarchical and repressive features of state power' will only be successful once they locate themselves within 'the broader forms of class struggle' aimed at 'creating a more humanely rational society' (p. 112). We could, of course, easily reverse this injunctive and suggest that it is only when the politics of class struggle takes seriously and locates *itself* within questions of racism and sexual oppression, homophobia and the politics of recognition, that a more democratic and humane society will become possible.[9] Paradoxically, Critcher and Gruneau end up with an analysis of sport's supposed innate conservatism that perhaps owes more to the pessimism of the Frankfurt School – because no obvious signs of class struggle can, apparently, be found anymore, due, presumably to sport's capitulation to the instrumental rationality of capital – than it does to cultural studies' optimism for engaged everyday struggles. William Morgan notes that critics such as Gruneau and Critcher, having failed to find effective forms of class contestation to dominant values, 'pessimistically conclude that sport has little emancipatory potential to speak of, and so deflect our attention to other forms of popular culture. In so arguing, however, they gloss over an important residue of freedom and emancipation embedded in the gratuitous rationality of sport' (1988: 834).

Harry Cleaver reminds us that there are undoubtedly millions of people who engage in athletic activities around the world outside of what he calls the 'capitalist management' of both professional and school sports. Such activity, Cleaver (2009: xxxii) concedes, 'may, effectively, simply reproduce labor power; no doubt some people exercise just to be able to continue working, which is one of the reasons why many businesses … have provided "physical fitness" facilities to their workers. However, some, perhaps a great deal, of athletic activity provides both physical and mental energy that bolsters struggle rather than work for business'. However, even these limited sport/work locales offer ways to rethink active worker struggles. Cleaver continues that when 'waged workers use corporate facilities to regain energy lost on the job so that they can struggle for better working conditions, higher wages or less work, it's a nice piece of *détournement* (as the Situationists might say)' (p. xxxii).

But, Cleaver suggests, most athletic activity that escapes capitalist management probably takes place beyond the walls of corporations. Rather than succumbing to the belief that sport no longer offers anything other than self-alienating activity, we should instead orientate radical accounts of sport towards those spaces that escape, defy and rearticulate the instrumental rationality of capital. Developing this broadly 'autonomist' reading of Marx, Cleaver concludes:

> Reversing Marx's analysis of the four kinds of alienation, we can postulate that non-alienated athletics would presumably involve: (1) athletes' control over their own activity in individual and collective self-expression, (2) activity that creates bonds among players, (3) activity whose 'product', whether immediate satisfaction or spectacle, would be under the control of the players and (4) be organized as a creative realization of human species-being. Have such non-alienated athletics existed? Can we find moments of such non-alienated activity? When, where and to what degree? Determining the answers to these questions requires finding and analyzing examples of self-organized sports … But does the absence of organized 'movements' mean the absence of self-organized athletic activity that contributes to social struggle, and potentially to revolutionary struggle? I don't think so. (2009: xxii–xxxiii)

Class-centric hegemony theorists miss out on precisely those forms of sporting resistance to the logics of contemporary commodified sport, that, for example, can often be found within black recreational sporting spaces through which sports become a modality for self-actualization and the reaffirmation of previously abject identities (Carrington 1998a, 1999). Thus, despite the always obligatory reference to C.L.R. James,[10] we end up with undoubtedly learned and in many ways theoretically sophisticated accounts of the formation of modern sports in the west, but accounts that can only achieve their degree of conceptual and theoretical precision by negating the historical reality of European colonialism that produced ideas about race and that saturated the very categories of 'class', 'the west' and even, as we shall see, 'sport' itself.

What is required, then, is a critical theory of sport that remains attuned to the fact that 'imperialism and the invention of race were fundamental aspects of Western, industrial modernity' (McClintock 1995: 5); a cultural theory of sport that can begin to think of race, gender and class as 'articulated categories' that come into existence in and through each other, rather than seeing them as discrete and distinct realms of social experience in which class is always understood, in the last instance, to be the primary category of analysis.

## Sport, Colonialism and the Primitives

Modern sport was born in the age of colonialism. The formal codification of many of the sports that would eventually achieve a dominant position within the global sports market took place during a period when European colonialism was at its height. While historians often trace the antecedents of modern sports back to sixteenth and seventeenth century Europe, and in some cases earlier still, the spectacular growth and institutionalization of the physically competitive activities that we recognize today as 'sports' occurred more recently. The period from the late eighteenth to the late nineteenth century witnessed the sportization of European folk games into an assemblage of rule-governed and institutionally sanctioned cultural pursuits. Local and regional variations became increasingly regularized. By the end of the nineteenth century, national, and soon after international, sets of standardized rules and codes of conduct had been established for most sports. This was seen as a desirable principle (if not quite yet universally practiced and not without dispute as to *which* set of rules would prevail) that reshaped how sport would and should be played. Thus the Enlightenment urge to map, demarcate and master both the physical and social environment was reflected in sport's material development. The heterogeneity of disparate, sometimes chaotic and often unruly pastimes largely gave way to the formalization of homogenous, ordered competitive sports that in turn would provide the locus for modern forms of identity and identification.[11]

National sporting institutions, as Barry Smart suggests, 'brought order and coherence to competitive sport within the territorial boundaries of the nation state. They introduced and regulated local, regional and national competitions and in turn promoted the prospect of international sport' (2005: 36).

This moment saw the rapid establishment of bureaucracies that would assert their rights as 'governing bodies' to oversee how actual bodies would in fact be allowed to play. This process was most clearly evident in the extraordinarily large numbers of sports that were codified and institutionalized within Britain alone during this period. Significant examples included the Royal and Ancient Golf Club of St Andrews (1834), the Football Association (1863), the Rugby Football Union (1871), the Amateur Athletic Association (1880), the Amateur Boxing Association (1881), the Lawn Tennis Association (1888) and the Rugby League (1895), among others.

This sporting history, of course, maps directly onto the period, as Edward Said puts it, 'of unparalleled European expansion' (1978/2003: 41) when, from around 1815 until 1914, European direct colonial rule dramatically increased from 35 to 85 percent of the world's surface. The two great imperial powers of that time, namely Britain and France, are also the two countries that did most to institute the national and international codes of sporting conduct and governance. This has led many historians to argue that sports are an example of western cultural diffusionism *par excellence*. Where the Empire went, so did the sports of the colonizers. This dominant historical narrative of sport's evolution tends to locate it as a singularly European and modern invention. The origins of the many forms of competitive team games found across the globe today are more often than not traced back to Victorian Britain. Here, special attention is given to the role of school masters and the graduates of Britain's leading public schools in shaping not just the formal rules but the very ethos of modern sports that became defined by a logic of muscular Christianity and codes of martial masculinity that sought to produce virile and physically supreme white Christian imperialists of healthy mind and strong body (Mangan 1998). Thus, an 'imperial masculinity consonant with empire-building became a gender imperative' (Mangan 2008: 1083).[12] The historian J.A. Mangan notes:

> With some justification, it may be claimed that the New Imperial Britain of the late Victorian and Edwardian eras attempted to socialize a young elite into attitudes fundamental to the ambitions of the respective political regimes. This conditioning involved values based on four interlocking spheres of sociopolitical consciousness: the need to establish an ideal of selfless service to the state; the need to establish a sense of racial superiority as a cornerstone of this selflessness; the need to establish and maintain an imperial chauvinism; and the need to engender uncritical conformity to the values of the group. A major purpose of this interlinked set of values was to create a 'martial middle-class' ready to serve the nation in the plethora of its imperial struggles in both societies ... In the late Victorian and Edwardian eras, games in schooldays and hunting in post-school days represented, ensured and institutionalized upper-class support for martial imperialization. (2008: 1101)

Even sports that are now perceived as largely or uniquely American affairs are still regarded in their inception as reactions to or extensions of a more general European/British diffusionist trend. Thus games formerly played in Britain were often modified in the colonies to produce new 'national pastimes' as an explicit rejection of Anglophile associations (in America rounders becomes baseball). Or, conversely, certain sports were taken up by colonial settler communities precisely to maintain a link to the motherland, even where such adaptations at once functioned to produce national mores that were connected to but distinct from notions of Englishness (such as the embrace of cricket in Australia). Thus, the varied global reactions to cricket, that most symbolically English of sports, is seen as a shorthand way to chart the entire history of Britain's imperial successes and failures. 'From the remnants of wickets and bats,' Allen Guttmann asserts, 'future archeologists of material culture will be able to reconstruct the boundaries of the British Empire' (2004: 77).

Sports are seen to have 'diffused', largely unmodified, from the European center outward. Where non-western sporting forms were found by the colonizers these were either 'supplanted' and displaced or subjected to a process of 'modernization' such that 'traditional games' eventually conformed to the logic of modern sport (Guttmann 1994: 3–4). Although there is debate as to what the key motivators were for this process, be it (economic) capitalism or (rational) modernity, or some combination of the two, and latterly whether such cultural process should properly be labeled cultural *imperialism* (read as imposition) or cultural *hegemony* (read as negotiation), the underlying concept of *sporting diffusionism* from which these debates spring (see Guttmann 1994) is itself rarely challenged.

Even when there is a questioning of the sports diffusionist model this is largely done from *within* an avowedly European-centric framework. While there is much discussion as to *how far back* we can trace the antecedents of modern sport – seventeenth century France rather than Victorian Britain, or further to the period from the Middle Ages to the Renaissance, or even to classical antiquity – and disputes as to the role of various European states in shaping these developments, these debates rely on a more or less self-enclosed theory of endogenous European cultural development. Mention of athletic pursuits in other parts of the world, normally Japan, India and China, is sometimes made and occasionally an acknowledgment is given that similar forms of physical culture can be seen in the ancient civilizations of Central America, but these tend to be treated as discrete local variants that do not directly affect, except as interesting points of comparison, the central story of *the* history of sport which is read as a largely internal European affair.[13]

Allen Guttmann's (1978) Weberian typology of modern sports, first expounded in *From Ritual to Record: The Nature of Modern Sports* which defined sport not so much in terms of chronology but rather by a set of interrelated formal-structural characteristics, has become the standard, if occasionally contested, definition within sport history and beyond.[14] Drawing on anthropological work on the relationship between play and social structure, an account is offered of different types of play that range from basic games of chance and mimicry to more complex forms of competition that involve various levels of skill and strategy. It is suggested that 'primitive' societies are marked by simple forms of spontaneous play, whereas advanced societies develop more complex forms of rule-bound play. Historical change occurs through a latent evolutionary progression from the primitive, to the ancient and medieval, and eventually to the modern. Thus, as societies become more complex so do their forms of play. 'Structured games mirror structured society', as Guttmann (1978: 10) summarizes it. This structuralist account is then used to provide a set of seven core characteristics that are claimed to define and distinguish 'modern sport' from that which came before: these characteristics are secularism, equality of opportunity, specialization of roles, rationalization, bureaucratic organization, quantification and the quest for records (1978: 16).

On this basis, Guttmann implies that the 'primitive' (never clearly defined and left somewhat vague as to its precise meaning) is incapable of producing sport.[15] 'Primitive cultures', suggests Guttmann, 'rarely have a word for sport in our sense. If we hold strictly to our definition of sport as a nonutilitarian physical contest, we may be tempted to say that primitive men had no sports at all' (1978: 16). This argument is based on the notion that 'primitive cultures' are ontologically incapable of producing sports due to their assumed inability to make adequate distinctions between the profane and the sacred within the social structures of their societies, hence their lack of 'secularism' renders them incompletely modern. However, Guttmann pulls back from this 'temptation' to permanently expunge the primitive from the domain of sport. Guttmann (1978: 19) suggests that such '[d]ogmatic proclamations of negative universals ("Primitive peoples have *no* secular sports") are unwise'. In the very next sentence, Guttmann continues to suggest that, nonetheless, 'sports, as opposed to "physical exercises", may indeed have entered the lives of primitive adults primarily in conjunction with some form of religious significance. It is a fault of our own pervasive secularism that we tend to underestimate the cultic aspects of primitive sports' (p. 19).

Despite such cautions, underpinning Guttmann's framework, a framework that has been foundational to much sociological work on sport, is a series of problematic binaries. These operate to distinguish the modern from the traditional, the west and the rest, Europe and its Others, and ultimately the rational civilized moderns contrasted against the irrational violent primitives who, we are told, can barely even speak the language of sport. Rather than contesting whether or not these particular seven characteristics really do define and distinguish modern sports, I want instead to critically assess the preconditional assumptions and tropes of alterity that infuse the approach itself.[16]

Within the logic of such modernization theories, the primitives are located outside of modern time and space (and by extension sport). The primitives are not simply pre-Enlightenment European subjects, as these are separately designated as the ancients (which can therefore include the Aztecs as much as the Athenians, as both have complex if not fully developed civilizations unlike, presumably, the primitives) and the medievalists.

Defining modern sport is not just a question of chronology. Sport signifies something deeper about the very meaning of western modernity and its constitution. Modernity is cleansed of violence and violence itself is read as a characteristic of the primitive. So a sport such as American football, with its ritualistic, linguistic, symbolic and actual forms of bodily violence that would otherwise render it 'primitive', is instead reframed as an example of a civilizing practice that helps to dissipate latent forms of evolutionary violence that still reside within the modern subject, allowing for a relatively harmless cathartic release of aggression. Thus, since 'football combines primitive elements with a sophisticated complex of teamwork and strategy, it seems especially well suited for its dual function as a model of modern social organization and as an occasion for atavistic release' (Guttmann 1978: 135). The complex patterning of rule-governed behavior that makes sport possible, combined with the techniques and strategies that are prereq-uisites for success, indicate that what appears to be a primitive activity of barely concealed violent excess is in fact an example of how the modern western subject defines itself via the very notion of emotional control, cog-nitive calculation and bodily mastery: 'football requires a complex strategy. It is more than neanderthalic mayhem' (Guttmann 1978: 124).[17]

We get a clearer sense as to who 'the primitives' are when Guttmann describes *modern day* 'Zulu soccer players of Durban, South Africa' (1978: 18) as exhibiting some of these anti-modern tendencies. Guttmann qualifies his attempt to project contemporary black Africans back into pre-history by suggesting that such athletes are 'not, strictly speaking, drawn from a primitive society' (p. 18). Instead, Zulu football players are 'members of a transitional culture between tribal and modern social organization' (p. 18). From this we can deduce that African 'tribespeople' are the real primitives, while Zulu players with their superstitious pre- and post-game rituals are caught in a 'transitional culture' between western modernity and African tradition – neither fully primitive any more since they have discovered football, but not fully westernized either, as they still cling to their irrational forms of witchcraft and sorcery.[18] Thus, South African Zulus, standing in for the (semi-)primitive, manage to turn even something as thoroughly modern (read British) as Association Football into an object almost unrecognizable to the western eye: 'Their game, soccer, is the most widespread of modern ballgames, but their perception of the game assimilates it to a way of life anything but modern' (p. 18).

The primitive thus becomes the Other through and against which the modern sporting self is defined. Primitive games can never be sports and the closer an activity is to that which the primitives play, the less it becomes sport. Thus Guttmann contrasts ancient Greek athletic contests not so much by their distance *from* modern sports but rather by their very *closeness to* primitive games: 'Although Greek sports may be conceived of as the ancestors of modern sports, the physical contests of Olympia and Delphi were culturally closer to those of primitive peoples than to our own Olympics' (1978: 20).

Even children of the Enlightened west (including here the supposedly economically advanced and civilizationally complex Japanese) are better able to grasp the requirements and core characteristics of modern sport than those doomed to socialization within primitive culture, where counting and even numeracy itself are, apparently, so weak as to barely figure within the primitive's developmentally truncated society. Thus the teleological impulse of the modern subject to rationalize, master and quantify, that is, *to be able to reason*, is simply lacking in the underdeveloped primitive who is destined never to understand let alone appreciate sport:

> There can hardly be an American, a Frenchman, or a Japanese who did not, as a child, while playing alone, count the numbers of consecutive times that he or she tossed a ball into the air and caught it again. If one can throw, one can count. One *must* count. It is a childish game that is far more typical of modern than of primitive society, where quantification is not a *modus vivendi*. (Guttmann 1978: 47)

In short, the primitive mind is incapable of complex thought, hence the primitive produces a simple social structure wherein the play of the primitive remains underdeveloped, lacking the complex, multi-dimensional elements of calculation, quantification, secularism, specialization of roles and so on, that are claimed to define western, and hence modern, sport. This in turn means that there is little possibility for 'sport' for the primitive, who even when shown how to play the game distorts sport into something irredeemably Other.

### Sporting Diffusionism: Rethinking the Myth of Modern Sport

Some critical reflections on this theory of sport are in order. J.M. Blaut (1993) has convincingly argued that 'rationalist' accounts of the modern versus the primitive are based on a series of problematic and in some cases simply erroneous historical, anthropological and geographical claims. Blaut demonstrates how 'rationality' itself, as a discourse, was central to the justification of colonialism. Far from being a neutral description of objective social forces, relations and ways of thinking, the invocation of rationality operated as an ideological framework for explaining the 'superiority' of European economic and political progress compared to the rest of the world. The rationality of western science was at the same time a defining feature of its own self-definition (how science came to know itself) and also an important way to allocate and sanction social inequalities both between the 'west and the rest' as well as within western liberal democracies.

Hence 'rationality' was used during the eighteenth and nineteenth centuries to construct the very concept of the white, western, masculine self and became one of the key justifications, as was argued earlier, for why certain subjects, more often women, Native peoples and blacks, should be restricted from the public sphere and hence from citizenship due to their supposed inherent *irrationality*. Enlightenment scholars thus made rationality into a defining characteristic of European history. As Blaut (1993: 96) puts it, European thinkers unquestionably accepted and propagated this myth: 'Europeans became more rational as history progressed, just as children acquire rationality in the course of ontogenetic development. Ancient people had been not merely less intelligent, but also much more governed by emotions and passions than by intellect, just as is the case with modern children.' For the non-European, colonial tutelage would be the mechanism through which the colonized could eventually achieve some level of parity with the colonizer. Revolts by the colonized, who decided that they neither wanted nor required such paternalistic overseeing, were seen as irrational, violent outbursts, further confirming their stunted cognitive growth and limited ability to learn from the master.

The 'primitive mind' was deemed incapable of abstract thought, being driven instead by emotion. The primitive's own language was an outward sign of the fundamentally child-like mind. Blaut argues that this barely concealed racist doctrine underwent important changes during the middle of the twentieth century as 'modernization' theory sought to displace the cruder versions of this account. Thus:

> 'Colonial tutelage' gave way to 'diffusion of modernizing innovations'. Non-Europeans no longer were 'natives', and no longer were described as 'childlike'. In place of the notions of 'primitive mind' and 'primitive language' came the notion of *traditional mentality*. Non-Europeans are 'traditional' in two senses: they lack 'modern cognitive abilities', that is the ability to think theoretically and scientifically, and they lack 'modern attitudes' of the sort that push a person to achieve higher things, to reject the old, and so on. (1993: 98)

Rationality becomes not simply a descriptor of Modern Man but more importantly a way to explain social change itself. Non-Europe is stagnant and traditional because it *lacks the agent of change*, that is rationality. Today this sense of superiority is rarely attributed to racial or biological difference but, Blaut suggests, in the background of modernization theories lies the old colonial assumption of simple ontological difference: 'causality is consigned to the impenetrable mists of ancient history, with perhaps an occasional speculation about ancient free-living European peasants or the evils of Oriental despotism, or with ritual citation of Max Weber. For many historians, I suspect, the idea of European rationality is simply axiomatic. Europeans, for whatever reason, are just built that way' (1993: 104).

This way of understanding world events was not simply an account of colonialism and its effects but was a part of the colonial project itself; it was, as Blaut's title puts it, *the colonizer's model of the world*. This model assumes that Europeans are the makers of history, that Europe shapes, dictates and drives forward social change while the rest of the world stagnates and is dragged along. The world is thus imagined as having a center and a periphery, an Inside and Outside. The Inside leads, the Outside follows, the Inside innovates, the Outside imitates (Blaut 1993: 1). Diffusionism, or rather what Blaut terms *Eurocentric diffusionism*, establishes itself as a theory to explain the way cultural processes move across and over the world's surface as a whole, flowing 'out' of the European sector and towards the non-European: 'This is the natural, normal, logical, and ethical flow of culture, of innovation, of human causality. Europe, eternally, is Inside. Non-Europe is Outside. Europe is the source of most diffusions; non-Europe is the recipient' (p. 1).

Underlying this worldview are a series of linked claims that suggest that the largely autonomous rise of Europe, or the 'European miracle', occurred largely because Europe was more advanced and progressive compared to the other regions of the world prior to 1492. Blaut (1993: 59) defines the myth of the European miracle as:

> the doctrine that the rise of Europe resulted, essentially, from historical forces generated within Europe itself; that Europe's rise above other civilizations, in terms of level of development or rate of development or both, began before the dawn of the modern era, before 1492; that the post-1492 modernization of Europe came about essentially because of the working out of these older internal forces, not because of the inflowing of wealth and innovations from non-Europe; and that the post-1492 history of the non-European (colonial) world was essentially an outflowing of modernization from Europe. The core of the myth is the set of arguments about ancient and medieval Europe that allow the claim to be made, as truth, that Europe in 1492 was more modernized, or was modernizing more rapidly, than the rest of the world.

Europe's internal qualities and unique characteristics are seen to have enabled it to achieve its dominant world position, thus Europe's 'modernization' starts from within (unique innovation) and spreads outwards (diffusion). Modernity itself becomes a singularly European achievement, such that modernity is European, Europe is modernity. Colonialism is seen to be exterior to this formation, therefore 'colonialism must mean, for the Africans, Asians, and Americans, not spoliation and cultural destruction but, rather, the receipt-by-diffusion of European civilization: modernization' (1993: 2).

Drawing on and critiquing extensive data on issues such as supposed biological differences between the 'races', demographic rates of population growth, environmental factors, differences in technology, through to accounts of the state, class and family structures, Blaut shows that such issues cannot in fact be shown to have 'caused' the dominance of Europe. Instead Blaut argues that the key factors were the huge increase in wealth that flowed into Europe from the sixteenth century onwards as a result of colonization, married to fortuitous circumstances of Europe's geographical location in the midst of the expansion of both trade routes and emerging capital markets.[19] Blaut further suggests that although the model of essential European uniqueness and racial superiority has been challenged over the years, and the more overtly racist versions have been discredited and rejected, there still remains a general framework of imagining human history that falls back upon this narrative. Blaut describes it as a form of 'tunnel history' that relies on the idea that the world does in fact have an Inside and an Outside, and that what really counts (historically speaking) is what has occurred Inside.

This model is then used to explain cultural diffusionism. Diffusionism in and of itself is not necessarily problematic when taken simply to refer to the spread and movement of ideas from one place to another that leads to cultural development and change. But there is still the prior issue as to when and where certain innovations came about, the problem of 'independent invention'. Diffusionism becomes Eurocentric when it is premised on the notion that true invention tends to occur in one place (Europe) where innovation and change are seen as a natural state and that similar forms of invention could not have happened elsewhere. The basic cause of this innovative progress is the sense of European spirit or special intellect (the muscular Christians of Britain's public schools) 'that leads to creativity, imagination, invention, innovation, rationality, and a sense of honor and ethics: "European values"' (1993: 15). Non-Europe's 'stalled progress' is thus seen to be a result of this intellectual and spiritual lack. Other regions are sometimes acknowledged to have been 'rational' to some degree at certain points in their history, such as the Middle East during biblical times, China, Japan and India at moments, although other parts of the world such as Africa 'are unqualifiedly lacking in rationality' (1993: 15). The only way for such backward regions to progress out of their stagnant traditionalism is to come into contact with and benefit from European ingenuity: colonialism.

Another key proposition that underlies the Eurocentric diffusionist model is the claim that ideas that diffuse back into Europe must be uncivilized and atavistic – black magic, sorcery, witchcraft, vampires and the like. Moving farther away from civilized Europe is akin to traveling backwards in time: 'Thus the so-called "stone-age people" of the Antipodes are likened to the Paleolithic Europeans. The argument here is that diffusion works in successive waves, spreading outward, such that the farther outward we go the farther backward we go in terms of cultural evolution' (1993: 16–17).[20] The key characteristics of the European Inside come to be understood as inventiveness, rationality, abstract thought, theoretical reasoning, discipline, adulthood, sanity, science and progress. In contrast, the non-European periphery gets defined in terms of imitativeness, irrationality, emotion, instinct, practical reasoning, spontaneity, childhood, insanity and stagnation (1993: 17). Blaut argues that this classical form of European diffusionist thought materialized during the nineteenth century largely to justify the exploitation of colonized lands and to explain why Europe held such dominance:

> The era of classical diffusionism was the era of classical colonialism, the era when European expansion was so swift and so profitable that European superiority seemed almost to be a law of nature. Diffusionism, in its essence, codified this apparent fact into a general theory about European historical, cultural, and psychological superiority, non-European inferiority, and the inevitability

and absolute righteousness of the process by which Europe and its traits diffused to non-Europe. Diffusionism then ramified the general theory into innumerable empirical beliefs in all the human sciences, in philosophy, in the arts. (Blaut 1993: 26)

It could be argued therefore that the history of sport (as dominant narrative) and sports history (as discipline) are indebted to a model of Eurocentric diffusionist thought and logic. In tautological fashion, Europe is seen as the unique incubator of all forms of meaningful physical activity that can be properly understood as sport, and sport is defined in such a way as to preclude other forms of physical culture from being sport. Europe is the place where sport 'starts' and then 'spreads' on the wings of colonialism. There is little cross-cultural diffusion (Blaut 1993: 167) in the development of sports themselves and the influence of sporting forms from outside of Europe on 'modern' sports is either downplayed or ignored altogether. Deeply racialized and gendered colonial tropes of social development infuse the narrative. Binaries, often invoked unproblematically, of modernity/tradition, the rational/irrational and the civilized/primitive, work to structure how modern sport is defined and understood. Barry Smart, for example, drawing on the work of Michael Oriard, notes that 'the process of transformation from pre-modern, disorganized and disorderly recreational activities to formalized modern sports has been described as an evolution from "primitive physicality" to "reason and order"' (2005: 31).

Sporting modernity becomes reliant upon a notion of 'tradition' in order to produce itself. That the irrational is often an outcome of rationality itself and further how the civilized only comes into being through acts of great savagery (genocidal war, systemic torture, colonial subjugation) is disavowed so as to produce a clear line of ontological distinction between the (masculine) modern and the (feminine) primitive. As Sandra Harding notes, '[t]radition is always represented as feminine, primitive, in modernity's past. Modernity is obsessively preoccupied with contrasting itself and its distinctive features with these Others; the feminine and the primitive always appear in modernity's narratives as the negatives to modernity's positives' (2008: 202).

We might better formulate sport, then, as embodying not so much modernity and its self-declared properties – secularization, rationality, meritocracy and so on – but rather the *incomplete, partial and paradoxical* elements of competing modernities that refuse to be disavowed. Much ideological work has been necessary to hide modern sport's supposedly premodern, anti-rational tendencies – gratuitous violence, unpredictability, emotional instability – while these very attributes are actually *constitutive elements* that help to create sport's appeal and to sustain its very possibility. Put another way, sport, like the claims of liberal democracy – cultural tolerance, ethical decency, civic nationalism and citizenship, deliberative philosophical reason – should be conceptualized more as a particular physical manifestation and representation of modernist myths born of colonial conflict than as the actual instantiation of the 'truth' of such claims. These are, as Robert Young following Jacques Derrida puts it, the colonizer's *white mythologies*: 'western philosophy, through which the west in part defines itself, operates by exactly this kind of double logic which conflates a myth with a universal truth, the myth of reason for Reason' (Young 2001: 421).

Just as 'citizenship' is imagined as a universal category somehow free from the colonial state from which it was produced, so 'sport' is magically removed from the conditions of white supremacy, patriarchy and colonial governance to which it is necessarily tied. The ideological work necessary to produce a de-racialized and genderless liberal theory of citizenship is the same work undertaken to fabricate sport as actually constituting a meritocratic and egalitarian space of 'fair play' and 'level playing fields', conflating in its own way sporting myth with universal truth, the myth of rationality for Modern Sport. Sport's 'power' comes as much from the ability of some to exclude others from rightful participation and ownership as it does from its own 'intrinsic' rules and characteristics. The non-sporting 'primitive' turns out to be, in the end, a fiction of the western imagination.

### Césaire and Fanon Played Football Too

Given both the centrality of sports to the cultural project of western colonialism and the deeply problematic way colonialism itself has been figured within much of the scholarship on sport, it might be expected that critical work on colonialism and race would have much to say about sport. But this is not so. It is not even the case that sport is discussed, analyzed and then found to be institutionally and/or politically deficient as regards the broader politics of subaltern resistance and colonial struggle. It is, simply put, that sport as a cultural practice and social institution is not considered or theorized at all. Students have to read long and hard to find even a cursory examination of sport within the texts of leading post/colonial theorists and critical scholars of race and culture.

Opportunities to theorize sport beyond a footnote mention tend to be missed within the work of contemporary post/colonial scholars. For example, Anne McClintock's *Imperial Leather: Race, Gender and Sexuality in the Colonial Contest*, expertly explores, in part, 'the historically different but persistent ways in which women served as the boundary markers of imperialism, the ambiguous mediators of what appeared to be – at least superficially – the predominantly male agon of empire' (1995: 24; see also 1995: 361). Agon, of course, implies a sense of contest, a gathering for the act of physical competition often associated with the sporting games of ancient Greece (Hawhee 2004: 15). However, agon here is stripped of its sporting connotations thus closing down the opportunity to theorize sport itself as distinct cultural practice that was immersed in deeply gendered forms of imperial boundary making. Hence there is little discussion within McClintock's hugely influential text of sport as a key aspect of colonial racial governance and the use of gender and race as markers of empire.

However sport is not completely absent. Sport is briefly mentioned in the context of describing the polyvocal and contradictory nature of fetishes, including 'national fetishes such as flags, team colors and sport mascots' (1995: 202). This is later followed up in a discussion of the ways in which racist nationalist movements in South Africa, adopting the Nazi use of fetish political symbols, used 'spectacle' as a way to produce racial narratives of white hyper-nationalism. Challenging Benedict Anderson's argument that print technology was the key factor in the mass mobilization of, and identification with, nationalism, as the access to such print forms was limited to a relatively small literate elite, McClintock instead suggests that national collectivity has been primarily mobilized and managed via certain forms of mass commodity spectacle:

> nationalism inhabits the realm of fetishism. Despite the commitment of European nationalism to the idea of the nation-state as the embodiment of rational progress, nationalism has been experienced and transmitted primarily through fetishism – precisely the cultural form that the Enlightenment denigrated as the antithesis of Reason. More often than not, nationalism takes shape through the visible, ritual organization of fetish objects – flags, uniforms, airplane logos, maps, anthems, national flowers, national cuisines and architectures as well as through the organization of collective fetish spectacle – in team sports, military displays, mass rallies, the myriad forms of popular culture and so on. (1995: 374–375)

These are all provocative and suggestive observations but are left at that. In a later section McClintock discusses the historical marginalization of women within the political activities of the African National Congress and women's struggles to express their political agency, quoting one activist as saying: 'We women can no longer remain in the background or concern ourselves only with domestic and sport affairs. The time has arrived for women to enter the political field and stand shoulder to shoulder with their men in the struggle' (1995: 381). It is interesting that sport is relegated, alongside the domestic sphere, to the realm of the *non-political*. 'Sport' and 'domestic' coupled as standing against and outside the 'political field'. We might begin to rethink the politics of sport, space and colonialism in light of an important aspect of McClintock's general argument that the 'domestic sphere', far from being a space of apolitical private activity, was in fact infused with the tensions of imperialism while domesticity itself denoted a particular social relation to power, or as she puts it, 'as domestic space became racialized, colonial space became domesticated' (1995: 36). In other words, and as I explore in more detail in the following chapter, we perhaps need to consider further how sport's assumed apolitical location paradoxically allowed it to become the site for politicized contestations over the permissible limits to black freedom.

When sport is occasionally mentioned within the texts of critical theorists, this is largely done by way of a passing comment that is rarely theorized or expanded upon or via the almost obligatory engagement with C.L.R. James and his work *Beyond a Boundary*.[21] The latter, in and of itself, is not necessarily a problem. James's work and ideas remain indispensable for any critical approach to sport and colonialism. The problem lies in that *simply invoking James is seen to be sufficient*, as though that in and of itself completed the intellectual work necessary to think of sport and the colonial. The totality of what can be learned about the sport/race/colonialism conjuncture starts and ends with *Beyond a Boundary*. It is as if cricket in the Caribbean *circa* 1950–63 constituted and exhausted the possibilities to talk about sport, colonialism and politics.

The intellectual project that might *start* with questions of biography and politics, embodiment and freedom, sport as art versus sport as social control, is stymied by the repetitive and perfunctory 'Jamesian nod'. Sport is recognized as somehow important. James's weaving of the wider socio-historical forces that frame cricket is duly and respectfully acknowledged, and with that the critical theorist can leave the murky, populist waters of sport and get back to reading eighteenth century novels and nineteenth century poetry. And all this despite James's emphatic declaration that such bourgeois pursuits and cultural products merely filled space in 'print but not in minds' (1963/1994: 64). It would seem that post/colonial theory's over-reliance upon reading culture as text and treating literary texts as the sum of culture itself, derived largely because the field is so dominated by literary theorists, means that 'culture' often gets reduced to a purely linguistic frame, rendering forms of *physical* culture problematic, and hence largely ignored.

This is a problem not just for post/colonial theory but for cultural studies in general. That is, despite claims that such inter-disciplinary fields have developed a post-Leavisite model of understanding culture that embraces and takes seriously 'the popular', there is still a reluctance and inability to read certain popular cultural forms like sport on their own terms. Put differently, film, music (including popular music), fashion, television and so on, can all be rendered as signifying texts that can then be 'read' by simply reworking the familiar tropes of literary criticism in order to make sense of the play of ideology, power, politics and identity found within the contested spaces of popular culture and everyday life. However, sport's very physicality, the emphatically embodied nature of its performance, the sheer diversity of sporting forms and sites, and its assumed 'non-art' instrumental rationality, make it a distinct cultural type that cannot easily be 'read' in the same way as these other cultural practices. To analyze sport only as a 'text' means losing much of sport's power (both as spectacle and in terms of its ludic appeal) as a form of competitive human movement, embodied practice and emotional release. We still lack a conceptual language, in other words, with which to make sense of sport except by trying to apply ways of reading sport that have been developed elsewhere to sport.

In the 400 or so pages of Edward Said's (1994) *Culture and Imperialism*, sport hardly surfaces. There is a passing reference, though no analysis, to European football cultures (1994: 36), and then sport appears again via a brief engagement with C.L.R. James, who is variously described as a remarkable sportsman (p. 295) and athlete (p. 298), and a cricket correspondent (p. 299). But there is no analysis or even commentary on any aspect of sport, despite James's insistence on the necessity of such work. A strikingly similar absence, I would argue, can be observed in the works of other major post/colonial theorists such as Gayatri Spivak and Homi Bhabha.

It would be wrong, however, to claim that there are no writers engaged in developing a post/colonial theory of sport. Important exceptions would include the occasional writings on sport by the sociologist Brett St Louis and the literary theorist Grant Farred, both of whom, interestingly, completed their doctorates on C.L.R. James and who have both produced important books on James's work and life (see Farred 1996; St Louis 2007). The point, rather, is that such work, insightful as it is, remains sporadic and limited to a very small group of scholars. Writings on sport and post/colonial theory remain marginal compared to, say, the field of post/colonial literary studies, or even other cultural areas such as film, music and art.

There is some indication that sport studies scholars are slowly becoming aware of the potentially important contributions of post/colonial theory in rethinking some of the established narratives of sport. For example, John Bale and Mike Cronin's (2003) edited collection *Sport and Postcolonialism* and Stephen Wagg's (2005) edited book *Cricket and National Identity in the Postcolonial Age* both make important contributions to the emerging literature. Yet even here the engagement remains limited. Many of the contributors to Bale and Cronin's volume use the term 'postcolonial' in a rather descriptive sense that simply refers to analyses of sport in societies that were once formally colonized, thus negating a deeper discussion that would require examining the ways in which, and as noted earlier, such societies are 'post/colonial' in different and significant ways (see Hall 1996; McClintock 1995: 12–13). The use of post/colonial theory is also limited, reduced in many of the chapters to simply quoting Edward Said in either the introduction or conclusion.

A similar approach structures Wagg's book, where the key figures and concepts within post/colonial theory are largely ignored: Homi Bhabha is cited once in a footnote in one chapter, Gayatri Spivak is quoted once, second hand, in the introduction, and Said does not appear at all (similarly Césaire and Fanon have a marginal presence in both books). While this is not necessarily problematic – there are many ways to engage in post/colonial critique without simply quoting lines from the theorists most associated with the post/colonial turn in social theory – it does suggest that the serious engagement of post/colonial theory *and* sport, that challenges some of the epistemic claims of both sport itself and sport theory as produced in the west – that is, the serious intellectual work of deconstructing and decolonizing ways of understanding sport – has yet to fully arrive.

Part of this reframing of post/colonial theory would require us to not skip over those moments when sport rudely inserts itself into the political narrative but rather to consider what is at stake if we take the academically debased subject of sport seriously as an object for analysis. Historians and biographers have tended simply to note without further exploration the impact of certain key anti-colonial theorists' engagement with sport. Thus even an historian as sophisticated and adept as Robin Kelley, and someone who has himself written well on C.L.R. James in the past (see Kelley 1996), mentions in passing, but does not analyze, the friendship between Aimé Césaire and Léon-Gontran Damas that was formed in part through their footballing encounters (Kelley 2000: 11). Thus we have no sense as to whether or how such a sporting *cum* political relationship resembled that, say, between James and Learie Constantine in another context, in the development of negritude, Francophone concepts of solidarity, and of their wider understandings of freedom and embodied struggle.

Similarly, David Macey (2000), in *Frantz Fanon: A Life*, notes Fanon's love of and passion for football, a sport that he would play weekly in La Savane, Martinique, and a space whose physical landscape Fanon describes in less than glowing terms in *Black Skin, White Masks* (1952/2008: 8). Yet, notes Macey (2000: 58), 'for the boy who played football there it was a space of freedom and offered a welcome escape from the choking grid of narrow streets'. We might want to further consider, then, these relationships between freedom and space, of escape and movement, of revolutionary violence both real and symbolic, and of embodied emancipation, themes that drive much of Fanon's analysis of the native's constant striving to break free. Just as scholars have spent considerable time, and rightly so, on analyzing James's understanding of politics and political struggle via a reading of cricket's impact on James's development as an intellectual, we might also want to remember that Césaire and Fanon played football too.

### Diasporizing Sociology

There are problems with even some of the more self-reflexive accounts of globalization (whether theorized in terms of the modernity or capitalist axis), which in their periodization and conceptualization adopt a Eurocentric viewpoint, disavowing the complex relationship between globalization and imperialism. Such accounts, it has been argued, are simply 'a theory of Westernization by another name, which replicates all the problems associated with Eurocentrism: a narrow window on the world, historically and culturally' (Pieterse 1995: 47; see also Hesse 1999). Further, one of the central problems in attempting to think through the issue of global cultural formation and identification across and beyond national borders is that sociology itself and the social sciences in general have been so closely tied to the development of colonial nation states. That is, sociology has too often taken, sometimes uncritically, the nation as its primary object for analysis, unproblematically equating 'society' with 'the nation state', thus neglecting the fact that the production of knowledge and the theories produced therein are as much tied to the nation state formation process as the world such theories tried to explain. Increasingly attempts have been made to re-position sociology in such a way that it problematizes the nation/society couplet and takes a wider, 'transnational', historical approach. As Jan Nederveen Pieterse (1995: 63) argues, such a rethinking requires a new sociology, based 'around notions such as social networks (rather than "societies"), border zones, boundary crossing and global society. In other words, a sociology conceived within the framework of nations/societies is making place for a post-inter/national sociology of hybrid formations, times and spaces' (see also Urry 2003).

One such move has been to utilize the concept of *diaspora* as a way to reconceptualize current sociological debates concerning 'the global' versus 'the local' and the related discussions on cultural change and identity formation. One of the effects of the 'turn to diaspora' has been that in trying to understand the processes of global cultural formation, conceptualizations of *space* have been radically rethought. Space is understood in this context as operating *between* and *within* the outer-national, national, regional and local – sometimes occupying all of these locations simultaneously. This way of considering forms of attachment, solidarity and identification has challenged the tendency towards 'natural', territorially fixed, notions of the relationship between culture, community and place.

This new approach can be seen in the attempts by various post-national writers to rethink these traditional categories in terms of the external *flows* through which local space is constructed and the multiple *routes* through which identity is produced. Examples from across the social sciences of this analytical shift that began to emerge during the late 1980s and 1990s would include Doreen Massey's (1994) invocation of what she terms a 'global sense of place', Jan Nederveen Pieterse's (1995) concept of 'translocal space', and Avtar Brah's (1996) 'diasporic space'. What all of these accounts have done is to loosen notions of space and place from necessarily being rooted to specific bounded notions of geographical location, and relatedly to show how culture and identity are constructed through complex political and ideological discourses. Space is rethought as a hegemonic site for the maintenance and challenging of power relations that regularly exceed the delimitations of the nation state. Thus our understanding of space is transformed 'when it is seen less through outmoded notions of fixity and place and more in terms of the ex-centric communicative circuitry that has enabled dispersed populations to converse, interact and even synchronize significant elements of their social and cultural lives' (Gilroy 1994a: 211). The claim to *diasporic* identifications can be seen as a way to re-articulate wider political struggles in order to re-claim localized and discrepant histories. This means that the term *diaspora* becomes 'a signifier, not simply of transnationality and movement, but of political struggles to define the local, as distinctive community, in historical contexts of displacement'

(Clifford 1994: 308). In short, the concept of diaspora helps to challenge static and at times Eurocentric models of history and place defined through predictable binaries such as inside/outside, internal/external and core/periphery.

The need to write such diasporic histories of global culture (Pieterse 1995: 63) can be seen most readily in the evocative writings of Paul Gilroy, who has worked to transcend the national(ist) paradigm that dominates social science theorizing. Instead, Gilroy proposes a counter-history of modernity based on the inter-cultural and transnational formation of an alternative black public sphere, or what he calls 'the black Atlantic' (Gilroy 1993a). Seeking to introduce 'new intermediate concepts, between the local and the global' (Gilroy 1992: 188), he takes the Atlantic as a unit of analysis in order to 'produce an explicitly transnational perspective' (1992: 192). Gilroy uses the ship as a metaphor, or what he refers to as a 'chronotope', as the conceptual link to think through the travels between Africa, Europe and the Americas that literally and figuratively framed the black Atlantic world – the moving location from where black moderns made the transition from slave ship to citizenship. The image of the ship as a 'living, micro-cultural, micro-political system in motion' (Gilroy 1993a: 4) helps to focus our attention on 'the middle passage, on the various projects for redemptive return to an African homeland, on the circulation of ideas and activists as well as the movement of key cultural and political artefacts: tracts, books, gramophone records, and choirs' (p. 4).

In attempting to extend 'existing formulations of the diaspora idea' (1996: 22), Gilroy further defines the black Atlantic as 'a deterritorialized, multiplex and anti-national basis for the affinity or "identity of passions" between diverse black populations' (1996: 18). The concept of the 'black Atlantic' thus 'provides an invitation to move into the contested spaces between the local and the global in ways that do not privilege the modern nation state and its institutional order over the sub-national and supra-national networks and patterns of power, communication and conflict that they work to discipline, regulate and govern' (1996: 22). Black Atlantic intellectuals from Phillis Wheatley to Fredrick Douglass, and W.E.B. Du Bois to Richard Wright, have challenged western myths of progress and the tropes of European civilization that denied the importance of slavery, colonialism and white supremacy in the very founding of the west, while developing a deep scepticism towards the pull of racial nationalisms as the primary basis for modern identity formation. Historically speaking, Gilroy contends, the black Atlantic has been propelled by the need to 'supply a counter-narrative of modernity that could offset the wilful innocence of those Eurocentric theories that ignored the complicity of terror and rationality and in so doing denied that modern racial slavery could have anything to do with the sometimes brutal practice of modernisation or the conceits of enlightenment' (Gilroy 1996: 25).[22]

As with the field of post/colonial studies, sport has rarely figured within diaspora studies and African diasporic scholarship in particular (for example, on the non-analysis of sport within key texts see Clarke and Thomas 2006;

Cohen 2008; Dufoix 2008; Edwards 2003; Kanneh 1998; Okpewho et al. 2001). The focus, up until now, has tended to be on the exchanges and movements of writers and intellectuals (but rarely athletes) and within the cultural sphere on cultural practices such as music, film, dance and literature (but seldom sport).[23] If diaspora theorists have neglected *sport* as an object worthy of study then, similarly, the concept of *diaspora* has been surprisingly overlooked within the sociology of sport. With the exception of the occasional reference to the Irish diaspora, key theorists within the sociology of sport have largely failed to engage the expansive literature on diaspora as a way to consider sporting identifications, flows and processes that exceed nation state frameworks, instead relying on traditional approaches found within globalization theory that are then simply applied to sport (see Bairner 2001; Giulianotti and Robertson 2007; Maguire 1999, 2005; Miller et al. 2001).[24]

In contrast, I want to suggest that the notion of the *sporting black Atlantic* can be productively used as a way to comprehend the lives, travels, migrations and significances of black athletes over the past two hundred years or so, in the shaping of a sporting black diasporic space. This approach allows us to comprehend the *political* connections between athletes, intellectuals, writers and political leaders, the historical role of sport within black politics, the reasons why black Atlantic athletes could invoke forms of racial and inter-racial solidarity across and beyond national lines, and why, when such athletes achieved a degree of fame and power, they were able to pose threats to the racial order of the day, be they located in Europe, North America, the Caribbean or elsewhere within the African diaspora.

## Towards a Genealogy of the Sporting Black Atlantic

Peter Fryer notes that Africans were living in Britain during the third century, as part of the Roman imperial army, long before the 'English' arrived (1984: 1). Later, during the sixteenth century, as British imperialism and the mechanisms of slavery gathered pace, a sizeable, though disparate, black population began to emerge – most working as servants – as it became fashionable in some quarters to have black slaves amongst the household servants (1984: 9). By the middle of the eighteenth century, particularly in the 'slave-ports' of Liverpool, Bristol and London, it was possible to talk of an emerging self-conscious, and politicized, black community living and working in Britain and engaged with the radical working-class politics of the time. It is into this history of migration that we need to locate black Atlantic athletes, as they formed an important part of these emerging communities. As Peter Linebaugh and Marcus Rediker observed, during the eighteenth century black men and women arrived in increasing numbers in London where they found various forms of work as 'cooks, boxers, writers, and especially domestic servants, day labourers, and seamen' (1990: 243; see also Linebaugh and Rediker 2000). Black athletes, primarily as boxers, and often as freed-slaves, became central icons in publicly symbolizing the fraught transition of black people from former slave subjects to nascent public citizens. Extending this connection between sport and politics, play and freedom, and as I pursue in more detail in the following chapter, Fryer makes an interesting and suggestive connection between the political significance of black radicals such as William Cuffay, William Davidson and Robert Wedderburn, and black pugilists of the eighteenth century: 'It is hardly surprising that, of the black people living in Britain in this period whose names are known, so many were fighters of one sort or another: political activists or prize-fighters' (1984: 227).

Early figures who exemplified many of the key characteristics of the sporting black Atlantic world would include boxers such as Bill Richmond and Tom Molineaux. Born in Staten Island, New York in 1763, the son of Georgia-born slaves, Richmond was brought to England aged fourteen in 1777 as a servant by a British General. Richmond attended school in Yorkshire where he took up many sports, including boxing both as a fighter and later as a trainer, becoming 'the first black athlete to receive international acclaim' (Rhodes 2006: 47). Richmond became a well-known and liked figure in London's social circles, finishing his days as a publican in London's West End and running a boxing academy until his death in 1829 (Fryer 1984: 445–454; See also Rhoden 2006, ch. 2).

Following Richmond in winning his freedom through boxing, Tom Molineaux, born on a Virginia plantation in 1784, came to England in 1803 working as a deckhand on a ship. Molineaux eventually met Richmond who helped to establish him on the boxing circuit. Record crowds turned out to see Molineaux fight and he became a popular figure in early nineteenth century British sporting life, referred to in the press at the time as 'the American Othello' and 'the Great American Moor' (Rhodes 2006: 40). He eventually died in poverty, aged only 34, in Ireland (Fryer 1984: 445–454). Although Molineaux's life was short (although not unexceptional for the time), his impact was significant. The American journalist William Rhoden notes in *Forty Million Dollar Slaves: The Rise, Fall and Redemption of the Black Athlete*, that while Richmond had stumbled into professional sports, Molineaux's decision to pursue a career as a professional athlete was a deliberate one: 'Molineaux was a pioneer in many ways, not least of which was in showing how the tools of enslavement could become the tools of liberation' (2006: 47). The arena of sports enabled such men to momentarily transgress some of the racial constraints imposed on their lives and in so doing they began to redefine black political claims to freedom. By publicly challenging western racial sciences' proclamations concerning the supposed inherent degeneracy and weaknesses (moral, intellectual *and* physical) of the 'black race', and by performing on a national and increasingly international stage that was largely unattainable for blacks in any other cultural sphere at that time, their sporting achievements acquired a symbolic and therefore political significance that transcended the circumscribed space of the sporting arena.

The Atlantic, and the role of ships, remained central for this emerging 'transnational' athlete. As a mode of transportation, sometimes as a form of early employment, and as a way of practicing the skills needed to compete in Europe's boxing arenas, these black men quite literally fought their way across the Atlantic. Indeed, the hidden history of not only black boxers, but footballers, rugby players, cricketers, cyclists and athletes in Britain, from the eighteenth century through to the Victorian and Edwardian periods, is only now beginning to become recognized (see Fryer 1984; Green 1998; Vasili 1996, 1998), helping to complement the more extensive histories already available on African American athletes (see Bass 2005; Miller and Wiggins 2004; Sammons 1994; Shropshire 1996; Wiggins 1997; Wiggins and Miller 2003). This work is important in connecting questions of imperialism to the cultural, political and economic development of modern Britain, and the positioning of blacks as agents within that history, as well as in helping to establish the empirical basis for a broader, inter-connected global history of the sporting black Atlantic.[25]

Thus, the sporting black Atlantic can be defined as a complex, transnational cultural and political space, that exceeds the boundaries of nation states, whereby the migrations and achievements of black athletes have come to assume a heightened *political significance* for the dispersed peoples of the black diaspora: the sports arena thus operates as an important symbolic space in the struggles of black peoples for freedom and liberty, cultural recognition and civic rights, against the ideologies and practices of white supremacy. For black peoples throughout the African diaspora, such cosmopolitan formations and outer-national identifications operate as powerful counter-claims against nation state nationalisms and conservative mono-cultural ideologies, with their associated assimilationist drives. Such self-consciously selected identifications often cut across national borders, reconfiguring what it means to be a national subject, providing transnational routes of identity formation. Contemporary diasporic identifications with transnational stars such as Serena and Venus Williams, Kobe Bryant, Lewis Hamilton, Tiger Woods and Usain Bolt challenge narrow, prescriptive ways of thinking about national identity in the context of sport. These sporting identifications re-articulate elements of the black Atlantic sporting world alongside figures from music, fashion, film and television, and occasionally with black political icons too, in the production of new forms of black identity.

It is important to note that the cultural configurations of the sporting black Atlantic are not merely a reflection of underlying economic determinants driven by the circuits of global capitalism. Rather, such diasporic formations move between and beyond the processes of corporate sports globalization, though they can never, of course, be entirely divorced from them. They exist in productive tension with the logic of late capital, sometimes complicit, sometimes critical. As James Clifford (1994: 302) notes, 'contemporary diasporic practices cannot be reduced to epiphenomena of the nation-state or of global capitalism. While defined and constrained by these structures, they also exceed and criticize them'.

Although the antecedents of the sporting black Atlantic stretch back centuries, we can perhaps date the emergence of the first truly global and internationally known 'star' of the black diaspora to the appearance of the African American boxer Jack Johnson in the first decade of the twentieth century. When Johnson beat his fellow American Jim Jeffries in 1910 to retain the world heavyweight championship its international significance, which attracted front page headlines across the world, could be seen not only in the racial uprisings that took place in many American cities as jubilant blacks celebrating in the streets were attacked by whites, but throughout the British colonies too where similar forms of unrest were reported (Green 1998: 177).

Such was the fear of Johnson's impact on the white racial order that an exhibition match between Johnson and the British boxer William 'Bombardier Billy' Wells in 1911 was eventually banned by the then Home Secretary Winston Churchill, due in part to fears about the effects of a Johnson victory in instigating further demands for political equality throughout the British empire. While the campaign, led by the Baptist pastor F.B. Meyer and supported by religious elites and Edwardian moralists, to prevent the Johnson versus Wells bout was publicly framed as an ethical concern about the barbarism of boxing itself, the underlying racial significance was apparent to many at the time. Jeffrey Green notes that the very fabric of the British imperial order was deemed to be at risk should Johnson be allowed to fight the British champion: 'A huge empire would come close to collapse if a British soldier met a Texan labourer in west London. The empire was indeed a confidence trick' (Green 1998: 176). Similarly, as Phil Vasili points out, the success of sporting black Atlantic figures, such as Johnson, struck directly at the core fears of white supremacist logic, namely: 'Black athletic success as symbolic expression of the degeneracy of the White "race"; the consequent rewards of this success as a threat to White economic (and social) superiority; that the collective confidence and spiritual sustenance given to Black communities by Johnson as an heroic model may inspire emulation' (1998: 185).

Johnson is important as a diasporic figure precisely because, as a boxer, his sport was located within the colonial routes that reshaped the world, thus his impact on racial formation was global and not just national. This is not to deny the importance of Johnson as an African American figure but simply to note that many of his major bouts occurred *outside* the United States, their significance impacting black communities 'locally', be that in Australia, Europe, Canada, the Caribbean or Central America, as much as in the United States itself. William Rhoden notes that American baseball was in fact 'unofficially' integrated in 1945 when Jackie Robinson signed for the Montreal Royals, *two years before* Robinson would famously step onto the field for the Brooklyn Dodgers. Rhoden (2006: 119) continues: 'Interestingly, three of the greatest landmarks of African American sports history took place outside the United States, a testament to this country's

# The Daily Mirror

THE MORNING JOURNAL WITH THE SECOND LARGEST NET SALE

| No. 2,087. | Registered at the G. P. O. as a Newspaper. | TUESDAY, JULY 5, 1910 | One Halfpenny. |

## JOHNSON, THE NEGRO PUGILIST WHO BEAT JEFFRIES, THUS RETAINING THE TITLE OF HEAVY-WEIGHT CHAMPION OF THE WORLD.

Yesterday's great boxing contest at Reno, Nevada, between Jack Johnson and James J. Jeffries, resulted in a victory for the negro, who thus retains the title of heavy-weight champion of the world. Born thirty-two years ago, the giant negro won his present title in December, 1908, when he defeated Burns, at Sydney. Last October Ketchell made an attempt to regain the title for the white race, but was beaten by Johnson, at San Francisco. Above is a recent photograph of Johnson.

Figure 1.1    *Jack Johnson: The 'Giant Negro' (1910) The Daily Mirror (reproduced courtesy of Mirrorpix)*

57

racist response to the emergence of black sports figures: Tom Molineaux fought for the boxing championship in England; Jack Johnson won the championship in Australia; and Jackie Robinson integrated baseball in Canada.'

We might go further and note that, in addition to the three examples identified by Rhoden, many of the most iconic moments in African American sporting history occurred *outside* of the United States, the African American athlete often associated more with international geographical markers than with American ones. We think, for example, of Jesse Owens in Berlin, Althea Gibson winning the French Open and Wimbledon, Wilma Rudolph in Rome, Tommie Smith and John Carlos in Mexico City, and Muhammad Ali in the Congo and Manila. This is why it is important to read the politics of race and sport diasporically in order to understand how nominally 'national' star athletes come to have a global significance that both alters their relationship to their countries of origin and enables transnational forms of identification to be established within the broader cultural circuits of the black Atlantic. Historically, for many African American athletes, leaving the United States enabled their development as athletes and provided a means to obtain status, fame and wider social significance that was often curtailed in their 'home' country.

Many contemporary accounts significantly underplay this aspect of Jack Johnson's career and his diasporic impact. Similarly, Johnson's time abroad is often overlooked or downplayed, seen simply as time spent 'in exile' rather than a formative period in defining his own identity as a thoroughly modern subject. Johnson thus gets reduced to simply being an African American athlete who bravely fought Jim Crow racism and became an iconic (if sometimes overlooked) figure within the self-enclosed story of America's long journey from the 'original sin' of slavery through to historic election of the nation's first African American President. This is of course all true. But it is not all that Johnson is and was. As I examine in more detail in the following chapter, Johnson also helped to challenge and change the meaning of race itself, in America and throughout the western world, and in so doing helps us to understand the complex *diasporic relations* between race, sport and politics.

## Notes

1 David Rowe describes Gruneau's text as an 'influential early study' (2004: 105) and Hargreaves's later work as '[o]ne of the most cited sociological works deploying Gramsci' (2004: 106). Other key texts from this period that pursued similar themes would include Jennifer Hargreaves's (1982) edited collection *Sport, Culture and Ideology* and John Clarke and Chas Critcher's (1985) *The Devil Makes Work*.

2 In contrast, Alan Bairner argues that many of the key works mentioned here *do not* in fact rely on Gramsci and his writings but on a somewhat watered down, cultural studies version of hegemony theory that owes more to the ideas of Raymond Williams and Stuart Hall than to the Italian revolutionary Marxist

himself. As Bairner (2009) notes, 'Gruneau's ... only direct reference to Gramsci is in a footnote where his role in the development of the concept of hegemony is acknowledged but it is made apparent that Gruneau's particular concept owes more to Williams and Stuart Hall. Interestingly, neither Gramsci's *Prison Notebooks* nor any of his other writings appear in the book's bibliography' (2009: 200); and '[w]hile it is true that Hargreaves is frequently cited in this context, his work contains little direct reference to Gramsci' (p. 200). Thus Bairner argues that Gramsci's ideas have been misused and abused by sociologists of sport, and others, who have placed too great an emphasis on notions of domination by consent rather than by coercion and have been too eager to find examples of resistance in sporting cultures that are focused on non-class identities instead of material economic struggle. Bairner calls for a return to a more orthodox reading of Gramsci and the sublimation of cultural struggles around identity to material class struggles over the economic: 'there is a real need for the rehabilitation of Marxism at the level of theory, as well as for Marxist sociologists to stand up and pronounce publicly on the economic injustices of our age. As for Marxist sociologists of sport, the time has surely come for fewer apologies and for a more robust defense of the subtleties of historical materialism as properly understood. If that means retrieving the argument that our identities can best be understood in terms of economics, then so be it' (2007a: 33; see also Bairner 2007b). For a critique of Bairner's 'back to basics' position see Andrews (2007) and Carrington (2007).

3   I focus on Gruneau's text not because I think it is uniquely flawed (it is, rather, symptomatic) nor that that book's omissions render it without merit. It is arguably the most important theoretical exegesis of sport and society produced in the last thirty years and has rightly remained an essential reference point for anyone interested in developing a critical sociology of sport. My critique, rather, is an attempt to supplement and not supplant Gruneau's analysis by identifying what I take to be a fundamental omission of the 'hegemony theorists' of this period, and who continue to exert a strong influence over contemporary debates, without seeking to repudiate the entire framework, as William Morgan (1994) attempts to do.

4   We should note too that depending on the context women and the 'lower classes', especially those without property, could be similarly excluded. While white working-class men could, under certain conditions, gain entry into the sphere of citizenship, the barriers to women and to blacks remained more fundamental. David Theo Goldberg notes: 'Lacking the necessary degree of rational capacity to underpin self-determination, blacks and women accordingly lack the possibility of self-directed labor and so of self-mastery. Reduced rationally to working for white men, blacks and women are incapable accordingly of modern state citizenship. It must follow, *of course*, that to imagine it otherwise presumptively would be to take on that irrationality rendering one at once illegitimate and so unqualified for citizenship. The struggle of women and people characterized as not white to acquire voting rights in the first half of the twentieth century as a consequence was as much about clearing away these insidious background assumptions as about the formalities of legal change' (2002: 48–49).

5   J.M. Blaut makes a stronger claim with regard to the demand for commodities and other goods that colonialism both produced and itself needed: 'there would not have been an Industrial Revolution had it not been for the immense demand that Europeans were able to generate in the colonies, and it was this

fact that, more than anything else, pushed the Industrial Revolution forward' (1993: 206).

6   Gruneau himself, in a reflexive postscript to the 1999 reissue of his book, concedes this point: 'my appeal to "classical" sociology in *Class, Sports and Social Development* largely precluded any discussion of global core–periphery relations beyond Europe and North America, as well as racial and gender oppression. The die was cast the moment I linked the idea of "classical" sociology as a distinctive style of analysis to a more specific set of "classical" sociological problems associated with agency, freedom, and constraint in the development of industrial capitalism, defined primarily with respect to social class. The focus on "internal" social dynamics and struggles arising in conjunction with industrial capitalism was undertaken with progressive intentions, but it nonetheless reproduced many of the Eurocentric and Androcentric assumptions implicit in the canonical foundation of sociological history' (1983/1999: 123).

7   Again, see Thobani (2007: 25): 'Likewise, the Canadian state can be accurately characterized as having been an overt racial dictatorship up until the mid-twentieth century, as it organized the governance of Aboriginal populations through the Indian Act and upheld racialized immigration and citizenship legislation to produce a homogenous and dominant white majority.'

8   Critcher's own conceptual commitment to reading questions of ideology and politics almost exclusively through a de-racialized class lens is all the more striking (and in some ways disappointing) given his role as a co-author of *Policing the Crisis* (Hall et al. 1978). It could be argued that while that text marks an important and pivotal moment within British cultural studies in opening up a space to think seriously about racism in British politics, it is not until the 1982 publication of the CCCS's *The Empire Strikes Back* that a complete rethinking of the race and class conjunctural is produced, and that provides an adequate account of autonomous black political struggles against racism (Carrington 2010; Harris 2009).

9   Gruneau (1983/1999: 127) acknowledges this problem in his 1999 postscript when he writes: 'my discussion of class and sports actually would have been far stronger if I had explored the mutually constitutive relations between class and such things as masculinity, internal colonialism, overt and subtle racism, and racial nationalism'.

10  Gruneau, in a footnote, summarizes *Beyond a Boundary* as 'a study of sport, class forces, and third world development' (1983/1999: 132), thus reducing both the politics of James's anti-colonialism into a neutered framework of development theory and collapsing the specificity of race itself back into class. C.L.R. James makes it into Hargreaves's text (1986: 42) with a single, passing, unreferenced quote.

11  There were, of course, other forms of embodied activity that attempted to offer an alternative ethics and performative physicality to this particular model of sport such as the *Turner* movement that stressed exercise and a concept of physical culture more grounded in expressive gymnastics than competitive, score-driven sports. We might also consider in this context, as a critical form of resistance and challenge to the logic of colonial sport discourse, the development of *Capoeira*, a cultural form that continues to exceed western definitional boundaries separating sport, art, dance and music.

12  It should be noted that there is some disagreement among historians as to whether muscular Christianity *or* martial masculinity was the dominant ethical

code among British elites during this period. This dispute is not central to my argument here.

13 Occasionally mention is made of pre-Hellenic sporting antecedents in ancient Egypt. But sporting time is really seen to 'start' with ancient Greece, thus relegating Egypt to a pre-historical moment that also serves to underplay the extent to which Egypt influenced the political, intellectual and cultural formations of the period that is seen as the 'birth of civilization'. Ancient Greeks are nearly always read as the true 'ancestors of modern sports' (Guttmann 1978: 20). Thus, as Allen Guttmann (2004) phrases it in his 400-plus page historical overview of sport, *Sports: The First Five Millennia*, the chapter discussing Egyptian sports is titled 'Before the Greeks'. Discussions on ancient Greece rarely start by framing them as 'After the Egyptians'.

14 Some classicists have questioned the distinction often made between the sporting pursuits of antiquity and those of modernity. For example, Tom Hubbard (2008) suggests that Guttmann's modernization theory of sport's historical development that sharply contrasts modern sports with the games found in antiquity is a difference based on degree rather than substance, with many of the 'modern' features of sport also found in the games of ancient Greece.

15 The primitives, for Guttmann, appear to include Native Peoples defined by land and location, such as the 'Ifugao of the Philippine Islands' (1978: 43) and the 'Polynesians of Tikopia' (p. 47) and other 'tribespeople'.

16 See Richard Giulianotti (2005: 22–24), who suggests that all of the core characteristics of modern sports are empirically questionable. For example, sports in the west, and particularly in the United States, remain deeply inscribed with forms of religiosity, social stratification rather than meritocracy still largely determines access to and involvement in sport, and sports themselves are valued by many according to autotelic pleasures and a sense of the aesthetic that often negates the desire for records and extrinsic reward.

17 Although Guttmann's rhetorical flourish is presumably not meant to be taken literally, the invocation of Neanderthals nevertheless suggests that the modern subject is not just being contrasted with the primitive but quite literally the pre-human.

18 We might usefully compare this with Ann McClintock's fascinating discussion of nineteenth century commodity racism and the Pears' soap advertisements wherein the native, having found a bar of soap, is seen to have discovered modernity itself: 'The Birth of Civilization' as one advertisement put it (McClintock 1995: 223–224).

19 The structure and 'uniqueness' of European modernization, the extent to which different European countries modernized at different times and speeds, and the primary factors behind the so-called 'rise of the west' continue to be debated by historians and historical sociologists. For example, see the exchange between Bryant (2008), Elvin (2008), Goldstone (2008) and Langlois (2008).

20 See also McClintock when she notes: 'colonized people – like women and the working class in the metropolis – do not inhabit history proper but exist in a permanently anterior time, within the geographic space of the modern empire as anachronistic humans, atavistic, irrational, bereft of human agency – the living embodiment of the archaic "primitive"' (1995: 30).

21 For example, Neil Lazarus (1999) discusses sport in a chapter in *Nationalism and Cultural Practice in the Postcolonial World*, but largely in the context of cricket via James and *Beyond a Boundary*, E. San Juan, Jr (1999) mentions

cricket in passing, via James, in *Beyond Postcolonial Theory*, as does Timothy Brennan (1997) in *At Home in the World: Cosmopolitanism Now*.

22  Brent Hayes Edwards (2001) provides a useful genealogical mapping of the concept of diaspora within black studies. Edwards suggests that the term 'African diaspora' emerges in the 1960s and is coterminous with the institutionalization of black studies departments in the United States. Edwards suggests that, 'as a frame for knowledge production, the "African diaspora" … inaugurates an ambitious and radically decentered analysis of transnational circuits of culture and politics that are resistant or exorbitant to the frames of nations and continents' (2001: 52).

23  Gilroy himself is perhaps an exception here. Although music remains Gilroy's paradigmatic cultural form of choice, his more recent work shows a more sustained attempt to think critically about sport.

24  There are some recent exceptions to this. For examples of sociological work on sport that does engage the concept of diaspora and the black Atlantic, see Burdsey (2006), Andersson (2007) and McNeil (2009). See also the historical work of Runstedtler (2009).

25  Another early twentieth century figure whose life exemplifies the passage and transnational movement of black Atlantic athletes is the boxer Larry Gains. Born in Toronto, Canada, at the turn of the twentieth century, Gains travelled to Europe to pursue his career as a boxer (after being inspired by meeting Jack Johnson when he was a teenager), and moved throughout Europe fighting in Paris (where he met a young Ernest Hemmingway), Stockholm, Milan and Berlin, before he finally settled in England, where he became British Empire champion (he was prevented from fighting for the British heavyweight championship because of his color). Ironically, despite being inspired to become a boxer after meeting Johnson, it was Johnson's very success in challenging the ideology of white supremacy, and the subsequent drawing of the 'color line', that prevented Gains from competing for the official world heavyweight championship. In Gains's autobiography he provides an interesting account of how the passage across the Atlantic was more than just a means of transportation, and a chance to practice the skills he would later require, but importantly a way of gaining acceptance into male working-class culture, through his ability and status as a boxer. In a chapter headed 'Slow Boat to England', Gains writes: 'every time I trained on deck, a big, tough-looking stoker who had done a bit of fighting would stand watching me … Well, eventually he came over and said he would like to spar with me. I was grateful for the chance of a work-out. But I soon realised that this was to be a little more than that. All work on the boat came to a standstill, and everyone came crowding around … His intention quite clearly was to knock me out. He came in, swinging with both hands. He was really a brawler and nothing more. I couldn't miss him and eventually I stretched him out on the deck. They carried him below. After that, the attitude of the crew changed drastically. Overnight, I became everybody's friend, a man of respect. Their judgements were simple, almost primitive. If you were the best fighting man aboard, the boat belonged to you' (Gains, no date: 27–28).

# 2

## Sporting Redemption: Violence, Desire and the Politics of Freedom

The first thing the colonial subject learns is to remain in his place and not overstep its limits. Hence the dreams of the colonial subject are muscular dreams, dreams of action, dreams of aggressive vitality. I dream I am jumping, swimming, running, and climbing. I dream I burst out laughing, I am leaping across a river and chased by a pack of cars that never catches up with me. During colonization, the colonial subject frees himself night after night between nine in the evening and six in the morning. (Frantz Fanon)

It has often been suggested that there are intrinsic links between racism and sexuality. What has not been emphasized is that the debates about theories of race in the nineteenth century, by settling on the possibility or impossibility of hybridity, focused explicitly on the issue of sexuality and the issue of sexual unions between whites and blacks. Theories of race were thus also covert theories of desire. (Robert Young)

I have endeavored to show that, though there are both scientific and religious reasons for not believing in a plurality of origins of our species, the various branches of the human family are distinguished by permanent and irradicable differences, both mentally and physically. They are unequal in intellectual capacity, in personal beauty, and in physical strength. (Arthur de Gobineau)

For, in the end, in the tense tussle between interlocking sociocorporeal forces twirling in the pugilistic crucible, boxing remakes race more than race shapes boxing. (Loïc Wacquant)

### Great Last Hope: The Black Athlete as Savior

In the 1920s and 1930s, states in the American south began to introduce the gas chamber rather than the gallows as a way to more 'humanely' execute prisoners. The authorities decided, in the name of science, to record the final words of the condemned in order to judge how this rational if novel form of state murder affected the soon-to-be-dead. One such victim was a young black man. As the cyanide pellet dropped and gas quickly filled the room causing the prisoner's strapped-down body to begin its collapse into a state of hypoxia, the microphone picked up his last, desperate words: 'Save me, Joe Louis. Save me, Joe Louis. Save me, Joe Louis …'

Dr Martin Luther King Jr recalls this tragic account in his 1963 book *Why We Can't Wait*. King uses the story to illustrate the desperate state of the black struggle during the inter-war years. King describes the young man's cry for help, for redemption and salvation, as 'bizarre and naïve' (1963/2000: 101) symbolizing the wider sense of helplessness that marked that particular period in African American history. The young man's own personal 'loneliness' and 'despair' are reflective of the deeper trauma of the wider black community:

> The condemned young Negro, groping for someone who might care for him, and had power enough to rescue him, found only the heavyweight boxing champion of the world. Joe Louis would care because he was a Negro. Joe Louis could do something because he was a fighter. In a few words the dying man had written a social commentary. Not God, not government, not charitably minded white men, but a Negro who was the world's most expert fighter, in his last extremity, was the last hope. (King 1963/2000: 100)

There are many instructive aspects to this story, and King's telling of it, that are worth pondering for a moment. While the historical specificity of this particular story may be questioned and while we must remain cautious about over-reading any particular episode, however provocative, this account, nonetheless, reveals something important about the perceived role and place of athletes within the cultural life-world of blacks, and of the intricate relationship between race, sport and black politics more generally. It invites us to at least consider how such pronouncements could even have come to be uttered and what the ethical and political implications are in imagining black athletes as the last hope for black freedom. How and why was it that Joe Louis in particular was endowed with such prophetic power, deemed able to save the condemned when all else had failed?

The black (criminal) subject who had presumably committed the most heinous and uncivil of acts, the monstrous black figure so threatening and dangerous that it must be violently expunged from society, is reduced to a desperate and passive object: stripped of all power, his body immobile, organs failing, unable to do anything but summon some final inner strength to utter a few last words. The black masculine menace not only tamed but reduced of all agency by the physical straps pinning his body to the chair, the technological advances of modern bio-chemistry waiting to expunge the air, quite literally, from the black body. Beyond the scope of liberal tolerance, beyond the legal authority of the state itself to intervene, and even beyond the power of the Almighty to provide religious deliverance stood the only figure of redemption and black salvation capable of rescuing the souls of black folks: *the black athlete*.

We should consider, as well, that the prisoner did not call for Duke Ellington or Bessie Smith, not Claude McKay or James Weldon Johnson, nor even Marcus Garvey or W.E.B. Du Bois for help. In that very last moment, it was not jazz or blues, nor the novelists and poets of the Harlem

Renaissance, or the radical political voices of the age that could, possibly, maybe, save him. But the black athlete alone. And, we should note, not just any black athlete (it was not Jesse Owens either that was called upon), but the epitome of patriarchal manhood, power and prestige: the black, *male* heavyweight champion of the world, Joe Louis.

Rather than simply dismissing the prisoner's cry as delusional, I want to suggest that an account of the development of the black athlete within black life, and more specifically the role of the black heavyweight champion, can help us to better understand why in fact such a seemingly bizarre and naïve call may actually make sense. This requires us to go back in history to the key, foundational figure that came before Joe Louis, and who, I will suggest, decisively reshaped the racial context of America and the west more generally, as well as the very meaning of and contestation over the category of race itself, namely the boxer Jack Johnson. To do so is also to pursue the idea of the residue of freedom and emancipation embedded within the gratuitous rationality of sport itself, as Morgan phrased it in the previous chapter. It is to consider why sport becomes such an important, almost metaphysical, site for self-actualization at this particular historical moment for those black subjects whose post-slavery freedoms continued to be curtailed by white supremacy. For black people throughout the diaspora during this time, 'freedom' was not some esoteric abstraction that defined the nature of modernity under the domination of instrumental rationality. Rather, freedom represented something more fundamental for those whose ethical and political demands for liberty were premised upon the simple desire to occupy the status of the human.

Sport, as the structured pursuit of useless play, simultaneously serves to dramatize and accentuate the very conditions of racial subordination and freedom from constraint that race itself also inscribes onto black bodies. There is, if you will, both a double *negation* and a double *emancipation* found in the autotelic pleasures of creativity and movement that sport produces for the racialized subaltern. The colonial subject's dreams of muscular prowess, as Fanon puts it, imbue the category of sport with a form of physical release and symbolic power that resonates far beyond the playing fields and boxing rings from where they come. In this context we might suggest that sport becomes articulated with discourses of freedom and hope in the refiguring of the category of 'the human'.

Thus, contrary to those such as Guttmann (1978: 32) who have suggested that exclusionary practices from modern sport on the basis of race are 'clearly anomalous', I argue that sports were born out of and from classed, gendered and racial inequalities. Just as we have shown that it is a mistake to contend that citizenship had 'anomalies' of exclusion when in fact such exclusions were foundational in producing the very notion of citizenship itself, so too are the same social inequalities constitutive of modern sport. Guttmann needs to make social divisions of race, class and gender *exterior* to sport in order to maintain his schematic account of sport as defined by 'equality'. But this is to confuse, as was argued earlier, the rhetorics of sport with its materiality, to succumb to the Myth of Modern Sport. This does not mean that sport is forever 'determined' by these exclusions. In fact, the opposite becomes the case. Sport is understood as a contested cultural terrain wherein these struggles are formally linked to wider social structures and contestations over the meaning of race. That is to say, it is useful to *think of sport as a racial project that both changes and is changed by political struggles in and through race.*

### Sporting Racial Projects and the Meaning of Race

Race, as Michael Omi and Howard Winant have suggested, is an important dimension of social organization and cultural meaning (1994: viii). Race is a structured and structuring feature of western societies that shapes social institutions, economic relations, political ideologies and cultural practices. These racial meanings, however, are not static and fixed. They change over time as a result of political struggles. What Omi and Winant call *racial formation* (see also CCCS 1982; Gilroy 1987) refers to the socio-historical process through which 'racial categories are created, inhabited, transformed, and destroyed' (1994: 55). Racial formations come into being through the linkage of structure and representation. Racial projects are then seen as doing the ideological work in 'linking' what we might term *social structures* and *cultural representations*:

> A racial project is simultaneously an interpretation, representation, or explanation of racial dynamics, and an effort to reorganize and redistribute resources along particular racial lines. Racial projects connect what race *means* in a particular discursive practice and the ways in which both social structures and everyday experiences are racially organized, based upon that meaning. (1994: 56, emphasis in the original)

Although Omi and Winant spend little time unpacking and delineating exactly *how* such 'representations' manifest themselves *and relate back* to social structures, I want to suggest that this is a useful starting point for conceptualizing what I want to term *sporting racial projects*. That is, to consider sport as a particular racial project (that would include the rules of the game, the actions of the players, fans and coaches, the sports media, institutional governing bodies, as well as sports discourse itself) that has effects in changing racial discourse more generally and that therefore reshapes wider social structures. Sports become productive, and not merely receptive, of racial discourse and this discourse has material effects both within sport and beyond. *Sport helps to make race make sense and sport then works to reshape race.*

Although an analysis of sport *per se* does not figure within Omi and Winant's arguments, they do note in passing the role of sporting racial stereotypes as a micro-social site for the reproduction of racialized common sense understandings of social structure:

The black banker harassed by police while walking in casual clothes through his own well-off neighborhood, the Latino or white kid rapping in perfect Afro patois, the unending *faux pas* committed by whites who assume that the non-whites they encounter are servants or tradespeople, the belief that non-white colleagues are less qualified persons hired to fulfill affirmative action guidelines, indeed the whole gamut of racial stereotypes – that 'white men can't jump', that Asians can't dance, etc., etc. – all testify to the way a racialized social structure shapes racial experience and conditions meaning. (1994: 59)

Thus, racial projects, large and small, are at the center of the racial formation process helping to mediate between the discursive and representational aspects of race and their organizational and institutional forms that result in the patterning and structuring of social relations. Central to the process of 'linking' race and sport is the dominant role of the body that in a sense 'creates' both sport (as practice) and race (as ideology). The body serves to make sport *possible* and race *'real'*. If Paul Spickard (2007: 19) is right in his observation that race is a story about power that is written onto the body, then sport is a powerful, and perhaps at certain moments even a pivotal, narrator in that story.

Among historians of racism it is now commonly understood that it was not until the nineteenth century, with the development of a specific set of scientific discourses, that our contemporary understanding of race as immutable biological type emerged into a coherent, self-sustaining theory displacing a range of religious discourses concerning the darker-skinned heathens. Although various definitions of 'race' as family, as class and as nation, remained in usage throughout the eighteenth and nineteenth centuries, by the early twentieth century the scientific definition of race as implying absolute racial difference and hierarchy was widely accepted (Fredrikson 2002; Montagu 1997). The fact of the inequality of the human races, with occasional notable exceptions (see Firmin 1885/2002), was barely contested. The only point for debate concerned whether or not the lower races, with appropriate levels of European tutelage, could perhaps be lifted from their sorry state. White supremacy became a social fact that was buttressed by the scientific data of phrenology and craniometry and the supporting grand philosophical theories of race, culture and civilization (Gould, 1996; Graves, 2005). It is important, though, to map more precisely the 'historical flexibility of racial meanings and categories' (Omi and Winant 1994: 4) as these were shifting and reforming during this time.

As racial discourse cohered during the nineteenth century from a 'disorganized and inconsistent inventory of racial attributes' (McClintock 1995: 50) into the 'classical' form of racial science, three core ideas became dominant components in defining the racial order and therefore whiteness itself. These characteristics were, of course, relational. Whiteness became defined in relation to what it was not and could not be as much as any 'positive', intrinsic features. A key belief, however, was that whites were *intellectually, aesthetically and physically* superior to blacks, regardless of whether black people were living in Africa or 'the new world'. White people's supposed innate *intellectual superiority* was a fact of such obviousness that its truth was often merely asserted using random examples from the world as it was known at the time as opposed to being systematically demonstrated. As Emanuel Eze (2001) has shown, as far as major European intellectuals such as David Hume, Georg W.F. Hegel and Immanuel Kant were concerned, blacks were savages who were constitutionally incapable of producing higher thought and anything other than basic technology, and therefore were as removed from the domain of 'civilization' as the animals with whom they were supposedly most closely related. Hegel, for instance, notes, in a passage from *Lectures on the Philosophy of World History*, that:

> man as we find him in Africa has not progressed beyond his immediate existence. As soon as man emerges as a human being, he stands in opposition to nature, and it is this alone which makes him a human being. But if he has merely made a distinction between himself and nature, he is still at the first stage of his development: he is dominated by passion, and is nothing more than a savage. All our observations of African man show him as living in a state of savagery and barbarism, and he remains in this state to the present day. The negro is an example of animal man in all his savagery and lawlessness, and if we wish to understand him at all, we must put aside all our European attitudes ... nothing consonant with humanity is to be found in his character. (1830/1975: 128)

As such, blacks apparently lacked not only the ability to make judgments of taste and distinction but were themselves visually grotesque specimens whose peculiar form and shape rendered them *aesthetically displeasing*. While some aspects of their physique might occasionally be admired just as we might marvel, from an anthropological position of curiosity, at an animal's spectacular physicality, the true epitome of human beauty was to be found in the white European, the standard for which derived from a neoclassical conception of physical perfection based on Greek and Roman statuary (Fredrikson 2002: 59). Thus, as George Fredrikson notes, the 'milky whiteness of marble and the facial features and bodily form of the Apollos and Venuses that were coming to light during the seventeenth and eighteenth centuries created a standard from which Africans were bound to deviate' (2002: 59–60).

And finally, completing the tripartite structure of racial discourse, whites were held to be *physically superior* to blacks. This later notion became increasingly important towards the end of the nineteenth century as social Darwinism's influence spread as a way to explain social development more generally, underpinned by the notion of the separate sub-species of Man locked in battle for race survival from which only the fittest and strongest would emerge. The physicality of the body was not so much divorced from the intelligence of the mind and the beauty of the form but conversely was an outward manifestation of the superior inner developmental state that allowed for forms of higher cognition and even for aesthetic appreciation.

Arthur de Gobineau spelled this out clearly in his 1856 text *The Moral and Intellectual Diversity of Races*, volume one of *Essay on the Inequality of the Human Races*, in which a latent religiosity is combined with the absolute certainty of racial difference in bodily type, thus demonstrating that even though the negro's soul may be worthy in the eyes of the Lord, the negro's own limited physicality ultimately prevents the attainment of both abstract thought and artistic understanding:

> A person with dull auditory organs can never appreciate music, and whatever his talents otherwise may be, can never become a Meyerbeer or a Mozart. Upon quickness of perception, power of analysis and combination, perseverance and endurance, depend our intellectual faculties, both in their degree and their kind; and are not they blunted or otherwise modified in a morbid state of the body? I consider it therefore established beyond dispute, that a certain general physical conformation is productive of corresponding mental characteristics. A human being, whom God has created with a negro's skull and general *physique*, can never equal one with a Newton's or a Humboldt's cranial development, though the soul of both is equally precious in the eyes of the Lord, and should be in the eyes of all his followers. (1856: 91, emphasis in the original)[1]

The 'negro's skull' and 'general physique' provided evidential proof of black people's *inferior physical status* to whites. Within the discourse of the Family of Man this meant that whites' dominant position within the various branches of the human family as Gobineau put it, rendered the black race 'feminine'. McClintock suggests that as a result, the 'white race was figured as the male of the species and the black race as the female' (1995: 55), the 'pendulous belly' of African males, for example, deemed comparable to the bodies of white women who had borne too many children. In other words, just as women and children remained physically 'underdeveloped' compared to men, so too were blacks as a 'race' locked in a state of perpetual familial subordination. This logic resulted, of course, in black women being seen as the most atavistic of all, as the demonstrable 'proof' of Saartjie Baartman's abject and anachronistic body was meant to show.[2]

The belief in the physical superiority of whites was embraced by both white Europeans and North Americans, becoming a defining principle for whiteness itself. For example, Thomas Jefferson, in *Notes on the State of Virginia*, cautiously advanced the proposition that:

> the blacks, whether originally a distinct race, or made distinct by time and circumstances, are *inferior to the whites in the endowments both of body and mind*. It is not against experience to suppose that different species of the same genus, or varieties of the same species, may possess different qualifications ... This unfortunate difference of color, and perhaps of faculty, is a powerful obstacle to the emancipation of these people. (1787/1982: 143, emphasis added)

So, by the end of the nineteenth century, we have a set of cultural, political and economic forces that converge to produce a particular logic of racial formation and understanding of human difference. The precise causal mechanisms, if indeed they exist in any autonomous sense, are not a key concern here. Indeed, it may be better, conceptually speaking, to think of these dimensions as mutually reinforcing so that over time they become not only interconnected but *co-articulating*, regardless of the 'originatory moment' of racial formation.

Racial formation during this period is defined by the expansion of European colonial capitalist states that dramatically re-shape panoptical time and geo-political space across ever-increasing parts of the globe. A set of scientific doctrines and philosophies try to account for and explain these processes that rely on a deeply racialized understanding of human difference and capabilities that are rooted in a Eurocentric framework and that find expression in the form of white supremacy. Part of the ideological work of the white colonial frame is to deny or play down the brutal violence that is enacted as a result of colonial expansion, including slavery, and to develop a set of discourses wherein the subjugation and exploitation of 'non-Europeans' can be justified as the inalienable march of Progress and Civilization, driven by the putatively objective and rational process of 'modernization'.

Culture is fundamental to the colonial project, serving to accelerate and enable colonial 'penetration' of 'virgin' lands, that are either deemed to be 'empty' and can therefore be legitimately occupied, or populated by primitive savages who lie outside of or on the very edge of the category 'the human' and thereby subject to either literal ownership (slavery), political governance (colonization), or ultimately extermination (genocide). This is achieved, in part, via the use of cultural practices, such as sports, as modes of colonial control and instruction, and through a more general process of the creation of a 'European culture'. This serves to bind European elites and the general populace together in a way that naturalizes European domination and invents a shared sense of pan-European white identity that sits alongside and increasingly supersedes questions of nation and class.

The production of white supremacy as a coherent philosophy rests upon the belief in the *intellectual, aesthetic and physical* superiority of whites over all others and in so doing centers the body as a crucial site for the production of racialized identities. Racial ideology becomes manifest in the body. As such, questions of hygiene, strength and, above all, sexual virility become increasingly important. Muscular Christians are seen to represent both the successful mastery of the body over its own atavistic impulses and the development of a refined intellect, all in the service of Empire. Gendered tropes suffuse the imperial project, with the control of sexuality becoming a key fault line connecting the practices of colonialism in the metropole with those 'overseas'. For the colonial racial order to be maintained, and for racial degeneration to be avoided, strict codes of conduct and legal sanctions on sexual practices become necessary to safeguard the imperial project. Unsurprisingly, then, racial formation during this time is replete with sexual anxieties and gendered fissures that can never be fully contained, resulting in a deeply ambivalent racial discourse. Robert Young (2001: 326) argues that:

> Imperial culture was … augmented in the nineteenth century by racial theories that portrayed Europeans as masculine and non-Europeans as feminine races; the cult of masculinity became hegemonic. British public schools, the emphasis on sport, on game hunting, the outlawing of homosexuality, the founding of the Boy Scouts, even the fashionableness of male circumcision, all bear witness to a restrictive narrowing of gender identity during the era of militaristic imperialism.

However, during the first few decades of the twentieth century a dramatic and profound change occurs that challenges, and in one respect completely reverses, a central tenant of nineteenth century racial science. I want to suggest that sport played a pivotal role in effecting a shift in the structure of racial formation during the first half of the twentieth century. We can further and more precisely locate the decisive moment as connected to the emergence onto the world stage during the first decades of the twentieth century of a young black boxer from Galveston, Texas. Such a claim requires further substantiation.

### Jack Johnson and the Remaking of Race

In *Imperial Leather*, Ann McClintock presents a persuasive argument that while racial science proved important in constructing ideas of 'race' and of human difference more generally, such discussions remained largely the preserve of educated elites. McClintock suggests that a far more powerful and effective reproduction of racist ideologies occurred as a result not of the writings of French aristocratic idealists, British public-school headmasters, nor of American political figures, but from the everyday, mundane forms of *commodity spectacle* that the newly emerging leisure mass market was able to produce. What she refers to as 'commodity racism' meant that the widespread dissemination of ideas of white supremacy and black degeneracy, of the myths of imperial Progress, was largely achieved through the literal packaging of racist tropes onto the products that people bought and consumed. The powerful images and discourses of advertising and marketing interpellated individuals into a new, respectable, civilized, British subjectivity.

> Commodity racism became distinct from scientific racism in its capacity to expand beyond the literate, propertied elite through the marketing of commodity spectacle. If, after the 1850s, scientific racism saturated anthropological, scientific and medical journals, travel writing and novels, these cultural forms were still relatively class-bound and inaccessible to most Victorians, who had neither the means nor the education to read such material. Imperial kitsch as consumer spectacle, by contrast, could package, market and distribute evolutionary racism on a hitherto

unimagined scale. No preexisting form of organized racism had ever before been able to reach so large and so differentiated a mass of the populace. (1995: 209)

It becomes apparent then, that any serious attempt to trace the centrality of forms of late nineteenth and early twentieth century popular culture as a space for the transmission of ideas of racial difference must take into account the dominant position of organized sport. Sport, during the first half of the twentieth century, is an increasingly powerful, and perhaps the most powerful, form of *racial spectacle*. We might suggest that sport becomes the modality through which popular racism is lived, embodied and challenged, and the most dramatic example of this is boxing.

When Jack Johnson defeated Tommy Burns, in Sydney, Australia, in December 1908 in front of 20,000 spectators, he became the first black heavyweight champion of the world. This cultural milestone had repercussions that extended far beyond the sport of boxing. Up until then white fighters had usually declined to fight black boxers for world championship titles, ensuring the continuation of white superiority over blacks in matters sporting as elsewhere. Johnson, after years of being denied an opportunity to fight for the world title, quite literally chased Burns around the world in order to secure his chance to compete for the title. He followed Burns to London, and then eventually to Australia, where the promoter Hugh D. 'Huge Deal' McIntosh was finally able to come up with the $30,000 that Burns had decided was money enough for him to break the color line. Johnson would receive $5,000 as the challenger.

News that the fight would go ahead was greeted with dismay among white Australians, who feared the repercussions of a Johnson win, especially as Aboriginal Australians had taken to supporting Johnson as a symbol of their own struggle against Australian genocidal racism, and among many white Americans who similarly worried about the immense damage to the racial order that would result from a Johnson victory. A letter to the *Australian Star* solemnly noted that 'this battle may in the future be looked back upon as the first great battle of an inevitable race war ... There is more in this fight to be considered than the mere title of pugilistic champion of the world' (Roberts 1983: 58). As the campaign to stop the fight floundered and arrangements were made for the contest to go ahead, the former champion, John L. Sullivan, attacked Burns for agreeing to fight Johnson, declaring, 'Shame on the money-mad Champion! Shame on the man who upsets good American precedents because there are Dollars, Dollars, Dollars in it' (Roberts 1983: 54).

Just as many whites had feared, the bout itself turned out to be a rather one-sided affair. Burns went down twice within the first two rounds as it became apparent that Johnson was by far the better fighter. The early betting quickly swung in Johnson's favor. The utter disdain for black deference towards white authority, and an example as to why Johnson would prove so destabilizing a force for the boundaries of white supremacy, was indicated by the way in which Johnson, self-aware of his own technical and physical superiority, would mock his white opponents *during* the bouts themselves. It is difficult to imagine a greater insult to the white male ego than a black boxer of the time not simply being 'allowed' to compete against a white boxer in public (thus implying some level of equality between the races), but the white fighter actually being dominated by the black Other, all the while being verbally reminded, *in real time*, of the ensuing beating. The *New York Times* (December 26, 1908) noted that during the sixth round Burns managed to land some strong punches into Johnson's stomach and rib cage. The report continued, 'Johnson, however, treated these blows as a joke, laughing at the crowd and making sarcastic remarks to his opponent as he pushed Burns into a corner and scored a couple of rights to the body'.

Burns continued to call Johnson a 'yellow dog' throughout the fight, a reference to the widespread belief among whites that black boxers, like animals in general, lacked courage and could easily be startled when confronted with superior force. It was clear, as each round passed and as Burns's battered, bloodied and bruised face continued to be probed by Johnson's accurate punches, that the Texan was merely taking his time as he savored his impending victory. At the end of the thirteenth round the police informed the referee and Burns's corner that if the now one-sided assault continued they would step in and end the fight. Burns insisted that he was fit to continue and could still win. Johnson unleashed a barrage of shots in the fourteenth round, Burns went down again and the police, as they had warned, entered the ring to bring the bout to a close. The referee (who was none other than Hugh McIntosh himself) immediately awarded the fight to Johnson, declaring later that it was one of the best fights he had ever witnessed.

The news of this shock result (Burns, despite being smaller and lighter than Johnson, was still a pre-fight favorite) was immediately communicated across the globe via the newswires. The December 26, 1908 edition of the *New York Times* announced 'JACK JOHNSON WINS: POLICE STOP FIGHT: Negro's Punishment of Champion Burns Causes Authorities to End Bout'. The paper informed its readers that 'the big negro from Galveston, Texas' was now the heavyweight champion of the world. The article continued, quoting Burns after the fight:

> 'I did the best I could and fought hard. Johnson was too big and his reach was too great.' Johnson appeared fresh after the fight, while Burns's eyes were badly puffed and his mouth swollen to twice its normal size. The Canadian fought a game battle and showed indomitable pluck, but he was no match for the big black Texan.

The monumental nature of Johnson's victory was felt across the black diaspora; celebrated by Aboriginal Australians and blacks throughout the new world, as much as by African Americans themselves. The *Richmond Planet*, a black newspaper from Charlottesville, Virginia, reported that 'no event in forty years has given more genuine satisfaction to the colored people of this country than has the signal victory of Jack Johnson' (Roberts 1983: 55). As euphoric was the reaction of blacks, so was the deep and near utter despair of white commentators, troubled not only by the significance of Johnson's win but also the manner in which he had defeated his white opponent. The writer Jack London described the fight, in his usual understated way, by hinting at the wider implications for the white race: 'The fight, there was no fight. No Armenian massacre could compare with the hopeless slaughter that took place in the Sydney Stadium' (Roberts 1983: 61).[3]

It is worth recalling that subscription to the racial ideology of the day had material effects in shaping sporting outcomes. As Randy Roberts notes, the conventional wisdom at the time alleged that blacks lacked stamina and physical endurance. Thus it was widely believed that while black boxers might score a knock-out blow if they got lucky, they could not 'go the distance' and would eventually tire, lacking too 'the will' to push themselves to the limit. Blacks were thought to have thick skulls that made it more difficult to knock them out, but their 'yellow streak' was a deficiency that manifested itself in black fighters' supposedly weak stomachs. A few strong blows to the body, so it was thought, and the black boxer would likely collapse and concede.

Remarkably, many white boxers duly trained for and fought tactically against blacks based on these 'scientific facts'. Black boxers themselves, aware of this white sporting mythology, could duly develop their midriff in order to sustain the inevitable barrage of blows, while knowing that they were less likely to receive far more damaging shots to the head, and able to practice effective counter-punches as white fighters 'came in low'. Burns, somewhat disastrously, pursued such a strategy against Johnson. Johnson taunted Burns during their bout calling him 'Tommy Boy' and 'little Tommy' and at one point saying to Burns, 'Go on Tommy, hit me here' while gesturing to his highly conditioned midsection. As Burns pointlessly went for Johnson's supposed 'weak spot', Johnson laughed and asked him to hit him again, only harder (Roberts 1983: 63). On this point Roberts notes:

> Burns's strategy was thus founded on the racist belief that scientists, armed with physiological and climatological evidence, had proved that blacks were either inferior to whites, or – as in the case of harder heads – superior because of some greater physiological inferiority; that is to say, blacks had thicker skulls because they had smaller brains. Burns never questioned that his abdominal strength and his endurance were superior to Johnson's. Nor did he doubt that his white skin meant that his desire to win and willingness to accept pain were greater than Johnson's. But above all, he was convinced that as a white he could outthink Johnson, that he could solve the problems of defense and offense more quickly than his black opponent. Burns's faith, in short, rested ultimately on the color of his skin. (1983: 62)

While this sporting aberration was clearly a shock, it was assumed at the time that the Texas negro would shortly be dispatched back to

Galveston by the next available white boxer, enabling the so-called 'color line' to be quickly redrawn so as to prevent any such mistakes from occurring again. Unfortunately for the racial order, Johnson proved to be one of the best boxers of all time, and certainly one of the most skilled boxing technicians of his era. In short, he was too strong and too quick for any boxer, regardless of color.

The search for what became known after the Johnson/Burns fight as 'The Great White Hope' to reclaim the title from Johnson brought to the fore a number of issues. It demonstrated the fragility of the racial order itself that rested, in part, on the notion of white physical superiority. The growth of organized sports during the early twentieth century, as a popular form of competitive physical culture, meant that sport in general and boxing in particular became an important site for objectively and publicly 'proving' the superiority of certain bodies (be they marked by gender, age, region, nationality or race) over others. The racial signification of sports thus ensured that sporting encounters between black and white athletes quickly took on broader, symbolic significance in terms of popular understandings of racial difference.

The problem posed by Johnson, put simply, was how could whites continue to make claims of innate superiority over blacks when the very epitome of muscular physicality as represented by the heavyweight champion of the world was a negro, born of slaves, from East Texas? If that central aspect of racial ideology proved to be false, then where did that leave the theory of white supremacy itself, founded as it was, in part, upon the 'facts' of physical preeminence? What were the wider political implications of Johnson's continued victories in terms of black emancipation, and even the potential reversal of the racial order itself? 'Flamboyant and powerful,' writes Michael Kimmel, 'Johnson was the black specter that had haunted white workingmen since antebellum days – the fear that unskilled free blacks would triumph over skilled white workers in the workplace, the bedroom, and now, in the sporting world' (2006: 94). Thus Johnson's victories – a kind of racial blasphemy – provoked profound anxiety concerning the very meaning of whiteness and the future of the imperial project.

As Johnson successfully dispatched challenger after challenger to the canvas, the national and international search for a white fighter to reclaim the mantle of masculinity and therefore restore the racial order became increasingly frenetic. The 'white boxer's burden' eventually fell to the previously retired Jim Jeffries. Widely regarded by most whites at the time as the true champion on account that he had retired from the ring undefeated, it was assumed that Jefferies would, as he put it himself, prove to the world that the white man was superior to the black man. Jeffries was quoted as saying, 'I fully realize what depends upon me, and won't disappoint the public. That portion of the white race which is looking to me to defend its athletic supremacy may feel assured that I am fit to do my very best. I'll win as quickly as I can' (*Daily Mirror*, July 5, 1910, p. 3). Johnson could not consider himself a true champion, it was suggested, until he had fought Jeffries. The fight, which was dubbed 'The Fight of the Century', was arranged for the suitably patriotic date of July 4, 1910 in the city of Reno, Nevada.

The plan was simple: Jeffries would win, the racial order would be restored, black hopes of freedom within and beyond the ring that had become embodied in Johnson himself would be dashed, and the dominance of white masculinity would once again be secured. Things did not turn out that way. As with Burns two years before, the fight simply proved that Johnson's technique and ability were far superior to that of his challengers. During round fifteen of the sun-baked and one-sided contest, Jeffries's corner finally threw in the white towel to concede defeat. The battered imago of the superior white athlete that had been dented two years earlier in Sydney was now severely and irrevocably damaged.

Jeffries was too old and slow to compete with the younger Johnson, although he would later admit that he doubted he could have beaten Johnson even in his prime. Even John L. Sullivan, who had been hired by the *New York Times* to cover the lead-up to the fight, had to acknowledge Johnson's superiority. The opening line of Sullivan's *Times* report simply stated: 'RENO, Nev., July 4. – The fight of the century is over and a black man is the undisputed champion of the world.' Sullivan went on to note that 'Johnson got scarcely a knock during the whole encounter, and was never bothered by Jeffries's actions one little bit'.

### Sport Science and the Invention of the Black Athlete

Many commentators have, of course, noted that Johnson's win challenged the general notion of white supremacy not just in the United States but globally, but I want to suggest that something else resulted from the encounter. While the widespread white belief in the physically superior white man was being undercut by Johnson's powerful uppercuts, Johnson was also, inadvertently, creating a new racial type. From the slow but unmistakable burial of white physical superiority, that had been a largely unquestioned fact of racial difference for more than two centuries prior to the Burns and Jeffries encounters, a new racial trope emerged: *the black athlete*.

While racial ideologies (as with all such worldviews) can often contain contradictory elements, indeed are sometimes founded upon them, there remains a limit to how much work ideology alone can do in subverting 'common sense' understandings of the world. Theoretical frameworks are sometimes able to overcome that which is deemed 'obvious', Galileo's eventual usurping of geocentric models of the universe for example, yet even the white colonial frame had trouble accounting for the public and demonstrable beatings that Johnson produced. It is hard to claim physical ascendancy over the cowardly yellow-streak negroes when at the end of every fight the negro is left smiling, barely bruised and having mercilessly mocked his opponent's weaknesses, laughing at the 'joke' punches thrown against his body, as the supposed white *Übermensch* is carried from the ring freshly painted in his own blood.

Of course, racial ideology has always had to account for the 'racial exception' in order to explain observable human differences *within* racial groups as well as the occasional overlaps *between* them. Even Gobineau, that most eloquent of nineteenth century proto-Eugenicist racists, conceded this point while trying to argue (as his latter day intellectual heirs such as Jon Entine, Charles Murray and John Phillippe Rushton would also) that to do otherwise would be to succumb to irrational prejudice, an affliction that Gobineau truly believed himself to be free from:

> With regard to intellectual capacity, I emphatically protest against that mode of arguing which consists in saying, 'every negro is a dunce'; because, by the same logic, I should be compelled to admit that 'every white man is intelligent'; and I shall take good care to commit no such absurdity. I shall not even wait for the vindicators of the absolute equality of all races, to adduce to me such and such a passage in some missionary's or navigator's journal, wherefrom it appears that some Yolof has become a skillful carpenter, that some Hottentot has made an excellent domestic, that some Caffre plays well on the violin, or that some Bambarra has made very respectable progress in arithmetic. I am prepared to admit – and to admit without proof – anything of that sort, however remarkable, that may be related of the most degraded savages ... Nay, I go further than my opponents, and am not in the least disposed to doubt that, among the chiefs of the rude negroes of Africa, there could be found a considerable number of active and vigorous minds, greatly surpassing in fertility of ideas and mental resources, the average of our peasantry, and even of some of our middle classes. But the unfairness of deductions based upon a comparison of the most intelligent blacks and the least intelligent whites, must be obvious to every candid mind. Once for all, such arguments seem to me unworthy of real science, and I do not wish to place myself upon so narrow and unsafe a ground. (1856: 440–441)

Of course, part of this argument related to the fear among white elites that the absolute invocation of racial hierarchy logically led to the suggestion of internal white 'equality'. Especially as the eugenics movement gathered pace during the first three decades of the twentieth century, many eugenicist supporters tried to avoid a Manichean racial worldview, precisely in order to separate themselves from any biological connections to the degenerate white lower classes. Hence the belief that certain members of the black middle class could be regarded as more 'developed' than sections of the white working class.

Gobineau is again worth quoting at length as he makes the direct connection between the different elements of white racial supremacy (intelligence, beauty and physique). Interestingly, he develops his argument by citing sport itself as space where individual black achievement that matched that of whites could, conceivably, be found:

Taking the white race as the standard of beauty, we perceive all the others more or less receding from that model. There is, then, an inequality in point of beauty among the various races of men, and this inequality is permanent and indelible. The next question to be decided is, whether there is also an inequality of physical strength. It cannot be denied that the American Indians and the Hindoos are greatly inferior to us in this respect. Of the Australians, the same may safely be asserted. It is necessary, however, to distinguish between purely muscular force – that which exerts itself suddenly at a given moment – and the force of resistance or capacity for endurance. The degree of the former is measured by its intensity, that of the other by its duration. Of the two, the latter is the typical – the standard by which to judge the capabilities of races. Great muscular strength is found among races notoriously weak. Among the lowest of the negro tribes, for instance, it would not be difficult to find individuals that could match an experienced European wrestler or English boxer. This is equally true of the Lascars and Malays. But we must take the masses, and judge according to the amount of long-continued, persevering toil and fatigue they are capable of. In this respect, the white races are undoubtedly entitled to pre-eminence. (1856: 380–382)

We note here, and almost prefiguring the arrival of a 'Jack Johnson', the acknowledgment that some *individual blacks* might, on rare occasions, be as strong as elements of the white English working classes when it came to sports such as boxing. And also, what we might call the founding discourse of racial sport science, in the distinction between the explosive power of 'muscular force' and the 'capacity for endurance'. A century later such arguments would reappear as a distinction between 'fast twitch' and 'slow twitch' muscle fibers that are supposedly unevenly distributed among racial groups and therefore indicators of performance differences. The key point to remember, however, was that nineteenth century racial logic insisted that while the odd black may occasionally rise above the lower-caste European and even more rarely a particularly stupid and under-developed middle-class citizen of the west, no negro could rise above *all whites*. It was this central, foundational belief that Johnson both undermined and ultimately helped to subvert.

To be clear, this is not to claim that ideas of black physical superiority only started with Johnson. As John Hoberman (1997, 2004) has shown, such ideas circulated for many decades before Johnson dispatched Burns to the canvas, and in various iterations can be found in the writings of European explorers and scientists from the very beginning of colonialism. Hoberman notes, for example, that the 'idea of racial athletic aptitude developed during the period of European imperial and colonial expansion, and such observed differences have often been presented in the context of an evolutionary narrative that has traditionally distinguished between the "savage" and the "civilized" races' (2004: 281). My point, rather, is that the ambiguity around black physical superiority begins to dramatically recede in the years after Johnson's 1908 victory and consolidates around a set of particular and absolute physical markers of not just racial difference but inherent black physical *advantage* that find their fullest expression in this idea of 'the black athlete'.

During the nineteenth century, isolated moments of sporting success – normally by black athletes who showed deference to their white benefactors, such as the boxer Peter Jackson who was often favorably contrasted by whites with Johnson – were not seen as problematic.[4] Even though black athletic aptitude was often acknowledged in certain sports among particular individuals, the dominant racial paradigm still asserted white physical dominance over the 'feminine' race. By the time we reach the 1930s this paradigm is collapsing, especially with the exploits of other black sporting stars such as Jesse Owens in athletics and then, once the heavyweight color line had been lifted, Joe Louis in boxing.

We thus see, particularly in the 1930s, a deluge of scientific studies, influenced by the eugenics movement, seeking to discover the reasons for black sporting success (Dyreson 2008a, 2008b; Wiggins, 1989). Black accomplishment in sport could not be understood as due to individual achievement, driven by dedication, hard work and perseverance in the context of a deeply racist social system that all but denied opportunities for self-actualization in most other areas. The individual athlete, racialized as black, could only be known through the category of 'the black athlete', their success becoming a 'problem' to be investigated. The particular (athlete) was rendered secondary and thus reduced to the universal (black). Even if the empirical problem of sporting success by black athletes required scientific investigation, the category of 'race' itself was rarely problematized. In fact, with each sporting victory, each successful punch thrown, each finish line crossed, each record broken, 'race' was further consolidated and embedded as a demonstrable fact of ontological difference. Thus modern sport science was born from the 1930s parents of eugenics and colonial racism, driven by the desperate search to find the physiological essence of the sporting black body in order to further the goals of elite sports performance (Spracklen 2008: 223). Patrick Miller (1998: 125) notes that early twentieth century academicians, drawing on the myths of nineteenth century racial science, 'became engrossed in the "scientific" analysis of racial difference, various anthropologists and anthropometrists reached for the calipers and tape measure in search of a gastrocnemius muscle with a certain diameter or of an elongated heel bone in order to explain the success of certain sprinters or jumpers'. Miller continues, arguing that explanations for sporting achievement became increasingly racialized; white accomplishments were defined in terms of 'diligence, forethought and application of the mind', those of blacks understood as 'natural' and 'innate' (1998: 125).

By reducing black athleticism to the body and the body alone, sports science discourse attempted to supply white supremacist logic with a much needed rationale that would disallow any suggestion that such sporting achievements be reflective of any deeper, cognitive and above all intellectual disposition. Having previously worked to demonstrate the *physical* basis for intellectual and aesthetic supremacy, sporting success (and the related mastery of the body) was now deemed to be an indicator of a certain *limitation of cognitive development*. 'During the interwar period,' Miller argues,

> anatomy and physiology were frequently invoked to explain the athletic success of African Americans and thus used to circumscribe any declarations that prowess in contests of speed, strength, and stamina bespoke fitness for other realms of endeavor. Simply stated in the idiom of sports, to deny the translation between athletics and other accomplishments (more profound and longstanding), numerous mainstream commentators began to 'move the goal posts'. (1998: 128–129)

The attributes of character building, personal discipline and hard work – that had been at the core of the sports ethic all the while white muscular British and American Christians and white French aristocrats were reshaping the world through sport – were now dispensed with as explanations for black sporting success. Such feats of spectacular athleticism would now be re-read as the atavistic attributes of the unthinking black body. So when black athletes 'outsprinted white runners, it was presented in the roundest terms that they were merely reenacting some primordial escape from a lion or tiger' (Miller 1998: 130), Gobineau's muscular Yolofs and Caffres merely finding evolutionary expression for their true animalistic propensities.[5]

This discourse, of course, would come to frame how black female athletes, as much as black male athletes, were viewed. In fact, the effect, it could be argued, was more damaging to black females as the masculine coded representation of 'the black athlete' simply heightened the centuries-old discourse that black females were already 'mannish amazons' and hence potential if not actual hermaphrodites. Put another way, whereas black male athletes came to be seen as *hyper*-masculine, black females athletes were seen as not female at all. Susan Cahn makes this point when she argues:

> The myth of the 'natural' black athlete lent further support to the perception that African-American women were biologically suited to masculine sport. Early-twentieth century education and social science journals, especially in the 1930s, were sprinkled with anthropometric studies of racially determined muscle length, limb size, head shape, and neurological responses. Experts in both science and sport labored to identify genetic factors, including a conditioned 'fear-response' and peculiar characteristics of African-American hands, tendons, muscles, joints, nerves, blood, thighs, and eye color, which might explain the fact that black athletes sometimes jumped higher or ran faster than whites. (2004: 221–222)

Thus, it is not so much that sport science attempted to discover the secrets encased within the black body (as ontological fact) but rather that the *belief* that there was such a thing as 'the black athlete' helped *constitute the object itself*. In other words, *race was made in the process of the search*, the object constituted by the scientific gaze. It is the very discourse that is generated through the work of biomechanics, physiologists, geneticists and others, that creates 'the black athlete' in the first place. Although this point is often lost on most contemporary sport scientists, the reason why study after study turns out conclusions that are tentative, incomplete and contradicting of other studies, and at their very best merely 'suggestive' of racio-performative *correlation*, is that there is no ontological black athletic body within which to find the scientific secrets outside of the laboratories themselves.

The fact that even those 'race realists' committed to establishing 'race' as a discrete and independent variable that is capable of producing differential athletic outcomes ultimately have to concede that the concept is 'fuzzy' (Entine 2000), does not lead them to consider the obvious point that the reason for race's indeterminable status is that there is no coherent racial object there to begin with. Thus such studies invariably conclude with calls for further research based upon more advanced technologies capable of measuring muscular strength and genetic variation, larger sample sizes of more 'black subjects', and sometimes an acknowledgment that greater attention needs to be paid to 'environmental factors' and their 'interplay' with the underlying black sporting genome. Of course, these environmental factors do not usually mean an analysis of the complexities of history, culture, identity and economics, but the literal geographical location and altitude of certain African countries in simply 'producing' the conditions within which the pre-wired black athletic body can find its fullest expression.[6] 'The environment' in this case simply acts as a surrogate way for an essentialist account of the 'primitive living conditions' of the black African to be smuggled back into supposedly objective, scientific accounts. The continuing western academic and journalistic fascination with 'Kenyan long distance runners', despite the record-breaking efforts of Paula Radcliffe to get them to call off the search, is simply the latest incarnation of white sports science mythologies.[7]

The 'black athlete' is less about 'its' inherent qualities and characteristics. The 'black athlete' does not exist in any meaningful ontological sense outside of the discourse of white sports science and popular imaginings. The 'black athlete' is a construction made from the repertoire of colonial fantasies about blackness that find their fullest expression in the shape of *sporting negritude*: the angry, wild, uncontrolled and almost uncontrollable, and ungrateful sporting subject that owes its success to innate animalistic physiology and that often requires a white male overseer to channel the naturally aggressive black body (male or female) towards disciplined, productive sporting ends; the white coach or trainer providing the necessary intelligence lacking in the inherently lazy but potentially dangerous black subject.

Historically, however, this construction of sporting negritude was ultimately concerned with trying to establish a coherent and tenable whiteness in the context of black demands for freedom and justice. *The black sporting Other becomes the means through which the white cognitive self is produced.* 'The Great White Hope' only becomes meaningful in the context of a supposedly intractable black sporting Other. 'White Men Can't Jump' does not need to mark blackness for us to know that the generative opposite is the 'fact' that Black Men *Can* Jump. It is not Asians, or Hispanics, 'yellows' or 'browns', but blacks and blackness itself that acts as the constitutive Other for whiteness. Indeed, embracing such racialized sporting tropes was one way, along with quickly learning anti-black racist words, that white European migrants to America, who might otherwise have shared common socio-economic cause with working-class blacks, could quickly and easily become 'white' (Roediger 2005). There was no better way to show your commitment to American nationhood, to move from being not quite white to fully white, than to identify with the call for a white person of any background or stock to recapture white masculine pride.[8]

We should also note here that it is white *men* who supposedly lack the ability to leave the ground with any great success. As I pursue in more detail in the following section, homosociality, as male on male agon, asserts itself in rendering the feminine spatially redundant yet symbolically central. Michael Messner (1992: 14) suggests that the rapid growth of organized sports during the nineteenth century can be seen 'as the creation of a homosocial institution which served to counter men's fears of feminization in the new industrial society' and helped to 'naturalize', by its overt emphasis on the 'obvious' facts of biological difference, men's collective power in society. The symbolic exclusion of femininity from sport allows for the reproduction of a supposedly non-sexual space from which the deepest sexualized desires for racialized (white) male on (black) male action can be sanctioned.

### The Black Athlete and the Production of Desire

A question remains as to why Jack Johnson, and not any other athlete of the time or before, was able to have the impact that he did. A number of factors came together that enabled Johnson to become the pivotal figure in the formation of the black athlete and the subsequent remaking of race.

An argument could reasonably be made that cinema was as powerful as sport as a form of racial spectacle during the first half of the twentieth century in terms of facilitating the production and dissemination of racial ideologies in easily and readily understandable narrative form. This is undoubtedly the case. But what is often overlooked is the importance of sport, and boxing in particular, in the making of modern cinema itself. Black athletes provided the form for what would become the archetype of muscular, threatening black physicality on the 'big screen'. In other words, it was not just that films of fights became popular but that, particularly in the United States, black athletes (meaning their bodies) were often and extensively used by Hollywood productions requiring black actors and extras.[9] Thus Johnson's rise to international 'stardom' coincided with the birth of modern cinema. Dan Streible suggests that Johnson's 'screen presence made him, in essence, the first black movie star' (2008: 195).

Charlene Regester (2004) has shown that, starting in the first decade of the twentieth century, black athletes, boxers and gridiron players in particular began to make the transition from sport into film. Few of these were lead roles, with most of the early black 'sports actors' hired primarily for their bodies. Even when 'talkies', films with speech, emerged in the late 1920s, the black athletes often remained silent, their bodies doing the talking for them, providing a dark vista against which the film's narrative would develop. What this further established, however, was the powerful figure of the *black athletic body*, sport and film working symbiotically to create, define and circulate what the 'true' black body looked like. This particular black body (athletic, toned, muscular, normally male) came to stand in for *all* black bodies, thus furthering a certain white fascination with the black Other that could shift from moment to moment, scene to scene, from fear of to desire for the black body itself.

Regester notes that black athletes' 'overwhelming size, physique, and aggressive behavior rendered them threatening, while at the same time, positioned them as desirable' (2004: 269). In other words, if sport produced the black athlete as a discernible figure within the white imagination, Hollywood went to work to embed the black athlete into the emerging mass public consciousness. You need not be a fan or follower of sport or of boxing to recognize and see the chiseled, muscular and powerful black athletic body: 'The African-American athlete as actor became an embodiment of sexuality, while at the same time he symbolically represented danger because of his imposing size, stature and blackness' (p. 271).[10] Whether or not black athletes were talented actors mattered little compared to how they looked. In this sense, black film actors held a similar position to female actresses, whose main function was to occupy the space of desirable objects, to be looked at and to be seen rather than to speak. By the 1940s black athletes were frequently used as extras for films in which they would often play the 'native', their dark and exotic bodies deemed perfect for such roles by white film makers. Professional football players such as Woody Strode, Al Duvall, Joe Lillard and Kenny Washington received such roles, as would later stars such as Jim Brown, Fred 'The Hammer' Williamson, Bernie Casey, O.J. Simpson and Carl Weathers.

In the 1920s and 1930s heavyweight boxers such as Joe Jeanette and John Lester Johnson found themselves in films such as *Wild Man from Borneo* (1933), *Ali Baba Goes to Town* (1937) and *Tarzan's Revenge* (1938). Regester (2004) notes that boxer Sam Baker landed a part in *The Mississippi Link* (1926) – playing the role of a gorilla. Later boxers such as Ken Norton would get roles in films such as *Mandingo* (1975). Unlike Paul Robeson, probably the most famous athlete turned actor of his generation, most of these athletes were given roles that were defined by and limited to their physicality and that served to reproduce a superficial, sexualized and primitive representation of blackness. Thus black athletes tended to fill 'muscle roles' (Regester 2004: 278), even when they were given more substantive parts, such as Woody Strode's role in *Spartacus*

(1960), for which he would receive a Golden Globe nomination for Best Supporting Actor, 'where he plays a gladiator who elicits the gaze of white women and is selected by them to engage in battle with Spartacus, played by Kirk Douglas, a less capable gladiator, but one to whom Strode concedes defeat' (p. 278).[11]

Jack Johnson, as one of the first black 'movie stars', thus helped to both usher in the figure of the black athlete and was himself helped by the growth in audiences for his fight films, even as the authorities, concerned about the incendiary nature of showing Johnson's victories on the big screen, sought to have his fights banned. Johnson's arrival onto the sporting landscape happened to occur at a precipitous moment in terms of wider economic and technological advances. Barry Smart (2005) suggests that international exchanges and competitions grew rapidly during the last decades of the nineteenth century and the start of the twentieth, driven by the establishment of international governing bodies and the international standardization of rules of play. Developments in transportation and mass media enabled athletes as well as fans to travel farther and more quickly than they had before, enabling sports to stage 'mega events' that could attract tens of thousands of spectators, many of whom were now increasingly aware of the leading athletes from other countries.

The emerging culture of individualism, tied to the growth in new media such as film (and later radio), the development of newswires and print, enabled the formation of what we would now call 'sports stars'. Media discourse, including the establishment of a distinct field of sports journalism, fueled Johnson's global profile such that he could reasonably be described as the world's first truly global sports star. It is difficult not to think of Jack Johnson himself when Smart describes the growth of the culture of individualism: 'The notion of the individual as an autonomous or self-constituting subject seeking personal development, fulfillment, identity affirmation and/or status enhancement through the exercise of self-interest … closely articulated with capitalist modes of production and consumption' (Smart 2005: 38).

Sport's emphasis on competition and individual achievement helped to make it an exemplar of this new, consumer-based social formation in which the spectacularization of everyday life led to the possibility for 'stars' and 'celebrities' to emerge. For those who already had 'charisma' and at least a discernible level of talent, this meant that their popular appeal could flow across and beyond national boundaries to reach thousands if not millions of new 'fans'. In many ways Johnson was able to go beyond the star status that either W.G. Grace before him and Babe Ruth after achieved in their time. For while Grace and Ruth's sporting achievements were significant and both transcended their respective sports in terms of their national fame, both were star players on team sports that were restricted by their own sport's limited geographical reach, baseball largely limited to North America and cricket to England and parts of the English-speaking British Empire. Although the latter, of course, still reflected a significant portion of the globe's surface, boxing had a deeper and farther reach than cricket, which during the nineteenth century decreased in popularity in certain parts of the Empire as settler colonial states, as was argued earlier, sought to distinguish themselves from the 'mother country' by the invention of new games, often at the expense of cricket itself.

Johnson's own personal characteristics – brash, funny, confident and charming – and his self-conscious flouting of the social conventions that he read as restrictions on his individual liberty, together with his intimidating physique that engendered powerful emotions, created a persona that was ripe for being commercially exploited. To this we must add the image of a black man, with gold capped teeth, a shaven head, dressed in the finest suits, speed driving the most expensive cars of the day when most people could not even drive let alone own one; a black man who complained that his white challengers in the ring did not hit hard enough, as outside the ring he slept with and married multiple white women at a time when the lynching of black men for less was commonplace. It is not difficult, then, to understand why Johnson had a bigger global profile and therefore impact than any other athlete, black or otherwise. And the 'moving picture machine', as papers of the day called it, caught nearly every moment it could of this new and unprecedented racial spectacle.

While it is true, as post/colonial theorists such as McClintock have pointed out, that the quintessentially Victorian institutions of the museum, the exhibition, photography and imperial advertising, served as important technologies of knowledge for displaying, in commoditized form, the narrative of Progress and the branches of the Family of Man, these remained largely static accounts, the frozen image as historical specimen. Sport, however, told a *moving, visual and contemporary* story that was not relegated to describing the past but revealed the flow of history into the present and even into the future. Part of what troubled white commentators so much was not just Johnson's disruption of past racial logics, important as they were in sustaining the present, but what he portended about *future* racial conflicts in which the future suddenly began to look black. Johnson emerged on to the scene just as the moving image was becoming embedded within western culture and thus was able to project apparent truths of racial difference in a way that even the most well-cropped photograph or carefully designed exhibit could not. If photography was both 'a technology of representation and a technology of power' (McClintock 1995: 126) then the moving image of the black athlete captured on film served to accelerate and deepen these processes even further.

The images, photographs, news and film reels, as well as the actual sporting contests themselves, became one of the most public forms of porno-tropics for the European imagination. Whereas the world exhibitions and fairs displayed eroticized specimens and human treasures 'discovered' by Europe's travelers, explorers and anthropologists, sports (and boxing in particular) provided a weekly, sometimes daily, and more accessible, showing of partially clothed, semi-naked, black bodies performing for the enjoyment of white eyes. The tall tales of Europe's writers that produced 'a fantastic magic lantern of the mind onto which Europe projected its forbidden sexual desires and fears' (McClintock 1995: 22) could be seen, live, and in real time by engaging the spectacle of the sporting primitive.[12]

In conceptualizing how the spectacle of the sporting primitive is produced we might consider sport as a theater for the invention of whiteness and a space for the pursuit of racialized homosocial fantasies, that reveals sport's 'inner libidinal logic' (Pronger 2000: 236).[13] Sport serves as a mechanism for the production of bounded space that is delimited by colonial desire itself. Or as Brian Pronger (2000: 235) phrases it, 'sport is a disciplinary practice that organizes the body and desire in time and space'. Thus, although sport is often defined by actual, material bodies in motion we should not underplay how it also operates as a site for fantasy play shaped by discourses of imagination, projection, dreaming, desire, yearning and longing. Even among the most aggressive and violent of sporting spaces, marked by sexism, homophobia, xenophobia and racism, we also find discourses of vulnerability and even love. Followers of British football will be familiar with the chant of fans towards their own team (in which the tune remains the same but the team's name changes) that goes: 'We love you Millwall, we do/We love you Millwall, we do/We love you Millwall, we do/Oh Millwall we love you'. This is sung repeatedly by groups of nominally straight, predominately working-class men for whom overt and public expressions of love in other contexts would likely be highly circumscribed.

The object of the projected love however is slightly ambiguous. At one level it is an expression of love for the players, the song sung in part to inspire and 'raise the game' of those on the pitch. It is a reassurance that the fans, deep down, love the players (just in case they were not sure). In a more Durkheimian sense we might also conclude that the object of desire is more general, referring to 'the club' itself, the institution that represents the local community, that is the stadium and the club's history, the directors and staff, the players and managers, and of course the fans themselves. Such songs become, in effect, a ritualistic display of public self-love projected outwards onto the 'totem' of 'the club' in order to sustain the group's own identity and sense of social solidarity. Sport thus becomes a space for desire and love as much as the utilitarian drive for results, victories and trophies. While undoubtedly caught between sentimental nostalgia and commercial opportunism, sport as fantasy play and dreaming can be seen in the marking of some of sport's most sacred spaces: baseball's 'field of dreams', Manchester United Football Club's 'theatre of dreams', 'la scala del calcio' in Milan.

I want to suggest then that the largely homosocial world of sport (and men's competitive sport in particular) has historically provided a fantasy space in which black bodies can be gazed upon, safe in the knowledge that the circumscribed arena of the sports field provides a legitimate modality for such racialized homosocial dreaming. As Elizabeth Alexander (1996: 170) observes in her analysis of the film *White Men Can't Jump*:

> What is the space of the basketball court, of black male theatrics in the white male imagination? … The basketball court is imagined as a classless, raceless, hypergendered space of transcendence. It is also, crucially, where white men can safely articulate and experience their desire for black men.

The black athlete, abject and feared, debased and reduced to the status of animal-like savagery, is *at the same* time imbued with certain hyper-masculine qualities of virility, strength, power and aggression. 'The black athlete' as object and as fetish thus serves as a boundary marker for white masculinity, or as R.W. Connell (2005: 80) puts it, 'in a white-suprema-cist context, black masculinities play symbolic roles for white gender construction … black sporting stars become exemplars of masculine toughness'. Colonial discourses about black physicality and sexuality reemerge with the fascination that is projected onto the 'tough' black ath-lete, turning the imagined *athletic black body* into a foundational object for white desires and fears about blackness more generally.[14]

In *Black Skin, White Masks* Frantz Fanon explores the deep psychological wounds that colonial racism inflicts upon the subjectivities of both the colonizer and the colonized. As a psychotherapist, Fanon was interested in the role of fear and desire in articulating forms of racial identity and iden-tification. In his Chapter 6, 'The black man and psychopathology', Fanon explores the phobias of some of his white patients. He notes:

> Over a three- or four-year period, we questioned about 500 individuals from France, Germany, England and Italy who were all white. We managed to create a certain trust, a relaxed air in which our subjects would not be afraid to con-fide in us or were convinced they would not offend us. Or else during the free association tests we would insert the word Negro among some twenty others. Almost sixty percent gave the following answers: Negro = biological, sex, strong, athletic, powerful, boxer, Joe Louis, Jesse Owens, Senegalese infantryman, savage, animal, devil, sin. (1952/2008: 143–144)

For Fanon, the black male was the imago of white fantasies, and of all of these constructions, one figure above all others held a central place within the white colonial imaginary: 'There is one expression that with time has become particularly eroticized: the black athlete. One woman confided in us that the very thought made her heart skip a beat' (p. 136). Thus, the black athlete is seen to be the embodiment of hyper-masculinity; ultravio-lent and the ultimate manifestation of phallic power, whose 'hyperbolic virility' signifies black masculinity, as Kaja Silverman (1996: 31) notes, as a *surplus* and therefore a threat to the 'white male corporeal ego' (p. 31). Fanon continues to suggest that blackness comes to signify biology itself:

'The Negro symbolizes the biological' (1952/2008: 144). The logical conclusion to this sexualized discourse is that, via the processes of visual objectification and white mythological discourses (scientific, filmic and literary), the black man is effectively reduced to the phallus: 'no longer do we see the black man; we see a penis; the black man has been occulted. He has been turned into a penis. He *is* a penis' (p. 147).[15]

The black athlete (as the quintessence of blackness) assumes the preeminent position as *the* 'penis-symbol' and becomes a fantasmatic trope through which anxieties concerning the fragility of western (male) sexuality are played out.[16] The black athlete is thus positioned as a site for voyeuristic admiration – the black athlete is idolized for its sheer super-human physicality – but also controlled by a complex process of objectification and sexualization that once again renders the threat of negritude controllable to white patriarchy. As I argue in more detail in the next chapter, the fear of the black athlete as a commodity-sign is thus appropriated, its political symbolic potential neutered, and finally 'domesticated' by its exploitation within contemporary consumer society and its attendant media culture. Thus the *very same* 'Joe Louis' that was a (political) signifier of redemption and salvation for the black American prisoner facing death in the gas chamber, here becomes a fetishized object producing both fearful dread *and* sexual release for the white European psyche. The black athlete is imagined in all of these iterations as containing and quite literally embodying *power* itself.

Developing this line of argument, McClintock (1995: 375) suggests that fetishes are not merely, or solely, phallic icons but become expressive of wider crises in social values that are then 'projected onto and embodied in, what can be called impassioned objects'. Paraphrasing McClintock, I want to further argue that the early twentieth century crisis of whiteness sought to resolve itself by turning the 'athletic black body' into an 'impassioned object' that throughout the twentieth century became a ubiquitous and highly profitable commodity. The display of black bodies within many professional sports thus becomes a contested fetishized ritual of racial spectacle and (homosocial) desire that is capable of producing both narratives of freedom as well as forms of subjugation.

### Terrible Strength: Sporting Violence and Black Freedom

There is a sense in which Jack Johnson has never been an easy figure to recuperate for mainstream African American history. His flaunting not only of white laws but also black expectations has led to a certain reluctance to elevate Johnson into the pantheon of great African American historical figures that might otherwise have been expected. He did not fit easily with the black political positions of his time. Johnson's 'politics' was profoundly individualistic and in many ways conservative, based on the premise that he had as much right to the spoils of the great American society as anyone else yet his public displays of brash assertiveness meant that he could not easily be accommodated with the assimilationist politics of a Booker T. Washington that he might otherwise have identified with. Similarly, his courageous strength to confront directly the inequities of white supremacy made him an icon of sorts for more radical forms of black nationalist politics, yet his notion of self often came at the expense of or with little regard for broader forms of collectivist politics thus making him a difficult figure for the likes of W.E.B. Du Bois to embrace without qualification. While it would be an exaggeration to say he has been ignored – and with the 2005 PBS documentary on his life and the accompanying biography by Geoffrey Ward, interest in his life and story has increased once again – it is undoubtedly the case that Johnson's impact on American life and African American culture tends to be downplayed when compared to the other three canonical Js of early African American sporting history: *Jesse, Joe and Jackie*.

For example, in Robin Kelley and Earl Lewis's (2000) nearly 700-page edited volume *To Make Our World Anew: A History of African Americans*, Johnson, astonishingly, does not receive a single mention, not even a footnote. While it is true that sport in general does not figure prominently in the book, despite its claim to provide a panoramic view of black life, other notable African American sporting greats are at least mentioned, albeit in rather cursory ways. Even the brief chronology of significant dates in African American history at the end of the book has room for Jackie Robinson's 1947 debut for the Brooklyn Dodgers, Joe Louis's 1938 defeat of Max Schleming and even the 1920 founding of the Negro National League in baseball, but not for Johnson's historic victories and his life as a thoroughly modern black subject.

For the emerging early twentieth century black bourgeoisie, Johnson embodied a series of contradictions. His sheer physicality, confidence and strength both impressed and unsettled them. He represented a version of negritude that was neither afraid of nor intimidated by whiteness. There were few, if any, public figures of the time that were so strident in their *public* disregard for white attempts at reducing blacks to the status of social inferior. In fact, it was not so much that Johnson refused to accept his subordinate position to whites but that he actively and willfully suggested *his superiority*.

Just as he had done with Tommy Burns before, when Johnson fought Jeffries – fully aware of the wider racial and political significance of the fight and surrounded by a white, largely hostile crowd – he goaded his opponent in the most provocative of ways. During the bout Johnson followed up his physical assaults on Jeffries's bloodied body with verbal assaults, asking after each punch, 'How do you like it?'. In the fourteenth round and after throwing three unanswered punches at the exhausted and weary Jeffries, Johnson enquired 'Does it hurt, Jim?' (Roberts 1983: 106). Johnson's contemptuous bravado exceeded the definitions of black pride that progressive black politics had mapped out as the permissible alternative to submissive, deferential incorporation. Johnson pointed instead to an as yet unobtainable and at times barely imaginable, post-racial social contract wherein the individual pursuit of freedom and happiness, unbounded by racial mores and ties, would be the only defining characteristic as to how a person would and should be judged. He was post-Civil Rights before there had even been a Civil Rights movement.

Johnson's radical provocations, not the least of which included his flagrant transgression of sleeping, repeatedly, across the color line, meant that a deep ambivalence ran through the judgments of the leading black intellectuals as regards Johnson's impact on black politics. Nevertheless, black leaders knew that Johnson's actions both inside and outside of the ring were profoundly important in the struggle for racial justice. The fanatical white reaction induced by each Johnson victory, the 'thrill of national disgust', as W.E.B. Du Bois (1914: 181) phrased it in an editorial in the journal *The Crisis*, was supposedly an objection aimed at Johnson's dubious 'character'. But, noted Du Bois, America had long put up with the philandering of white athletes and even statesmen without subjecting them to the same level of hostility that Johnson had faced. The truth was that Johnson was being punished for his 'unforgiveable blackness' (p.181).

The writer, academic and civil rights activist James Weldon Johnson, who was friends with Jack Johnson, described him as 'the most interesting person' (1933: 208) he had ever met. His descriptions of his 1905 encounters with the boxer, before he had fought for the world title, served to highlight Johnson's immense physicality in a way that bordered on a voyeuristic fascination with working-class, southern alterity:

> Jack often boxed with me playfully, like a good-natured big dog warding off the earnest attacks of a small one, but I could never get him to give me any serious instruction. Occasionally, he would bare his stomach to me as a mark and urge me to hit him with all my might. I found it an impossible thing to do; I always involuntarily pulled my punch. It was easy to like Jack Johnson; he is so likable a man, and I like him particularly well. I was, of course, impressed by his huge but perfect form, his terrible strength, and the supreme ease and grace of his every muscular movement; however, watching his face, sad until he smiled, listening to his soft Southern speech and laughter, and hearing him talk so wistfully about his big chance, yet to come, I found it difficult to think of him as a prize fighter. (1933: 208)

Sensing that such power had deeper political import, the writer and activist noted the symbolic and literal connections between the *sporting prizefighter* and the *political freedom fighter*. 'Frederick Douglass', James Weldon Johnson goes on to note, 'had a picture of Peter Jackson in his study and used to point to it and say, "Peter is doing a great deal with his fists to solve the Negro question." I think that Jack, even after the reckoning of his big and little failings has been made, may be said to have done his share' (1933: 208).

Douglass's connection between the freedom fighter and the pugilist should not be surprising. *Narrative of the Life of Fredrick Douglass, an*

*American Slave* establishes, as Saidiya Hartman notes, the centrality of violence in the making of not just slavery but the slave subject itself and 'identifies it as an original generative act equivalent to the statement "I was born"' (1997: 3). The blood-stained birth of the slave subject becomes a 'primal scene' in the formation of the enslaved. If this 'terrible spectacle' (p. 3) is used to dramatize the originatory moment of slave subjecthood and marks the brutal dialectical conditions of domination of the black subject/white master, then violence also marks *the moment of release* from subjugation both for the individual and, as Fanon would later argue, for the broader national consciousness of the colonial subject. The moment and act of physical struggle creates the conditions from which a post-slave consciousness, that is more fully and complexly human, can emerge. Douglass's (1845/2003) own recounting of the moment of metaphysical emancipation that resulted from his famous fight with Edward Covey, is worth quoting here:

> This battle with Mr. Covey was the turning-point in my career as a slave. It rekindled the few expiring embers of freedom, and revived within me a sense of my own manhood. It recalled the departed self-confidence, and inspired me again with determination to be free. The gratification afforded by the triumph was a full compensation for whatever else might follow, even death itself. He only can understand the deep satisfaction which I experienced who has himself repelled by force the bloody arm of slavery. I felt as I never felt before. It was a glorious resurrection, from the tomb of slavery, to the heaven of freedom. My long-crushed spirit rose, cowardice departed, bold defiance took its place; and I now resolved that, however long I might remain a slave in form, the day had passed forever when I could be a slave in fact. I did not hesitate to let it be known of me, that the white man who expected to succeed in whipping, must also succeed in killing me. (1845/2003: 69)

We might better understand now how the role of the boxer (and therefore of the black athlete) has come to be seen as a revolutionary agent of resistance to the most total forms of racial domination and white supremacy.[17] That such acts of violent resistance are contradictory should be immediately obvious. The 'productive' use of violence raises a number of profound ethical questions. We must avoid simply valorizing such instantiations of black politics as if they do not entail some deeply problematic outcomes. Such moments of violent anti-racist praxis bring to the fore the difficulties in trying to think through the contradictions of the gendered nature of struggle itself.

Indeed, as was earlier argued, sport, as a form of regulated play, contains within its very constitution the paradoxes of freedom and constraint. It should not be a surprise to find that the use of sport by the subaltern reproduces and in fact accentuates these paradoxical elements – a kind of doubling of the effects of freedom and domination. However, rather than dismissing sport's political praxis as inherently 'compromised', as many critical theorists have tended to do (the master's games cannot dismantle the master's rules) and seeking to avoid the oftentimes utopian embrace of black athletes as proto-revolutionaries often found in the writings of those desperate to defend the complicated actions and lives of black athletes – ghetto ball 'playas' seen as the new black revolutionary guard (Boyd 2003) – I want to suggest that we need to hold these constitutive contradictions in productive tension and to read them diachronically and dialectically against each other.

In her detailed exposition of the freedom claims contained within the pragmatic, strategic and performative acts of defiance that structured black leisure and cultural practices during and after slavery, Saidiya Hartman suggests that:

> since acts of resistance exist within the context of relations of domination and are not external to them, they acquire their character from these relations, and vice versa. At a dance, holiday fete, or corn shucking, the line between dominant and insurgent orchestrations of blackness could be effaced or fortified in the course of an evening, either because the enslaved utilized instrumental amusements for contrary purposes or because surveillance necessitated cautious forms of interaction and modes of expression. (1997: 8)

What Johnson threw into stark relief was the abject failure of American society to come true on its belated promises of freedom and emancipation. If the inter-war period was, as Martin Luther King, Jr had suggested, a dark time for black political claims for freedom, then the period after Reconstruction was just as, if not more, dispiriting. Under such conditions of domination (which we should remember framed the black experience throughout the colonial world and not just in the United States) the politics of everyday struggle, of infrapolitics, became central to both sustaining life itself as well as offering a utopian politics of transformation and transfiguration.

Writers such as James Scott (1985, 1990) and Paul Gilroy (1993a, 2000) have shown that the cultural, symbolic and linguistic weapons of the weak have provided a powerful alternative to the public scripts of domination that underwrote racial exploitation and genocide. Hartman too notes that under such conditions of domination, in which access to the formal institutions of state politics are greatly curtailed, such everyday political acts and cultural practices help to 'illuminate inchoate and utopian expressions of freedom that are not and perhaps cannot be actualized elsewhere. The desires and longings that exceed the frame of civil rights and political emancipation find expression in quotidian acts labeled "fanciful", "exorbitant", and "excessive" primarily because they express an understating or imagination of freedom quite at odds with bourgeois expectations' (1997: 13).

Put another way, sport enabled Johnson to 'get away' with what he did, precisely because sport was seen to be (and still is) apolitical; a space that sits outside of the formal demands of politics and therefore questions of power and ideology. Sport's putatively post-political framing enabled Johnson do things in the ring that would have been impossible in any other social or cultural arena at the time. The personal financial rewards accrued through his boxing success gave him a temporary degree of relative autonomy *outside of the ring* from the racial strictures of Jim Crow America and the wider colonial world. His wealth, gained from the newly emerging capitalist consumer culture and not insubstantial for the time, meant that he was able to largely circumvent the system of debt-bondage (Hartman 1997: 139) that came to replace slavery for most black laborers of his age. But Johnson's triumphs (as well as his failings) could never be read as simply personal achievements. Given the historical moment into which he came, his impact transcended the biographical to reshape broader social parameters. James Scott makes a relevant point here when he notes:

> Whenever a rare event legitimately allowed the black community to vicariously and publicly savor the physical victory of a black man over a white man, that event became an epoch-making one in folk memory. The fight between Jack Johnson and Jim Jeffries (the 'White Hope') in 1910 and Joe Louis's subsequent career, which was aided by instant radio transmission of the fights, were indelible moments of reversal and revenge for the black community … Lest such moments be seen purely as a safety valve reconciling blacks to their quotidian world of white domination, there were racial fights in every state in the South and in much of the North immediately after the 1910 fight. The proximate causes varied, but it is clear that in the flush of their jubilation, blacks became momentarily bolder in gesture, speech, and carriage, and this was seen by much of the white community as a provocation, a breach of the public transcript. Intoxication comes in many forms. (1990: 41)

Sport is able to symbolically impact the racial order precisely because it can simultaneously claim to be a space removed from politics. Sport also enabled black people to go beyond simple mimicry. While the rules of the game would have to be learned, and the tactics and strategies of success may have initially been copied from the public scripts provided by Victorian elites, over time the informal codes of behavior, *how the game was really to be played*, could, eventually be re-written. Before Johnson, most black athletes simply followed these permissible scripts that defined their social roles and engaged in cautious forms of interaction and modes of expression. Johnson took the play book, subverted it, and turned it upside down. White became black, black became white. He dismantled the racial logic, and added some lines of his own, as he struck out against Jim Crow itself: 'Does it hurt, *Jim?*'

Of course the reaction to this was furious and brought to the fore the naked virulence of white racism, exposing the pretensions of European bourgeois civility, that Césaire and Fanon would later so brilliantly debunk. Take, as an example, the writings of Bohun Lynch. Lynch epitomized the early twentieth century English upper-class view on Johnson and on racial difference more generally. Lynch studied at Haileybury (formerly the East India College set up to train civil servants heading to India) and University College, Oxford, where he boxed as a middle-weight and was, unsurprisingly, a big supporter of Tommy Burns during the 1908 bout (Roberts 1983: 63). Lynch was a refined, worldly, educated man of letters, a journalist who wrote on topics as diverse as boxing, antique furniture, drawings (he was himself a caricaturist) and the Italian Riviera. He even penned science fiction novels in his spare time.

Lynch outlines his views on the changing nature of the sport in his 1914 book *The Complete Boxer*, which also carried a preface by Hugh Lowther, the Earl of Lonsdale, the founding President of the National Sporting Club and the namesake for the Lonsdale Belt. So what did the book to which 'England's greatest sporting gentleman' had written the preface have to say about the role of the black boxer? Lynch is, unsurprisingly, concerned at the professionalization of boxing that is supposedly undermining the amateur spirit. The true craft of the noble sport is yearly being destroyed by the vulgarity of commerce. Lynch does not deny the more honorable prize fighters of old from earning an honest wage from their endeavors. In fact Lynch compares the 'good, old fashioned bruiser' (1914: 169) who at the end of his career quietly retires with his financial hoard to open a pub, with today's British 'young pugs'. These young impressionable white boxers, Lynch suggests, are being led astray by their black American peers who are implanting 'dizzier ambitions' in the young, naïve British boxers, impressed as they are with the Americans' 'diamonds' (post-Edwardian sporting 'bling') and general swagger. Lynch adds that, of course, 'if a man squarely earns his money, no one has the least right to dictate the method of its expenditure. If the young boxer tries to be swell, let him try. But it is a sad buffoonery: and the sadder from his own point of view – if he only knew it – because flashiness is so very characteristic of the black' (1914: 170).

The 'flashy blacks' are the least of Lynch's concerns, however. The very nature of the sport itself is being troubled by the new generation of black boxers who, unlike their fine predecessors (he mentions Bill Richmond) who fought with great skill and a sense of honor, now have elevated ideas about their station in life. Rehearsing some of the racial myths of the day concerning physical difference, Lynch complements the skills of some black boxers, before adding:

> But, as already said, a black man is not made in the same way as a white man. He is far less sensitive about the head and jaw: he can take, almost without knowing it, a blow which would knock out the toughest and most seasoned white pugilist. So that, other things being equal, the white man and the black enter the ring together upon a different footing. In some cases a negro's weakness in the stomach countervails the hardiness of his head, but not always. But these inequalities in physique are of small importance compared to the matter of temperament. Any triumph, of whatsoever nature, turns the head of the average black. It is bad for him because he behaves like a spoiled child, which is just what he is. And when that triumph is a personal one, over a white man, the nigger becomes an appalling creature, a devil. His insolence knows no bounds. His preposterous swagger excites the passionate hatred of ignorant white men, the disgust of their betters. There is no holding him until his money has run out, or he transgresses the law. It is far better that blacks should

be allowed to fight, exclusively, amongst themselves. There are good black boxers – reasonable men – with a sense of proportion, a sense of the fitness of things – good sportsmen with clear heads; Peter Jackson was one, but they are not sufficiently numerous to warrant mixed fighting. (1914/2007: 170–171)

Apart from the way in which such criticisms mirror contemporary moralists in their critique of professional black athletes for their ostentatious and 'vulgar' displays of sporting bling, what is important here is the shift that begins to take place in acknowledging that the absolutism of racial difference, that before was merely a matter for tactical circumvention by the white boxer but that still left the white man superior, is now in doubt. The fear is not just that both racial types may be entering the ring on a 'different footing' but that the black athlete may in fact have *an advantage*. That, in fact, blacks may be, in some strange as yet unproven way, *physically superior to whites*. And worse still, that such sporting victories are beginning to 'turn the heads' of the average blacks.

It is also interesting that Lynch, in this passage, does not directly mention Johnson by name. But it would have been apparent to readers of the time exactly who Lynch had in mind with those descriptions. In a sense, Johnson did not have to be named. Johnson had ushered in and created, by his own actions and the reactions of his detractors, the very modern image of the aggressive, muscular, brash, animalistic and above all powerful black Other: 'the black athlete'. The black boxer was merely the purest form of this new subjectivity. Johnson did not need to be named for the fear of the black athlete to be known.

When Johnson was finally defeated by Jess Willard on April 5, 1915 in Havana, Cuba, there was an immediate sense of relief among many whites and a hope that the racial order could be put back in place; that the aberration could and would be forgotten with time; that Johnson's victories were a historical blip, much like the Haitian Revolution. The nightmarish seven years of black pride and arrogance were at an end. Within weeks of the Johnson–Willard fight, American cinemas would also be showing *Birth of a Nation*. White supremacy was back, enabling even the least physically able of whites to once again lay claim to racial supremacy via their identification with the victorious pugilistic White Hope. *The Chicago Tribune* was explicit:

It is a point of pride with the ascendant race not to concede supremacy in anything, not even to a gorilla. The fact that Mr. Willard made it possible for many millions of his fellow citizens to sit down to their dinners last night with renewed confidence in their eight inch biceps, flexed, and their twenty-eight inch chests, expanded, is his peculiar triumph. (Ward 2004: 382)

Willard quickly announced that just as he had never fought a black man before the fight, so he would not in the future (p. 381). But things would not be the same. The racial scaffolding could not be put back. The master's house had been irrevocably damaged and changed. Jack Johnson could not be forgotten. His impact and imprint had been too great. As much as the white colonial frame tried, Johnson's 'unforgiveable blackness' and his 'terrible strength' had shattered the myth of physical white supremacy. The effect was to alter racial discourse itself.

When Joe Louis arrived on the heavyweight scene in the mid-1930s his management ensured that Louis would become acceptable to the broader American public by becoming the anti-Jack Johnson; no vulgarity of language, or mocking of whites, and certainly no public relationships with white women. Victories would now be met with a solemn respectfulness, the broad confident smile replaced with deferential modesty (Runstedtler 2005). However, the attempt by Louis to distance himself from Johnson, to move away from the image of 'the black athlete', served to constitute it once again. It was sustained in the public imaginary by the very attempt at denial.[18] The angry, rebellious black Other inhabits the space of the gracious, deferential black athlete, even as the good black athlete may personally attempt to shun any notion of rebelliousness. The crisis of whiteness and the fault lines of the colonial racial order ensured that Fanon's white patients would associate 'Joe Louis' with devil, sin, biology and sex, *regardless* of what he actually said and did, inside and out of the ring.

After the Second World War, with the slow retreat from overt theories of racial hierarchy and the profound discrediting of eugenics brought about by the revulsion to Hitlerism, the white colonial frame could no longer, or at least not so easily, lay claim to the same forms of white supremacy that it had before. Coupled with the piecemeal but steady desegregation of American sports in the late 1940s and through the 1950s, wherein blacks were now 'allowed' to compete with and against white athletes, the narrative of 'whites as physically superior' disappeared, alongside the collapse of the old colonial order. And yet, as one set of racial logics was displaced, another re-emerged to complete the ideological suturing necessary to maintain white supremacy in the moment after colonialism. The primitive would return within the definitional scaffolding of 'the black athlete'. Whereas it has increasingly become problematic to refer to non-Europeans as 'primitives', although very occasionally such language is still used, a metonymic signifier was created that worked just as well. The colonial tropes that once marked the primitive – savage, wild, uncontrolled, emotional, lazy – now provide a way to describe errant black athletes who, if left to their own devices, are wont to engage in acts of violent deviancy and to shirk their responsibilities unless disciplined by the appropriate white (father) figure who is able to tame and channel the bestial power that supposedly lurks inside the black athlete.[19]

At the end of the twentieth century the fantasmatic figure of the uncivilized and uncivilizable black athlete that Jack Johnson had helped to bring to birth once again found its expression in the shape of a boxer that came to be known across the globe as 'Mike Tyson'. And just as the arrogant American Johnson was often contrasted, as Bohun Lynch did earlier, with the good colonial sporting subject that was Peter Jackson, so too would the

British media create an anti-Mike Tyson; a good black sporting subject as a model for black Britons to follow, this time called 'Frank Bruno'.

## Notes

1 As Stephen Jay Gould notes, 'Gobineau was undoubtedly the most influential academic racist of the nineteenth century. His writings strongly affected such intellectuals as Wagner and Nietzsche and inspired a social movement known as Gobinism. Largely through his impact on the English zealot Houston Stewart Chamberlain, Gobineau's ideas served as a foundation for the racial theories espoused by Adolf Hitler. Gobineau, an aristocratic royalist by background, interspersed writing with a successful diplomatic career for the French government. He authored several novels and works of historical nonfiction (a history of the Persian people and of the European Renaissance, for example), but became most famous for his four-volume work on racial inequality, published between 1853 and 1855' (Gould 1996: 379–380).

2 See McClintock when she notes: 'In 1810, the exhibition of the African woman, Saartjie Baartman became the paradigm for the invention of the female body as an anachronism. The supposedly excessive genitalia of this woman (represented as they were as an excess of *clitoral* visibility in the figure of the "Hottentot apron") were overexposed and pathologized before the disciplinary gaze of male medical science and a voyeuristic public. [Georges] Cuvier, in his notorious medicalizing of her skeleton, compared the female of the "lowest" human species with the "highest ape" (the orangutan), seeing an atavistic affinity in the "anomalous" appearance of the black woman's "organ of generation"' (1995: 42). See also Lola Young's (1996) *Fear of the Dark: 'Race', Gender and Sexuality in the Cinema*, Sander Gilman's (1985) essay 'The Hottentot and the Prostitute' in *Difference and Pathology: Stereotypes of Sexuality, Race, and Madness*; and Anne Fausto-Sterling's (2000) essay 'Gender, Race, and Nation: The Comparative Anatomy of "Hottentot" Women in Europe, 1815–1817'.

3 In his autobiography *In and Out of the Ring*, Jack Johnson would later recount his feelings of the 1908 Burns fight: 'I had attained my life's ambition. The little Galveston colored boy had defeated the world's champion boxer, and for the first and only time in history, a black man held one of the greatest honors which exists in the field of sport and athletics – an honor for which white men had contested many times and which they held as a dear and most desirable one. Naturally I felt a high sense of exaltation. I was supremely glad I had attained the championship, but I kept this feeling to myself. I did not gloat over the fact that a white man had fallen. My satisfaction was only in the fact that one man had conquered another, and that I had been the conqueror. To me it was not a racial triumph, but there were those who were to take this view of the situation, and almost immediately a great hue and cry went up because a colored man was holding the championship' (1927/1992: 58).

4 Peter 'Black Prince' Jackson (1861–1901) was a black Australian fighter, originally born in the Caribbean Virgin Islands, and former deckhand in the Sydney docks, who went on to become the Australian, British Commonwealth and World Colored Heavyweight champion. He memorably fought a 61 round, four-hour bout with James Corbett in 1891 that ended in a draw after both boxers reached the point of exhaustion. John L. Sullivan and later Corbett himself

refused to allow Jackson to compete for the world title on the grounds of race (see Sammons 1988: 32–33). Jackson is regarded by boxing historians as one of the best boxers never to have been given a chance at the world heavyweight championship.

5 The heroic sporting qualities that would otherwise enhance the inherent *humanness* of the athlete become instead instantiations of the intrinsic reflexes of innate black athleticism. White writers and commentators thus strived to animalize and thereby discredit black sporting achievements. Paul Gallico, the then *New York Times* sports editor, described Joe Louis as 'the magnificent animal … He eats. He sleeps. He fights … Is he all instinct, all animal? Or have a hundred million years left a fold upon his brain? I see in this colored man something so cold, so hard, so cruel that I wonder as to his bravery. Courage in the animal is desperation. Courage in the human is something incalculable and divine' (cited in Coakley 1998: 258).

6 The biologist Joseph Graves, in rebutting biologically determinist accounts of sporting performance linked to 'race', notes that 'we can show that it takes very little migration to explain the small amount of genetic diversity we see among human populations. The long and short of this is that for most large populations, there is sufficient genetic variation to produce virtually any body type in conjunction with other specific physiological traits. This means that we could produce great athletes for virtually any sport, anywhere in the world, given the correct cultural and environmental input' (2005: 147).

7 On this point see, for example, the belated and rather inadequate *mea culpa* of the critical geographer John Bale: 'In 2004 I was invited to join a group of scientists at Glasgow University who had established an International Center for East African Running Science. I was impressed by the fact that the group consisted of scholars from the humanities and social sciences as well as from the "hard" sciences of biology, nutrition, and genetics … They had visited Kenya, examined hundreds of runners, taken blood and DNA samples, undertaken genetic analysis, established whether the boys they interviewed ran or walked to school, and checked the athletes' diets. The runners' bodies were measured and analyzed. I was reminded of the anthropological antics of the nineteenth-century explorers. Back in Glasgow a conference was held where the results were presented to an excited audience of trainers and scholars. Additionally, an international road race was held in which it was demonstrated that the first six finishers were from East Africa. A Kenyan runner of world-class standard was invited to make a short presentation to the conference and to answer questions from the audience. One of her responses was: "Why are you studying me? Why don't you study the British world-record marathon runner, Paula Radcliffe?" I felt uneasy about being one of the group's members' (2008: 340).

8 This form of sporting interpellation also, of course, provided a possible moment to construct an anti-racist white identity that rejected such hailing. Much of the research on Johnson, for example, has tended to ignore the fact that most of his entourage were actually white. Although Johnson's relationships with various white women are well known and widely discussed in the literature, Johnson clearly had large numbers of white supporters and friends who were invested in his success. No doubt much of this can be explained by the financial rewards that would have accompanied anyone in Johnson's circle, but a significant part would likely have also resulted from intra-class allegiances, friendship and respect that cut across racial lines even amidst deeply racialized social circumstances. We

might ponder too that, notwithstanding the violence of working-class racism at the time in the United States and elsewhere, Johnson remained a *popular* figure among thousands, perhaps millions, of working-class whites too, especially in Europe. The fact that middle-class elites were so concerned to ban fights involving Johnson and the *films* of those fights shows, perhaps, that Johnson actually had a degree of popular support among some sections of the white working-class that white elites had to work hard to negate. On this point see David Roediger (2005: 104–105).

9  Boxers of the era would often make as much money, if not more, from the sales of fight films as they would the fight fee itself, hence their self-interest in making sure bouts lasted at least ten rounds.

10  That 'the black athlete' was marked as male should not be surprising. Given the limited opportunities for women to play sport, and the barely existing professional careers for female athletes that relegated female sports to the margins of commercially viable activity, the space of the black athlete was largely occupied by black men. Although the black athlete is coded as masculine it is not inherently male. The later arrival of black female athletes on to the national and international stage would require them to be framed in relation to the dominant representation of the black athlete. Indeed, as I suggest, 'the black athlete' becomes a descriptor for all black people regardless of whether they are male or even an athlete.

11  Woody Strode, along with Kenny Washington, broke the 'color line' of American football when both athletes played for the Los Angeles Rams in 1946, ending the racist selection policies of NFL teams that had been reintroduced in 1934 (Marion Motley and Bill Willis would sign for the Cleveland Browns in the same year and, as younger players, would go on to have successful NFL careers). As football grew in popularity during the early decades of the twentieth century, blacks were slowly excluded from the professional ranks. As Alexander Wolff notes, 'in 1933 the NFL restructured itself into two divisions of five teams each, with a season-ending title game, which led to more media attention and presumably a desire to emulate baseball and its commercially successful formula of large markets and all-white rosters' (2009: 62). Interestingly, Strode and Washington played college football for UCLA with a young Jackie Robinson, who would himself go on to challenge racial segregation in baseball. For accounts of American football's history of racial segregation see Wolff's (2009) *Sports Illustrated* essay 'The NFL's Jackie Robinson' and Andy Piascik's (2009) book *Gridiron Gauntlet*.

12  This is a spectacle that was literally manifest with the 'Anthropological Days' that formed part of the 1904 Olympic Games in St Louis, wherein the scientists of the day and the public at large could watch the savages compete against each other in specially organized 'native games' inside the fairgrounds of the world fair. For an excellent account of this event see Brownell (2008).

13  On the 'erotic' in sport see Allen Guttmann's (1996) *The Erotic in Sports* and Toby Miller's (2001) *Sportsex*.

14  This racialized context of white desire for and envy of the black body is, of course, central to understanding the popularity of the *Rocky* films, wherein the white male psyche can project fantasies of both Great White Hope mastery through the identification with Rocky, while enjoying the spectacle of hyper-blackness that is in evidence with the array of black boxers on display. Indeed the physical and at times intimately playful relationship between

Rocky Balboa (played by Sylvester Stallone) and Apollo Creed (Carl Weathers) is surely one of modern cinema's most enduring but unconsummated homoerotic relationships.

15 Elsewhere (see Carrington 2000) I have analyzed the British media discourse surrounding the sprinter Linford Christie and how Christie, via the popular euphemism of 'Linford's lunch-box', came to quite literally embody Fanon's psychoanalytical reading of how the black man is turned into the phallus.

16 We should remember too that Jack Johnson was eventually stripped of his title and forced to flee the United States not because of a defeat in the ring but due to the criminal charges of 'white slavery' brought against him under the Mann Act, originally passed to protect the sexual exploitation of white women. That is, Johnson's relationships with white women (which many whites at the time believed must have been coercive and therefore illegal) were the basis upon which trumped-up charges of prostitution and 'pimping' were brought against Johnson and eventually led to his downfall. For accounts see Morgan (1999) and Johnson (2006).

17 See also Rhoden, who argues: 'For Douglass, the act of fighting, not winning was liberating. His liberation lay in having the courage to fight his oppressor. He translated the symbolism of confrontation in real terms. He fought a system of slavery, challenging it in a fundamental way by engaging his overseer in a life-or-death struggle. For many blacks, sports were similarly symbolic ways of physically transcending the system of bondage, a space of freedom' (2006: 49).

18 It is not surprising that Muhammad Ali would, unlike most athletes since, lay claim to Johnson's mantle. Ali is reported to have said that, if you replaced the issue of Johnson's relations with white women with the question of religion, Johnson's story of persecution outside of the ring and his figurative fight to be who he wanted to be on his own terms, was Ali's story as well (see Ward 2004: 429).

19 John Lee Hancock's (2009) film version of Michael Lewis's (2006) book *The Blind Side*, itself based on the life of the NFL player Michael Oher, provides a contemporary twist to this colonial trope. In the film version of the story, it is a white conservative matriarch (Leigh Anne Tuohy played by Sandra Bullock) who takes up the Christian obligation to 'save' Oher from the savagery of the black urban ghetto and the dysfunctionality of black family life (Oher is both figuratively and literally adopted by the Tuohy family and therefore into the space of white civility and domesticity), and in so doing – and as with Christian missionaries of the colonial period – able to save her own soul too. The film depicts Oher as a sheer mass of power (sporting negritude), unable to speak (for much of the film Oher does not talk, indicating his inner emotions through physical gestures and monosyllabic replies) and largely unaware of his own sporting potential. The 'inner athlete' is finally awoken in Oher by the gentle coaxing of Leigh Anne Tuohy who is able to use (female) empathy and analogy rather than (male) logical instruction, to get Oher to finally understand the rules and dynamics of American football, and hence to realize his destiny as a future offensive tackle.

# 3

# Sporting Negritude: Commodity Blackness and the Liberation of Failure

Professional sports have constituted an alternative work arena for many black men. In that world the black male body once used and abused in a world of labor based on brute force could be transformed; elegance and grace could become the identifying signifiers of one's labor. Historically entering the world of professional sports was a profoundly political endeavor for black men. If you wanted to enter that world you had to be willing to push against racial boundaries and there was no real way to escape the political. From Joe Louis to Muhammad Ali, from Wilt Chamberlin to Kareem Abdul-Jabbar, professional sports was a location where many black males received their education for critical consciousness about the politics of race and black male bodies. (bell hooks)

Colonialism returns at the moment of its disappearance. (Ann McClintock)

A black is not a man. (Frantz Fanon)

## Battle Royals and the Spectacle of Negritude

The startling sight of the naked, blonde-haired, young white woman caused some of the black boys to become aroused. One boy fainted, while the others started to cry as thick cigar-smoke filled the ballroom, choking the lungs of the young boys. The town's white male elite, drunk on beer and whisky, watched as the blonde began to dance. The music quickened and the atmosphere in the room grew darker as the old men attempted to grab her exposed body. She tried to flee but the white mob gave chase. 'It was mad. Chairs went crashing, drinks were spilt, as they ran laughing and howling after her. They caught her just as she reached a door, raised her from the floor, and tossed her as college boys are tossed at a hazing, and above her red, fixed-smiling lips I saw the terror and disgust in her eyes, almost like my own terror and that which I saw in some of the other boys.'

The woman managed to escape, and with that the attention of the old white men turned to the ten petrified boys. They were ordered into the ring for the start of the *battle royal*. Blindfolded and disorientated, the boys' job for the evening was to beat each other in blind fury for the entertainment of the on-lookers. 'Everyone fought hysterically. It was complete anarchy. Everybody fought everybody else. No group fought together for long. Two, three, four fought one, then turned to fight each other, were themselves attacked. Blows landed below the belt and in the kidney ... The smoke was agonizing and there were no rounds, no bells at three-minute intervals to relieve our exhaustion. The room spun around me, a swirl of light, smoke, sweating bodies surrounded by tense white faces. I bled from both nose and mouth, the blood spattering upon my chest. The men kept yelling, "Slug him, black boy! Knock his guts out!" "Uppercut him! Kill him! Kill that big boy!".'

Ralph Ellison's (1952) famous battle royal scene that opens *Invisible Man* is a powerful yet disturbing depiction of the chaos and fear felt by the book's unnamed protagonist that mixes together a range of conflicting, disjointed emotions from the various participants: sexual arousal, racist abuse, pain and torture, joy and laughter, fear and violence. We recall that after the grotesque spectacle of the fight itself the bloodied boys are left to scramble for coins upon an electrified rug as the white men sit laughing. Ellison skillfully captures, in a few short pages, a sense of the confused desperation that is produced by the complete sensual domination of the young boys' bodies. Both the black boys performing in their semi-naked state and the naked white women are served up as visual entertainment for the white, male gaze. Black athletic beasts and white blonde beauties. Ellison here teases out the psychological and troubling dynamics of that most sexually charged trope within the colonial racial imaginary. Black men with white women becomes *the* taboo sexual pairing that has invoked the deepest fears of white, male impotency and loss, even as that fear is then turned into a form of voyeuristic mastery and scopic control by the desire to watch and to see, turning both the black male body and white female form into sexualized objects. Within the literary, cultural and media tropes of the west, the black male becomes the predatory Other that throughout history is supposedly driven to defile and destroy white femininity: Othello, Jack Johnson, *King Kong*, O.J. Simpson, Tiger Woods'.[1] The white male thus has the authority to either intervene against the power of the hyper-masculine black Other – through technology, the law, the use of force – or, conversely, to engage the fetish play of the loss of masculine control by 'actively' allowing the black Other access to feminine whiteness, under the conditions and understanding, of course, that the white male can continue to watch, as in the set-up for numerous 'inter-racial' pornographic websites that allow for this (virtual) form of racial/masculine 'reversal' of power.

In Ellison's account the white men retain near absolute power to dictate the conditions under which the performances will be undertaken: the woman dances before being set upon, the boys fight before being electrified, the interventions of some of the more sober members of the white elite being the only thing keeping both from an even worse fate, thus casting white men as both instigators and saviors of the fate of the dependent Others. The black boys are drawn towards the unobtainable: the white woman's body. They are compelled to both look *at* and look *away* in fear and embarrassment. They are aroused and permitted to look (as men in the making) but immediately denied the 'right' to do so; white patriarchy setting the limits to black masculinity's access to the (white) female form. And, significantly, black femininity gets erased altogether from this primal scene of sporting negritude. An absent presence that is necessary for the scene to take place at all (as cooks, cleaners, mothers, domestics) but rendered invisible as actual bodies, not even there to not be seen.

We might also, perhaps, read this terrible scene as a somewhat pessimistic allegory for the fate of the black athlete in the world of modern sports. The black boys are given a chance to win their 'freedom' within this circumscribed (sporting) arena. They have a degree of agency for sure. But this comes at the expense of dominating each other. In the end the physical strength of the strongest and toughest of the boys counts for little. Real power, we are aware, lies outside the ring among the onlookers and patrons. The black boys' blows serve only to knock each other out, for the amusement of the white audience. Their own subjective violence towards each other serves, in the end, to both reproduce and therefore disguise the objective forms of violence (Žižek 2009) inherent within the system of white supremacist capitalist patriarchy. We are left with little doubt that anyone trapped for any length of time in such an environment of forbidden racialized sexual arousal, of physical assault and racial abuse, of false promises of freedom, and of the denial of humanity, would surely and eventually go mad.[2]

In her essay 'Chains of Madness, Chains of Colonialism: Fanon and Freedom' Françoise Vergès remarks that in *Black Skin, White Masks* Fanon had shown 'that colonialism had configured colonized masculinity as feminized and emasculated, and concluded that men in the colony had to reconstruct their manhood and their freedom through a rejection of colonial images' (1996: 60–61). Representation itself – the words, images, stories and depictions of the black Other – served to render the black male as a *failed* man, lacking the ability and power to exercise any form of patriarchal mastery even over his own body, let alone those of others. This provided a set of contradictory social conditions for the formation of black masculinity itself: it was at once acknowledged as a threat to systems of white supremacist patriarchy due to its (perceived) strength, power and virility, yet actual black men were denied the political and social authority that went along with this. Black masculinity finds itself in the position of being culturally 'hyper-masculine' yet socially 'powerless', a form of identity that Kobena Mercer has termed a *subordinated masculinity*:

> In racial terms, black men and women alike were subordinated to the power of the white master in hierarchical social relations of slavery, and for black men,

as *objects* of oppression, this also cancelled out their access to positions of power and prestige which in gender terms are regarded as the essence of masculinity in patriarchy. Shaped by this history, black masculinity is a highly contradictory formation of identity, as it is *subordinated* masculinity. (1994: 142–143)

The conditions of colonialism produced a space of denial for black self-hood; a denial of subjectivity, a denial of freedom and a denial of humanity. The black self that struggles to be recognized is therefore engaged in a struggle to be known, to be seen, to be free, to be human. Vergès suggests that Fanon's work as a psychotherapist was driven by the conviction that 'madness' itself was an obstacle to freedom, that the loss of consciousness and awareness reduced the capacity for breaking free from the chains of alienation and bondage. For Fanon, then, 'there is continuity between individual and political freedom and freedom from all that hinders full and free consciousness. Individual alienation and political alienation are related; both are the product of social, political, and cultural conditions that must be transformed' (Vergès 1996: 49). Colonialism itself, that is the attempt to develop a racialized institution of total social domination, produced a form of 'madness' that could only be cured through political (and not just personal) emancipation (Vergès 1996: 52), a politics that rejected the pathologizing discourses that rendered black women invisible and black men subordinate.

Indeed, as Melissa Nobles (2000; see also Gilman 1985: 137–142) has noted, defenders of Jim Crow racism argued that statistical studies derived from census data showed higher rates of insanity among northern blacks as compared to those living in the south, thus freedom itself was thought to lead to an *increase* in madness among blacks. 'The high insanity rates', notes Nobles, 'quickly became part of the larger racial discourse, confirming the view that Negroes were naturally inferior and thus uniquely suited for servitude and subjugation' (2000: 32). The underdeveloped black mind incapable of dealing with absolute freedom (just as a domesticated pet might not survive long outside their owner's control) supposedly demonstrated blacks' inability and unreadiness to deal with full emancipation and equality. Madness was thus seen to lurk just beneath the surface of all blacks, especially, paradoxically, those that were most free.

But the forms of emancipatory politics identified in the previous chapter that came to be associated with the bodies of athletes, the colonial subject's aggressive vitality as Fanon put it, served to create a form of freedom that in its very (physical) manifestation has now become intermeshed with highly profitable forms of commodity spectacle. In this chapter I argue that the black athletic body (male and female) has become a powerful signifier within contemporary media culture. This signifier has increasingly served to redefine and in some sense reduce the agency of embodied freedom into a narrow set of 'power' and 'performance' motifs that are radically decontextualized from broader political movements, thus separating the black body from any connection to social change and hence to a depoliticization of the black athlete itself.

The chapter concludes by reading the complex and changing post-sport lives of Frank Bruno and Mike Tyson. I show how various tropes of madness and savagery have infused the media representations of these high profile black men. However, I also argue that both of these public figures, in the very moment of their public demise, have been able to find a sense of *liberation from the space of failure*. Their 'new' public personas present us with ways to think about identity and gender politics that challenge and offer an alternative to the damaging logic of sporting competition and masculine domination.

## Commodifying Sporting Blackness

It was argued earlier that contemporary sports are increasingly hyper-commercialized, producing a form of commodity spectacle that is dominated by a profit-driven corporatization of sport to the virtual exclusion of other values and non-market ethics (Andrews 2009). Unsurprisingly, black athletes and their bodies have not been immune to these forces. In fact, it could well be argued that the black athlete has been the vanguard for these processes. The union of Michael Jordan and Nike, aided by the National Basketball Association's aggressive commercial drive in the late 1980s and throughout the 1990s, led to the perfect sport/capital synergy of the *in motion* but *speechless* figurine of the jumping basketball player: Air Jordan. As one British commentator put it, Michael 'the human billboard' Jordan 'is one of the best friends white American capitalism ever had' (Landesman, 1998: 1; see also Andrews 2001).

Of course the black athletic body as spectacle is not new. As was noted earlier, the convergence of film and sport at the beginning of the twentieth century was driven by just such intermeshed logics. As Regester notes, the 'black athlete, in all of his violence, aggressiveness, and threatening behavior, became a spectacle to be exploited for financial purposes, and there were repeated calls for the black athlete to return to the screen' (2004: 269). But what was then in nascent form has now become a dominant motif for defining blackness itself. The black athlete as sign currently has a ubiquitous presence across the media landscape, extending across not just film and sport but over and into all aspects of popular culture, from music and fashion, to advertising and beyond. The black athletic body is repeatedly used by contemporary advertisers to signify power and strength, the crouched black sprinter becoming a standard trope for 'performance', thus allowing those who 'buy into' the products a form of mastery and control over the black body itself (Carrington 2001/2002). bell hooks (1994: 131) suggests that it 'has taken contemporary commodification of blackness to teach the world that this perceived threat, whether real or symbolic, can be diffused by a process of fetishization that renders the black masculine "menace" feminine through a process of patriarchal objectification'.

A striking example of this can be seen in Intel's 2007 series of advertisements, that showed a white male boss, dressed in smart casual clothing, arms crossed, staring directly into the camera below a headline that
read 'Multiply Computing Performance And Maximize The Power Of
Your Employees'. The new 'Intel CORE 2 Duo Processor' was said to be
able to produce 40% greater performance, thus increasing the productivity and efficiency of the workforce. The 'workforce' were depicted as six
black male athletes, in the crouched sprinting position, heads bowed
with their ripped and muscled forearms and upper bodies primed for
explosive action, lined up at the feet of the boss, ready to 'work'. (Intel
also ran the same advertisement in India, this time featuring a South
Asian boss but with the same six black 'workers' bent over in subservient
fashion.)

Jamie Court (2007), writing at the Huffington Post, described it as the
'slave ship ad'. Faced with mounting protests and complaints about the
racist imagery, Intel quickly withdrew the advertisement and issued an
apology on their website (Richards 2007). Don MacDonald (2007), Intel's
Vice President of sales and director of global marketing, said the intent
behind their ad campaign 'was to convey the performance capabilities of
our processors through a number of visual metaphors. Unfortunately,
while we have used a visual of sprinters in the past appropriately, this ad
of using African-American sprinters did not deliver our intended message
and in fact proved to be culturally insensitive and insulting'.

What was most significant about the advertisement was that it attracted
such critical attention at all. As Intel noted, and as with many other companies, they had previously and repeatedly used images of (black) sprinters
in their advertisements. The 'mistake' that Intel made was to so straightfor-
wardly juxtapose the white 'boss' standing over the black workforce, in a
manner that invoked for many a slave–master relationship rather than the
image of the entrepreneurial capitalist merely seeking to maximize the
productivity of 'his' workers that Intel intended. In this moment the naturalized ideology of black athleticism became problematic. The racial under-
currents that normally make such ads 'work', the automatic associations
with power, performance and virility that marketers can routinely call
upon, unreflexively and without public comment, failed in this moment as
the signifiers overdetermined the message.

These contradictory representational processes continue to be played
out within the sign economy where 'blackness', and the black body, has
become a highly valued and traded commodity, at the very same time that
within the 'real economy' actual black bodies (largely divorced from their
own surplus sign value) struggle with the material disciplining effects of
late capitalism. Black people, once literal commodities, have, via the processes of the global spectacle of the black sporting body, been transformed
into mediated commodities to be bought and sold across the globalized
media market. Discussing the situation in the United States, although we

Figure 3.1    *'Performance' (2007) Intel advertisement*

might add that the analysis holds for the black diaspora more generally, Hazel Carby notes:

> In these days of what is referred to as 'global culture', the Nike corporation produces racialized images for the world by elevating the bodies of Michael Jordan and Tiger Woods to the status of international icons. Hollywood too now takes for granted that black bodies can be used to promote both products and style worldwide ... But despite the multimillion-dollar international trade in black male bodies, and encouragement to 'just do it', there is no equivalent international outrage, no marches or large-scale public protest, at the hundreds of thousands of black male bodies languishing out of sight of the media in the North American penal system. (1998: 1)

Carby suggests that despite the hyper-visibility of particular black bodies within the global media culture, there has been little comparative mobilization within the broader public sphere around questions related to black poverty and incarceration. Indeed some have argued that the allure of the 'spectacle of the black body' has not only served to obscure the social conditions of many black people, but has simultaneously diminished the space for progressive politics itself. The changing signification of black Atlantic athletes has not only mirrored, but often constituted, the form and formation of black politics more generally. For some, the possibilities for a politics of social transformation have shifted in a negative direction, the focus of black politics becoming reduced instead to the bodies of individual celebrities, musicians and athletes. The monetary advance of individuals via the selling of their own bodies now takes precedence over using such public positions as a space of oppositional speech. The 'agency' encapsulated by Jack Johnson's victories and his verbal taunts of protest and provocation, 'Does it hurt, Jim?', and Muhammad Ali's declarative political demands for recognition, 'What's my name?', make for a stark comparison to the static and voiceless icon of a Michael Jordan figurine stuck in mid-air clutching a ball, imploring us to 'Be like Mike' by consuming Nike. The radical and at times progressive, if contradictory, politics signified by Jack and Jesse, Joe and Jackie is seen to be all but lost in the Age of Jordan.

This shift in the culture of black politics can be seen in what Paul Gilroy has called the development of a form of bio-politics, 'in which the person is defined as the body and in which certain exemplary bodies, for example those of Mike Tyson and Michael Jordan, Naomi Campbell and Veronica Webb, become instantiations of community' (1994b: 29). The effect of such politics means that whereas previous attempts to transform the condition of black communities articulated around the 'liberation of the mind', today's bio-politics is only expressed via modalities of the body. Racialized bio-politics, therefore, establishes the boundaries of the authentic racial community through 'the visual representation of racial bodies – engaged in characteristic activities – usually sexual or sporting – that ground and solicit identification if not solidarity' (Gilroy 1994b: 29). For Gilroy this is problematic as 'it marks the racial community exclusively as a space of heterosexual activity and confirms the abandonment of any politics aside from the ongoing oppositional creativity of gendered self-cultivation … If it survives, politics becomes an exclusively aesthetic concern with all the perils that implies' (p. 29).

The formal and informal constraints that earlier black athletes tried to break free from in order to lay claim to a transfigurative politics of freedom have increasingly been displaced by media sponsors' requirements that athletes become first and foremost good corporate athletes. This theme, of the power and star status accorded to black athletes alongside their capitulation to forms of white corporate patronage, has, of course, been explored by a range of contemporary artists. The ambivalent tension that Jeff Koon's 1985 Nike ads ironically played with – using basketball player Moses Malone as a black sporting figure of salvation able to lead his people to the promised land of a NBA final – speaks to the often-times dialectical play between the corporatization of sporting spaces and the limited political agency of black athletic success.

In this context we might also consider other contemporary artists, who, following Jean-Michel Basquiat's sardonic series of paintings on 'Famous Negro Athletes', play with the complex and contradictory conjuncture of black fame in the context of the largely white-controlled cultural industries that serve to both limit the radical political potential of black athleticism while tying athletes to new forms of corporate bondage. On this point José Muñoz has noted that Basquiat's work 'reflects the problematic of being a famous black image that is immediately codified as trademark by a white entertainment industry. The deployment of the word *Negro* is a disidentification with the racist cultural history that surrounds the history of both sports in the United States and of the contested lives of African-Americans in general' (1999: 49).

Such themes, I would suggest, continue to frame the work of photographer Hank Willis Thomas and, in a somewhat different register, the challenging and provocative paintings of Michael Ray Charles. The power of the artistic work of Thomas, Charles and others lies in their ability to foreground the racial ideology of sport, to clarify and make explicit that which corporate marketers and advertisers, who also use similar images, work so hard to relegate to the background, even as they rely upon racial sporting tropes in order to sell their products. In Thomas's (2003) 'Basketball and Chain' the new forms of corporate servitude are depicted by a NBA branded basketball shackled via a chain to the ankle of a player whose actual body and face remain out of sight. Instead we simply see the legs and 'Nike'-adorned feet (the alienated body parts) of the iconic basketball player's 'jump shot' – a player that is apparently reluctant or unable to break free from the sports–industrial complex and its aligned institutional sponsors and partners. Similarly, Charles's (1997) 'After Black (To See or

Figure 3.2   *'Moses' (1985) Framed Nike poster (reproduced courtesy of the artist*
© *Jeff Koons)*

Figure 3.3 *'Basketball and Chain' (2003) (reproduced courtesy of the artist © Hank Willis Thomas)*

Figure 3.4    *'After Black (To See or Not to See)' (1997) (reproduced courtesy of the artist © Michael Ray Charles)*

Not to See)' plays with the ambiguous imagery of the blindfolded black subject, literally unable to see due to the dollar-sign-printed blindfold. The position of the 'basketball player' is again 'caught' in mid-air, underneath the hanging tree branches, metonymically invoking the specter of other types of 'hangings' that the literally darker companion piece 'Before Black' more directly plays on and off.[3]

bell hooks has argued for the need to differentiate between previous black athletes, such as Jack Johnson and Joe Louis, who symbolized a resistance to the racial oppression of their era, and those of today who, hooks suggests, have allowed their bodies to be reduced to the commodity form:

> Appropriated by market forces, the subversive potential of the displayed male body is countered. This has been especially the case for black male bodies whose radical political agency is often diffused by a process of commodification that strips those bodies of dignity. The bodies of Johnson and Louis were commodified, yet that process was one that exploited and sensationalized political issues like racial separatism and economic inequality. Rather than oppose those forms of commodification that reinvent the black male body in ways that subordinate and subjugate, today's black male athlete 'submits' to any objectified use of his person that brings huge monetary reward. Black male capitulation to a neo-colonial white supremacist patriarchal commodification signals the loss of political agency, the absence of radical politics. (hooks 1994: 133)

If this is the case, then what space, if any, is left for any alternative readings? Are black athletes today simply the silent messengers of global capital and the producers of racial spectacle? Is the black public sphere and the related 'black audience' suffering from false racial consciousness in identifying with and sometimes celebrating the artistry of black athleticism?

There is a danger in these radical critiques of replicating the analyses of orthodox Marxist accounts of the culture industries in which struggle, contestation and resistance is all but written out of the analysis. It is important to remember that, especially within the black diaspora, the processes of cultural consumption and identification cannot simply be reduced to the circuits and flows of commodity spectacle. There is always an element of creative consumption and reworking of cultural texts that need to be acknowledged if we are to avoid a 'top-down' ideological account of how cultural meanings are produced, decoded and then used. Indeed, the play of desire and fantasy always works to both reproduce *and* challenge dominant ideologies, thus it is important to carefully trace 'the creative use of desire and fantasy by young blacks to counter, and capitulate to, the forces of cultural dominance that attempt to reduce the black body to a commodity and text that is employed for entertainment, titillation or financial gain. Simply said, there is no easy correlation between commodification of black youth culture and the evidences of a completely dominated consciousness' (Dyson 1993: 69).

I want to suggest, however, that while the space for oppositional readings is indeed narrow and the scope for critical agency much reduced, sport retains within it elements of freedom and subversion, even among its most compromised practitioners, that are worth exploring. That possibilities for rearticulation around questions of gender and race remain, and open up, paradoxically, at precisely that moment when the racialized logic of sporting masculinity, inscribed in the identity of the all-powerful black athlete, is refused. hooks's epigraph to this chapter, while positioning sport as a central space for the production of political self-consciousness for black men through sporting labor, is written in the past tense. hooks argues that unlike the black sporting stars of the 1930s to the 1970s, the contemporary sporting arena 'has become so corrupted by the politics of materialist greed that it is rarely a location where an alternative masculinity rooted in dignity and selfhood can emerge' (2004: 22). As a general statement this is undoubtedly the case. Men's professional sports are replete with examples of hypermasculine excess where self-destructive and self-harming practices are normalized if not celebrated, the verbal and sometimes physical abuse of others is ignored if not excused, and a reflexive, politicized subjectivity is rarely present.

And yet, if we look a little closer, we can in fact recover alternative models of sporting negritude and counter-narratives of racialized masculinity. As yet these moments rarely appear at the center of the action. We have to look to the sidelines to find them, to the times when professional athletes have retired or are coming to the ends of their careers. But I want to suggest that alternative and progressive forms of black masculinity can indeed be found.[4] In a somewhat improbable gesture, and fully aware of the limitations and precarious political implications of such a move, I want to suggest that the boxers Franklyn Roy Bruno and Michael Gerard Tyson provide us with an insight into how black athletes might be able to offer more reflexive accounts of how white racism acts upon the black body as well as the destructive effects that black masculinist politics produces. In other words, I want to argue that the historical depiction of black men as 'primarily bodies ruled by brute strength and natural instincts, characteristics that allegedly fostered deviant behaviors of promiscuity and violence' (Collins 2004: 152) is both confirmed *and* challenged by these two men, whose very centrality to public discourse in Britain and the United States make them important subjects to understand. I also want to read these two figures against each other, to see how they have been defined as representing 'two sides' of black masculinity, particularly within the British media, as the good (British) negro set against the bad (American) savage, and how they themselves have responded to and challenged this media discourse.

The fact that the two, now retired, boxers, who fought each other twice during their professional careers – and who were, arguably, two of the most famous black men in their respective countries when they met in the ring – continue to occupy the newsstands, television and cinema screens, and public imaginations in both countries is significant. It suggests that 'Tyson' and 'Bruno' retain a presence as signifiers of deeper structures of feeling concerning black masculinity. Patricia Hill Collins suggests that:

> the contested images of Black male athletes, especially 'bad boy' Black athletes who mark the boundary between admiration and fear, speak to the tensions linking Western efforts to control Black men, and Black men's resistance to this same process. Athletics constitutes a modern version of historical practices that saw Black men's bodies as needing taming and training for practical use. Given the small numbers of Black men who actually make it to professional sports, the visibility of Black male athletes within mass media speaks to something more than the exploits of actual athletes. Instead, the intense scrutiny paid to sports in general ... operates as a morality play about American masculinity and race relations. (2004: 153)

The lives and careers of these boxers present us, then, with an important insight into contemporary formations of race and gender, and more generally into the nature of racism in both the United States and Britain, set alongside the commodification of blackness and depoliticizing of black politics previously discussed.

## When Frank Met Mike: Diasporic Masculinities

It would be difficult to think of two people who more closely approximate to the colonial binary stereotype of the good black/bad black than the former heavyweight boxing champions Frank Bruno and Mike Tyson. Throughout his career, the British media variously described Bruno as a kind, lovable, gentle giant. Bruno became a national hero; 'Our Frank', as he was affectionately called. Bruno came to embody permissible black British subjectivity. Tyson, by contrast, was more often framed as dangerous and deviant, a snarling animal-like creation of barely controlled black rage. If Bruno represented the acceptable face of black masculinity then Tyson constituted its intolerable Other.

During the 1980s and 1990s Frank Bruno was one of the best-known and popular black celebrities in Britain. While Thatcherism's conservative authoritarian populism (Hall 1988) sought to reshape the cultural, political and economic landscape of Britain, and as questions of race and immigration dominated national discussions concerning identity and belonging, Bruno came to be seen as the embodiment of black success, a visible sign of Britain's post/colonial meritocracy. Bruno seemed to move easily between the worlds of boxing, where he was a good, rather than a great, fighter, and the wider celebrity culture. He was a constant fixture on television throughout the 1980s and 1990s, appearing on game shows and in advertisements. He even appeared in pantomimes, where he would play roles such as the Genie in Aladdin, his over-sized muscular frame emphasized against the small costumes he would be given to wear, producing a comedic effect for the audience.

Bruno's slow, deeply pitched voice, together with his seemingly exaggerated laugh, served to endear him to much of the British public. His immense muscularity (Bruno is 6 foot 3 inches tall, with a fighting weight just under 250 lbs and one of the most physically defined boxers at his weight) was somehow rendered 'safe' and unthreatening by the ways in which Bruno would play up the character of 'Frank Bruno'. Bruno had his own catchphrase too – 'you know what I mean, Harry?' – derived from his numerous interviews with the sports commentator Harry Carpenter, that further helped to establish Bruno as a national icon. 'The adulation heaped on Frank', noted Paul Gilroy, 'is unprecedented for a black athlete' (1993b: 86).

Crucially Bruno's personal politics chimed with the conservative times. Bruno proclaimed himself as being unequivocally proud to be British while he rarely spoke out on issues of racism. In one of his earlier autobiographies, *Eye of the Tiger: My Life*, Bruno says that the reader 'will have gathered by now that I am a fiercely patriotic Royalist, and consider myself a Britisher to the bone' (1992: 140). At a time when the Conservative Party defined the choice for black British subjects as one between either being black or British (Gilroy 1987: 64), Bruno unashamedly chose the assimilationist route to national inclusion. Bruno was also a 'dedicated fan of Maggie Thatcher' (1992: 140). He defined himself as a conservative, family-orientated individualist who did not see race and believed that 'the world's problems would be settled if we could all be mixed together in a great big melting pot' (1992: 95). Unsurprisingly, he was widely embraced by the political right and had particularly strong support from Rupert Murdoch's tabloid newspaper *The Sun*, which more than any other media outlet helped to define Bruno's reputation within the national consciousness as 'Our Frank'. The 'paternalistic infantilization of Frank Bruno', as Kobena Mercer phrased it, rendered Bruno, in effect, a national mascot (1994: 178–179).

As much as Bruno was 'loved' by the white mainstream media, so he was viewed with deep suspicion by many blacks in Britain. 'Our Frank' seemed to remain the exclusive property of a certain white embrace and claim of ownership. By contrast, many black Britons remained wary of the extent to which Bruno seemed to embody a caricature of black masculinity, defined as the happy-go-lucky negro or Sambo figure, ever willing to please 'ol' massa'. He rarely showed awareness that racism did not just exist in the minds of blacks and anti-racist propagators, as the right alleged, but remained a structural feature of British society in reproducing social inequalities. Bruno tried to blend in, to assimilate and to downplay racism. He worked to distance himself from the wider black community (he rarely acknowledged or talked about his Caribbean heritage), who subsequently read Bruno's public persona as one of unconditional deference to the dominant white norms of British nationalism.

On September 3, 1995, aged 33 and after two previous failed attempts (including a previous title fight against Tyson in 1989), Bruno finally

Figure 3.5    *Mike Tyson versus Frank Bruno, Las Vegas 1989*

defeated Oliver McCall, in a twelve-round points decision, to become heavyweight champion of the world. It was to be the pinnacle of Bruno's long career since he had turned professional in the early 1980s. And he achieved it in front of his English fans on English soil. As 'Land of Hope and Glory' pumped out of the speakers at Wembley Stadium, his adoring fans let out a chorus of 'Bru-no'. The loyal servant had finally delivered.

What was most remarkable about that night was the immediate post-fight interview in which Bruno suddenly, and rather inexplicably, came out of the racial closet. Early on in the interview and to the bemusement of the Sky Sports interviewer, Bruno suddenly said: 'I'm not an Uncle Tom, I'm not an Uncle Tom, no way, I love my brother, I'm not an Uncle Tom …'. In the space of a few short minutes Bruno would say a version of 'I'm not an Uncle Tom', 'I'm not a sell-out', or 'I love my people' no fewer than eleven times (Carrington 2000). It was a significant moment in the cultural history of race and nation in Britain. Britain's favorite black athlete, on the verge of tears, his voice breaking, his huge frame struggling for breath, and having just achieved his lifetime's ambition, effectively broke down on national television (albeit via the satellite channel Sky Sports) to declare his love of black people and to let the black community know that he was, after all these years of 'denial', one of them. It was almost as if Bruno had had to keep his black side secret, submerged under the veneer of patriotic, conservative nationalism in order for him to be accepted: the unthreatening athlete who just happens to be black, rather than *the black athlete*. He was given the choice in the 1980s to be black *or* British, and he chose to be British. But now that he had finally won the world championship, he could 'come out' and announce, publicly, the secret he had long been carrying with him, that he was in fact *black British* and had been for a long time.

What was also significant about this most revelatory moment, when Britain's favorite black son suddenly and emphatically declared his pride in being black, was that the mainstream media largely *ignored* Bruno's emotional appeal, focusing simply on the fact that, at last, Bruno, the gentle giant who many thought lacked the 'killer instinct' to become champion, had finally done so. The awkward fact of race revealed itself within the fabric of British sporting culture and from within that one space – 'Frank Bruno' – where no one thought race existed. Rather than Bruno's emotional and powerful 'coming out' being the catalyst for a broader discussion about race and identity in Britain, the awkward moment was left untouched and ignored in the hope that the episode would be forgotten.[5]

Just six months later, Bruno would meet Tyson in Las Vegas for his title defense. Bruno, the ever-loyal servant, vowed that he would not let the nation down and that he would return from the United States with his title, and therefore British pride, still intact. Tyson, who had been released from prison just the year before after serving three years of his six-year sentence for the rape of Desiree Washington, easily out-fought a physically strong

Figure 3.6 *'Bruno: I Won't Let You Down' (1996) Daily Mirror (reproduced courtesy of © Mirrorpix)*

but as ever technically limited Bruno, winning by a stoppage in the third round. Bruno had held the title for just 197 days, losing to Tyson for the second time in his career. It would be Bruno's last professional fight. Curiously, much of the British press, who remained hugely supportive of Bruno, seemed to express a sense of satisfaction and relief that Bruno had lost to the brash and vulgar American that was Tyson. The *Daily Mail* leader noted:

> As Mike Tyson was pummeling Frank Bruno senseless, it is highly likely that he knew it wasn't just another British heavyweight he was rendering horizontal but a British institution … What he will not have realized is that by reducing Bruno to a blood-spattered ruin, he has restored him to a state of grace in his own land. America idolizes winners but Britain adores a certain kind of loser. Tyson has given us back the Bruno we know and cherish, an institution we almost lost when he outpointed the out-to-lunch Oliver McCall to win his world title six months ago. (Quoted in Bruno 1997: 194)

Thus, the good black British subject was returned to his rightful, 'senseless' place, as a worthy but plucky loser, who turned out to be no real match for the superior American fighter. There was a danger that Bruno (with his newly discovered black identity) may have gone on to become a successful world champion, but fortunately, the narrative seemed to suggest, that did not happen. Bruno could come back to being a light entertainer and part-time pantomime performer – the 'institution' Britain supposedly cherished – rather than a potentially cocky and racially conscious world champion. And maybe, presumably, to even open a pub one day. Bohun Lynch, the early twentieth century writer who had warned against British boxers following in the footsteps of the 'flashy' African American boxer, would no doubt have approved.

### Iron Mike: Return of the Savage

Tyson's 1996 victory signaled both Bruno's retirement and Tyson's reemergence as a boxing force. Albeit a fighter that lacked the ferocious intimidation of opponents that he had shown throughout the 1980s when, up until his first career loss to Buster Douglas in Tokyo in 1990, he was widely regarded as the finest boxer of his generation and possibly one of the greatest heavyweight fighters of all time. (Tyson remains the youngest ever heavyweight champion, unifying the titles while only twenty years of age.) If Bruno was a lovable and 'soft' national hero, then Tyson became an exaggerated parody of the anti-Bruno: a despised, hard anti-hero. bell hooks suggests that in order to 'counter the "soft" image created by subjugation via commodification, the black male body must refigure its hardness. For a hypermasculine athlete like Mike Tyson, that refiguring must be played out both in the boxing arena and via the assertion of sexual dominance over the female, even if it means one must rape' (1994: 135). 'Iron' Mike Tyson became the living embodiment of hypermasculine excess.

Shortly after his release from prison, Tyson gave an interview to the hip-hop magazine *The Source* in which he talked about his transformation while inside, where he read Machiavelli among other political philosophers, reflected on his turbulent life, converted to Islam and emerged with two new tattoos on each arm, one of Mao Tse Tung and the other of Arthur Ashe:

> I was attracted to the philosophy of Mao and Mr. Ashe because they were both incredible individuals. Mr. Ashe seemed to know a great deal about any issue and could debate anything. I respect somebody who knows a lot about any field. I never met him and I don't know if I would have liked him because I never considered him my kind of guy. But his outlook on life and certain issues and what he had to say were fascinating. (Cummings 1995: 84)

Thus Tyson attempted to reinvent himself as a more thoughtful and reflexive individual. The cover title for *The Source* interview read: 'The Rebirth of Mike Tyson: "I'm not good. I'm not bad. I'm just trying to survive in this world!"'. The reinvention was short-lived. If anything, by the end of the 1990s, Tyson's 'image' was arguably worse than it had been at any point in his career. When Tyson fought Evander Holyfield in June 1997 he infamously bit Holyfield's ear, earning himself a disqualification and subsequent ban. Tyson would later claim, as he had during their previous bout, that Holyfield had been intentionally head-butting him, thus Tyson's bites were merely retaliation for what he felt was dangerous and unsportsmanlike conduct on the part of Holyfield. Regardless, the reaction from the British print media was revealing if not surprising.

The incident was deemed to be of such global significance that accounts of the fight dominated not only the sports sections but the front pages of nearly all the British broadsheet and tabloid papers, often as the lead story, most with graphic color photographs of Holyfield's bloodied ear and a snarling, menacing Tyson. The *Daily Mirror* headline proclaimed 'Ban Beast Tyson', whilst the *Independent*'s Sport section counterposed a photo of a jubilant 'all-white' Tim Henman against a shot of Tyson, under the caption 'Beauty and the beast: Britain's Tim Henman brings a smile to Centre Court while Mike Tyson descends to new levels of savagery'. The *Express* avoided any ambiguity in its Sports Special and simply called Tyson a 'Monster', which contained a special pull-out section on 'boxing's night of shame'. The paper led with the story on its front page under the headline 'SAVAGE: Worldwide revulsion as Tyson bites off opponent's ear and takes boxing to new depths of depravity'. The lead story continued, 'When Mike Tyson's career started, it carried the mark of greatness. Effectively, it has ended with that of the beast'. The media depiction served to prove that Hegel's savage negro in all his lawlessness, the bestial animalism that was seen to lurk inside the black body, and the unrestrained negritude that haunted the imaginations of Fanon's patients, had once again found expression in the cannibal primitive that was 'Mike Tyson'.[6]

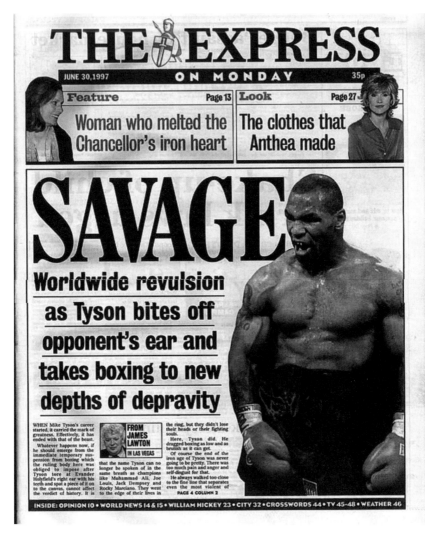

Figure 3.7   *Tyson: Savage (1997) The Express (reproduced courtesy of Express Newspapers)*

## Mad, Bad and Black

Whilst Tyson's life both inside and outside of the ring continued its downward spiral, Bruno's life was slowly collapsing. Although few knew this at the time, Bruno was diagnosed in 1998 as suffering from bi-polar disorder, or what was then more commonly called manic depression. Bruno had failed to adapt to life outside of the ring once his professional career ended in 1996. Amazingly, despite his retirement, Bruno continued to train every day and had maintained his fighting weight. His body remained as strong and as powerful as it had ever been. Yet Bruno was struggling to deal with the everyday realities of his post-boxing life. By 2000 Bruno started using cocaine and began to smoke cannabis on a regular basis. In 2002 he separated from his wife and manager, Laura Bruno, and a year later his close friend and former trainer, George Francis, committed suicide. Bruno's dramatic downfall was such that on September 22, 2003 Bruno was forcibly, and against his will, taken from his home to Goodmayes Hospital in Ilford, Essex, and 'sectioned' under the terms of the Mental Health Act of 1983. He had suffered a complete mental breakdown.

When news of Bruno's situation broke, the *Sun* led its early morning editions with the story under the title: 'Bonkers Bruno Locked Up'. The paper, misjudging its readership, was immediately inundated with complaints that it was not treating Bruno's condition and plight with the seriousness it deserved and that their coverage, complete with a photograph of a smiling Bruno in pantomime dress, was inappropriate. The *Sun*, realizing its mistake, changed the title for later editions to 'Sad Bruno in Mental Home', with a new photograph depicting a more somber-looking Bruno. One of Britain's favorite sports stars had gone from a 'national institution' to being 'institutionalized', from the world's most feared boxer to being labeled 'insane', in a few short years.[7]

However, from his darkest moment a 'new' Frank Bruno would emerge that appeared more reflexive and critically conscious than the Bruno of old. In 2005, Bruno published his latest autobiography titled *Frank: Fighting Back*, which marked an abrupt change from his smiling, happy-go-lucky, cliché-ridden accounts of before. The cover photo showed Bruno looking serious and somewhat stoic, looking the reader purposefully in the eye. The one-word title implied a more matter-of-fact approach, as though the laughter (at the old Frank Bruno) had now stopped. Bruno opens *Frank* with the following paragraph:

> My name is Frank Bruno. You probably know me as a fighter, the happy guy on the telly with the one-liners, the big guy in panto. Maybe you were there the night I won the world title. Maybe you shouted 'Broo-no!' at one of my fights. I was public property, a celebrity they say. And there wasn't much people didn't know about my life, about my wife and kids, the big house in the country, the MBE and all the other trappings. Strangers said hello in the

street. They still do. But one Monday in September 2003 I discovered another Frank Bruno – someone I didn't even know. (2005: 1)

Bruno then recounts, in a remarkably honest and revealing way, the events that led up to his breakdown and the pressures that he has lived with over the years in trying to be 'Frank Bruno'. The autobiography is largely devoid of the jovial one-liners and banal homilies of his previous books. Instead, the book provides a compelling portrait of a person struggling to come to terms with their mental illness, while being known in the public eye, for being somebody, that in Bruno's mind, no longer existed. Interestingly, Bruno dates his decline to March 1996 when he lost his world title to Tyson: 'he took the world title I had won only six months before; I'd hardly had a chance to enjoy it' (2005: 4). Tyson haunts Bruno's account of his life and career and his subsequent decline.

Bruno, perhaps for the first time publicly, also begins to recognize the precarious nature of his 'acceptance' by the British public, and particularly by the right-wing press who had done the most to promote Bruno as a 'national institution' during his career. Bruno comes to terms with the fact that the Frank Bruno that 'everyone' loved was not necessarily related to the real Bruno. That the mass media representation of 'Bruno' as 'public property', as he puts it, had more to do with the needs and desires of mainstream (white) society than it did with how Bruno perceived himself. Bruno reveals how he began to lose a sense of who he actually was outside of the discourse of 'Frank Bruno'. His embrace of the media-created identity that he played out simply served to cover up his underlying illness. In an interesting account of how even boxers have to play roles to convince others (and themselves) of their 'fearless' power, Bruno notes:

> As a boxer, I was used to deceiving myself. We spend most of our careers pretending, telling little white lies. You have to do it in the ring because you don't want your opponent to know if you're hurt or tired. You have to do it outside the ring when your manager shows you a deal you don't like. Most of my life I've been in a goldfish bowl – twenty-four hours a day, 365 days a year, you have to live up to an image someone else has created for you. My image had always been the happy-go-lucky joker. I found it hard to think of myself as mentally ill. (2005: 5)

This self-reflection extends beyond Bruno's belated awareness of his own mental health problems to a more critical reading of mainstream society's 'use' of him. Significant in this context is Bruno's reaction to how the *Sun* in particular initially reported his illness. Bruno writes:

> I wasn't fully aware of it at the time, but the papers – and one in particular – went to town on me after the breakdown. The *Sun*'s 'Bonkers Bruno Locked Up' headline said it all. It was obvious I'd become another disposable celebrity. It was as if all the good times I'd shared with *Sun* readers counted for nothing.

I wasn't naive enough to think it was always going to be roses. I just had no idea how vicious some of the papers could be. I didn't think they would care so little about the feelings of someone they'd once regarded as a hero. It was obvious I was now just a name that fitted a headline, something that went with 'bonkers'. It was a name people used to cheer. 'Broo-no!' Now I was a national joke. (2005: 208)

It is interesting that in these moments Bruno reflects upon his own media-created persona and the psychological costs he has had to bear for his contingent inclusion. The self-parody that he previously performed in order to be accepted as British, the Bruno of the HP sauce commercials and pantomime send-ups, returns to haunt him. Whereas for Ralph Ellison it was the phenomenology of racism that rendered black people, as social beings, invisible, for Bruno it was his blackness that *he* rendered invisible in order that he become accepted and recognized, and therefore visible in the eyes of whites. Bruno comes to terms with the fact that in so doing he had become trapped in an image that was not of his own making and over which he had little control. The pressures of performing this version of a black public self that was not allowed to speak for itself, proved unsustainable. The 'raceless mask' that Bruno wore could only be kept in place at great personal and psychological cost to the actual person trapped inside the caricature that was 'Frank Bruno'.

Once Bruno drops that mask, he begins to question the tropes of masculine bravado that demand that boxers engage in a performance of fearless masculinity, ready to deliver and receive violence without the hint of fear, as to show fear is to admit that the body is vulnerable and therefore weak. Bruno confesses that what really drives boxers is not aggression, arrogance or domineering violence (as is often assumed from the outside) but fear itself, and fear of losing in particular. Bruno notes that getting ready for a fight requires 'an act of faith' in yourself. But if that self has been produced exogenously, from a thousand distorted media images and discourses, then how do you know if your true self has what it takes to really go through with the act? What happens if you 'bottle it' in front of millions? Bruno suggests:

Boxers don't fear pain – although there can't be many who haven't thought about death or serious injury. What we fear is humiliation. We fear giving up our dignity, our reputation. We fear letting people down, people who put their faith in us. We fear the big L: Losing. (2005: 214)

### Failure as Liberation

Shortly after Bruno had been 'sectioned', the *Daily Mirror* carried a 'world exclusive' story on its front page, headlined 'My Tears For Frank'. The words were from Mike Tyson. In the article Tyson said that he had cried when he had first heard the news about Bruno's health problems, adding

'I always thought he did a good job walking away from boxing when he did. He got a good title and got a good pay day. But for us boxers fighting is just a way of making a living. That's the easy part. The hard part is making a life outside' (Harwood 2003: 4). Tyson went on to describe how he considered Bruno to be a national icon and a gentleman, adding, 'The English should have a "Frank Bruno Day". I used to love the way he spoke the Queen's English. He's an icon of London and England with all those typical mannerisms and conduct typical of an English gentleman. I consider Frank to be a very dignified and respectful man. I've seen how people make fun of him. But I have nothing but respect for him. He sets a fantastic example' (p. 4).[8]

During this same period, Tyson, shorn of the explosive power that had marked his boxing career, slowly descended into a mediocre fighter, still desperately longing for another chance to become world champion. His desire to fight was by now driven largely by the fact that despite career earnings since his professional début in 1986 of, reportedly, over $300 million, he still had debts in excess of $20 million. As Ellis Cashmore notes in his provocatively titled biography *Tyson: Nurture of the Beast*, 'Tyson's unexpected descent to the ranks of mere mortals was greeted with surprise spiced with some satisfaction, the satisfaction that comes from watching the world's most intimidating man's public humiliation' (2005: 6). Quite precisely which publics wanted to see Tyson's humiliation is not clear in Cashmore's account.[9] Nevertheless, there was something of this 'satisfaction' within much of the British press in witnessing the final chapters of Tyson's career as he lost first to the black British fighter Danny Williams in August 2004 ('Decked By A Briton – Tyson's Final Humiliation', *Sunday Telegraph*, August 1, 2004), and then again, in what would be his last professional bout, to the white Irishman Kevin McBride in June 2005 ('Tyson: from baddest man on the planet to sitting duck', *The Times*, June 13, 2005).

One of the most poignant moments in James Toback's (2009) documentary *Tyson* comes towards the end of the film, when Tyson gives an interview immediately after the McBride fight. Tyson seems, finally, at ease with himself and the decision he is about to take to retire from professional boxing. He appears almost relieved. He speaks much more freely – at other times in the film when Tyson becomes emotional he literally struggles to speak – and with a sense of humility, something that rarely existed in any of Tyson's previous interviews, post-fight or otherwise. Tyson concedes that he has not got 'the fight' in him anymore. He apologizes for letting people down, and he admits that he's only been fighting these past few years in order 'to take care of my bills basically'. The interviewer, momentarily shocked by the honest sincerity of Tyson's admission, is lost for words. A few awkward seconds pass as the interviewer, not expecting such a frank response, has no follow-up question ready.

Tyson eventually breaks the silence by suggesting that to continue to fake his interest in boxing would be to damage the sport itself and the courage of his opponents, and that now he wants to spend more time with his children. He declares that he's no longer capable of playing the game, of playing the black athlete: 'I don't have that ferocity. I'm not an animal anymore.' Asked what he'll do outside the ring, Tyson responds, 'Well I'm sure I'll find something to do. Boxing doesn't define me, I'm just sorry to disappoint the people in this city. I knew I didn't have it in my stomach no more but I was in dire needs to take care of my life … I'm just being honest. I'm not taking nothing away from him [McBride]. I don't love this no more, I don't love this no more …' He then, somewhat graciously, congratulates McBride on his victory and wishes him the best of luck with the rest of his career, and turns to leave the ring. The camera follows Tyson's final walk back to the dressing room, and as the screen slowly fades to black we hear a Tyson voice-over: 'I'm just tired of fighting. Boxing has no place in my heart anymore.'[10]

Numerous commentators have subsequently struggled to make sense of this 'new' Tyson. For example, in seeking to map and to get *inside* 'the beast' that is supposedly Mike Tyson, Cashmore's biography itself seems to get lost. Cashmore's literary flourishes, designed to tease out 'our' hidden fantasies and fears about Tyson, become worryingly indistinguishable from the discourses he is describing. The excess of Cashmore's *own* language serves, in the end, to reproduce the very discourses his analysis attempts to map. Put simply, the description ends up reproducing and confusing the *actual* Mike Tyson – as inherently, intrinsically and radically Other – with his *signifier*. Tyson, as heir to Jack Johnson's mantle, is described thus by Cashmore:

> Tyson was absolutely, certainly, undeniably different. He was bestial, horrific, repugnant, savage, beyond every known pale. He was to be feared, loathed, and rejected. And, yet, for two decades, we – and I mean everyone – remained in his thrall. The source of the fascination was, of course, the very quality that repulsed us. He was an ever-present reminder of difference. Tyson was the embodiment of black America, a monumental physical force which, left unfettered, would wreak havoc, disregarding all known rules of civilization and reverting to some atavistic state that generations of white domination had managed to submerge. Tyson terrified America as he gave the real reasons why racial equality was only an ideal, never a reality. It never would be. Tyson showed this. And, in this sense, he provided the comfort. No amount of social engineering could ever put right what nature had intended to be wrong. (2005: 254–255)

This type of analysis inadvertently collapses the gap between discourse/ representation and the actually existing human being that is Mike Tyson. Though not intended, the analysis ends up negating the dangerous play on words of the book's subtitle 'nurture of the beast', which clearly, if problematically, signals the socially created conditions of 'the beast'. Instead Cashmore ends up reintroducing a naturalized social Darwinian account by the back door by concluding that it is, after all, *nature*, black nature, black

**TIMES SPORT**

Monday June 13 2005

TENNIS
Roddick stands up to crash, bang and wallop of Karlovic
PAGE 60

RUGBY UNION
Another one bites the dust as revolving door spins mercilessly
PAGES 62-63

Tyson: from baddest man on the planet to sitting duck BOXING pages 64-65

Figure 3.8   *Tyson: Sitting Duck (2005) Times Sport (reproduced courtesy of © The Times)*

negritude, that lurks in the deepest recesses of Tyson's honed, deadly muscular body. That even the best of American social engineering and the civilizing processes of the west cannot in the end overcome the congenital alterity of the black athlete. Given this, it is logical that Cashmore (2005: 254) concludes by seeming to suggest that there is little if any chance of Tyson being recuperated within the mainstream media and wider (white) society due to his resolutely debased public persona, his unforgivable blackness we might say. Of course, the same was said of Jack Johnson and Muhammad Ali, two other boxers whose latter-day personas have remarkably, and by a profound act of historical amnesia, been recuperated as American heroes within the United States (Marqusee 2005).

Contra Cashmore, we might suggest that just such a process of re-imaging Tyson is already and slowly beginning to take place. Since his retirement Tyson has become a less maligned public figure, appearing in various films and media events, and not just those made by his most enthralled follower, James Toback. Indeed, with the tragic, accidental death of his daughter Exodus in May 2009 (just as Toback's 2009 film went on general release in the United States), Tyson has become a *sympathetic* character, invoking for some, though clearly not all, a sense of pity and understanding rather than (or perhaps as well as) disgust and outrage.

An important scene in *Tyson* shows the former boxer admitting to his own fear and his attempts to master his anxieties. The scene is difficult to follow as it is over-determined by Toback's insistence on depicting Tyson's 'inner madness' by the use of multiple shots of Tyson speaking simultaneously, his varied 'voices' thus 'talk over' each other at times, as we, the audience, struggle to make linear sense of the visual and auditory overflow. However, *Tyson* still manages to produce an intriguing insight into the question of *masculine failure* that is worth considering. When Tyson is asked to describe his feelings immediately before a bout, he says:

> As soon as I come into the ring I'm … No, stop it, that's not true. While I'm in the dressing room, five minutes before I come out, my gloves are laced up. I'm breaking my gloves down, I'm pushing the leather in the back of my gloves, I'm breaking the middle of the glove so my knuckle can *pierce* through the leather. I feel my knuckle piercing against the *tight* leather gloves on that Everlast boxing glove. When I come out I have supreme confidence but I'm scared to death. I'm totally afraid, I'm afraid of everything, I'm afraid of losing, I'm afraid of being humiliated, but I'm totally confident. The closer I get to the ring the more confidence I get. The closer, the more confidence I get, the closer the more confidence I get. All during my training I've been afraid of this man, I thought this man might be capable of beating me. I've *dreamed* of him beating me. I've always stayed afraid of him. The closer I get to the ring I'm more confident. Once I'm in the ring *I'm a God*, no one can beat me.

I want to suggest that such accounts, confusing and contradictory as they are, offer a potentially important way to 'create new tropes of black masculinity that challenge the most negative stereotypes associated with black masculinity' (Neal 2005: xx; see also Mutua 2006). We have an insight here into the anxieties and fears that are the necessary backstage work of hegemonic masculinity that enables the performance of the confident masculine self. Simply by revealing and exposing the actual anxiety that lies behind the front stage act of the tough, hyper-masculine black athlete, Tyson begins to engage the necessary deconstructionist work toward reconstructing a less damaging form of black masculinity.

But that fear of and anxiety about *failure* can never go away. What is striking about both Bruno and Tyson's accounts is how much they are driven by fear and how they compensate and deal with this by the strategic adoption of tropes of domination, using their bodies as violent tools in the process. Given the nature of their professions, this is hardly surprising nor particularly revealing. Yet, what is interesting is how both have somewhat belatedly, and in different ways, come to accept this space of vulnerability and to acknowledge their failures in a way that is not read as weakness but *as a site of learning and growth*. In that moment of admitting to 'failure', and in giving up on the identity of 'the black athlete', they become at last and simply human again. Bruno stops playing the happy-go-lucky negro; Tyson stops playing the animalistic negro. The dance of good black versus bad black, loyal colonial subject versus the rebellious racial agitator, Peter Jackson versus Jack Johnson, is negated by their refusal to play the colonial roles allotted to them. They find a way out of the Fanonion cycle of having to become white in order to be recognized as human by renouncing the white construction of the black athlete. They challenge the necessity of compulsory whiteness as the only way for blackness to exist by showing sporting negritude to be, in the end, a powerful and damaging myth.

In her short essay 'Notes on Failure', Judith Halberstam makes an argument for reclaiming 'failure' as a productive site of agency. Halberstam argues that the models of success and failure used within everyday encounters 'to determine social progress, individual achievement and political effectivity all derive in some measure from capitalist formulations of success and from economic notions of gain, profit, advantage and benefit. In order to make failure productive then, we need to link failure to a critique of capitalism and to a politics of negativity' (2007: 69). Perhaps, then, something useful can be retrieved from the morality tales, as Collins put it earlier, that both Bruno and Tyson provide us with in their post-sport lives. This would involve an attempt to produce a reading of their 'failure' in terms of what such a politics of negativity tells us about the recovery of their underlying humanity. A humanity that can only be revealed once the excesses of racialized hyper-masculinity, with its ideology of domination and material success, are relinquished.

I am suggesting, in other words, that sporting (and masculine) 'failure' becomes a site of agency allowing Bruno and Tyson to reject the patriarchal standards of 'success' that privilege the abuse of bodies and the celebration of power for its own sake. Instead the embrace of loss and disappointment are read as necessary and healthy constitutive elements of normal living as they begin to develop a critical, reflexive consciousness of themselves as black men, as fathers, as public figures and as complex human beings who are no longer defined by their physicality. Their 'failure' to live up to and to follow the public scripts of racialized nationalism (Bruno) and violent hegemonic masculinity (Tyson) is precisely the moment of a dialectical overcoming of the post/colonial trap that defines blackness as feminine loss and whiteness as masculine success. A moment when the expected performance is resisted and the representational work required to maintain the racial charade is exposed. From that moment of radical refusal, to refuse the 'freedom' of capitalistic domination, a more comfortable positioning for what it means to be 'black British' or 'a man' finally becomes possible.

In other words, Bruno and Tyson present an *alternative narrative* that even these hard, disciplined and most powerful of black bodies cannot be maintained, that they are prone to breakdown and failure. The morality tale concludes with the bodies of both Bruno and Tyson becoming disposable, weak bodies; 'Iron' Mike reduced to the analogy not of a tiger, lion or even a gorilla but that of a sitting, lame duck. In the end, however, Tyson could only be saved, could only begin to rebuild his own shattered life, to protect himself and his own body from the damage inflicted upon it, more outside the ring than in, by renouncing 'Mike Tyson', by giving up the specter of the black athlete. *No más, no más*, as Roberto Duran once famously declared. Who does the heavyweight champion of the world call in *his* last desperate moments? If *you* are Joe Louis, or Mike Tyson or Frank Bruno, who is left to engage the physical struggle for your freedom?[11]

It is at this point that Bruno comes to terms with the fact that 'Frank Bruno' is the one with whom he must do battle, the 'problem' that must be confronted. But in a way that *does not* require of him the physical strength he gained from boxing but rather the mental courage to confront his fears and now to acknowledge his illness:

> When my father gave me my first pair of gloves, I was hooked on a sport that is unlike any other. It's one on one. And it eats away at you even before you've thrown or taken a punch. What I learnt to do in a boxing ring was beat fear, to conquer my doubts. When I became ill, I had to do the same. Except the fears were far greater. And my opponent was a guy called Frank Bruno. (Bruno 2005: 213)

It is important to map the fissures, cracks and moments of existential crisis within the ambivalent spaces of racialized hegemonic masculinity. To move beyond glorifying the performances of sporting hyper-masculinity in order to see the psychic damage done to those individuals, and those around them, who are conditioned and expected to perform such identities. And to think imaginatively about how our readings of the politics of race and sport may provide the basis for more humane ways to perform black masculinity out of and from the very conditions of failure.[12]

Although I am not suggesting that Bruno and Tyson offer anything like a black feminist masculinity (White 2008), I do want to argue that the slow, uneven but demonstrable shift from their earlier debased and largely unreflexive commitments to patriarchal domination and capitalistic individualism towards a more reflexive and nuanced masculine self is worth understanding, especially given the central position of both men within the American and British popular consciousness over the past two decades or so. The fact that we can even begin to associate the values of humility, emotional openness and empathy, nurturing and dialogue (White 2008: 199) alongside the signifiers 'Tyson' and 'Bruno' may provide a way to 'establish alternative models for black manhood to offset conventional ones' (Ikard 2007: 175) that should not be ignored.

At the very end of his autobiography, in the final chapter, entitled 'Courage', Bruno returns, yet again, to Tyson, and says the following:

> The fighter I will always be linked to looks like he's finally called it a day. I hope so. Mike Tyson has had more than his fair share of troubles. In June 2005, Mike had his last fight. It wasn't the Tyson I fought twice. It was a 38-year old man who had nothing left except his name. Towards the end of the sixth round against a big Irishman called Kevin McBride, Mike was pushed backwards and fell to the canvas. He just sat there, lying against the ropes. He didn't look that hurt. But you could see the pain in his eyes. You could see he didn't want to get up. When he did, he wandered back to the stool in his corner, sat down and quit. Later, he said something that only Mike could say. 'I'm a cold and cruel and a hard person. I've been around the worst. You can't take away what's happened to me. I've been abused any way anyone can be abused. I'm not used to sensitivity anymore. Don't cry. I don't know how to handle people crying any more. I've lost my sensitivity.' It was the saddest thing I've ever heard. (Bruno 2005: 221–222)

In October 2009, Tyson appeared twice as a special guest on the Oprah Winfrey show. During an emotional interview he talked of his embarrassment at his own past behavior and how he was trying to become a better person, a better family man and a better human being. At the point of tears he discussed his daughter's ('my angel') accidental death. Tyson appeared contrite and reflective about his own forms of violence and the damage he had done both to himself and others. When Evander Holyfield joined Tyson and Winfrey, the two men embraced. Winfrey then asked Tyson what he wanted to say to Holyfield. Tyson said, 'This is a beautiful guy. Me and this guy both come from, basically, the sewage and we watched each other grow to become established and esteemed fighters, you know what I mean. And I just want to say it's been a pleasure passing through life and being acquainted with you'. Moved by Tyson's words, the two ex-fighters and former heavyweight champions shook hands, and then, in a brief but intimate moment, Tyson gently laid his hand on top of Holyfield's as a final gesture of loving friendship. Tyson added, simply, 'We need to love each other and treat each other better'.

## Notes

1 As I argue in Chapter 4, the allegations that came to light in late 2009, that Tiger Woods had had a series of extra-marital affairs, resulted in frenzied international media coverage that allowed for a voyeuristic spectacle of salacious stories concerning Woods' supposed insatiable 'sexual appetite' with a variety of alleged mistresses, all of whom were white. In this sense, I would argue, Woods was instantly reduced to the colonial stereotype of the lascivious moor unable to prevent himself from tupping white ewes. Thus the post-racial 'non-black' Tiger Woods that, up until that point, had been so marketable for corporate America, suddenly became black again, and therefore linked by association to the threatening signifier of 'the black athlete'. While in some sports, such as boxing and basketball, elements of the 'rebellious' black athlete can remain marketable, providing 'edge' to certain products aimed at youth markets, golf's inherent conservatism meant that many of Woods' key sponsors were quick to drop him as that particular construction of the black athlete cannot be easily reconciled with the neo-liberal, 'family values' conservative image of leading Fortune 500 companies (especially financial, insurance and management consultancy companies) aimed, predominantly, at white and upper-middle class markets. Similarly, Orlando Patterson suggests that media fascination with O.J. Simpson derived in large part from the fact that Simpson 'conflated the two extremes of "Otherness" projected onto the Afro-American male: that of the superhuman athlete and that of the demonized killer' (1998: 249).

2 Interestingly Ralph Ellison spoke positively, and with a sense of masculinist admiration, about Jack Johnson and the political agency that he inspired: 'that old dancing master, wit, and bull-balled stud, Jack Johnson is really *my* mentor, because he knew that if you operated with skill and style you could rise above all that-being-a-credit-to-your-race-crap because he was a credit to the human race and because if he could make that much body and bone move with such precision to his command all other men had a chance to beat the laws of probability and anything else that struck up its head and if he liked a woman he took her and told those who didn't like it to lump it and that is the way true studs have always acted' (cited in Murray and Callahan 2000: 132, emphasis in original).

3 'After Black' is essentially one half of a two-piece work. In the mirror work, entitled 'Before Black (To See or Not to See)', the same image is used but 'reversed' so that the tree appears on the left of the image. However, the black subject now appears to be running in a state of shock away from the house in the background, the smile replaced with fear. The daylight of 'After Black' has also been replaced by nighttime darkness and the basketball and blindfold have disappeared, allowing, nominally, the black subject to 'see' again, though as it is now nighttime whether either of the figures can truly see remains, as the title suggests, unknown. But the composition of the subject in both paintings remains essentially the same, caught in mid-stride hanging/running through the wooded area.

4   We might want to consider here athletes who have developed a critical political consciousness around questions of race, class, gender and sexuality and who have been outspoken in challenging forms of domination inside and outside of sport (Zirin 2007). I'm thinking here of basketball players such as Etan Thomas (Thomas 2004) and John Amaechi (Amaechi 2008) and the football player Lilian Thuram (Lapchick 2009).

5   This was in contrast to the black press in Britain where the incident and Bruno's comments were widely discussed (Carrington 2000).

6   To be clear, I do not wish to deny that Tyson's actions were illegitimate. What is significant is the readiness and extent to which Tyson's transgression allowed for the familiar tropes of savagery, cannibalism and bestiality to be effortlessly replayed. This was made clearer when, in January 1998 during a rugby union match, the London Scottish flanker Simon Fenn had part of his ear bitten off by Bath's Kevin Yates, requiring 25 stitches. Yates was heavily criticised, though largely only within the sporting media, for having 'gone too far' and for breaking the ethical codes, as well as the formal rules, of rugby union. His violent excess was thus seen as a regrettable but ultimately insignificant exception that did not require tropes of bestial savagery to explain it. Tyson, however, standing in for black masculinity within the white imagination, was reverting to 'type' and thus had to be morally and publicly denounced.

7   The *Sun*, desperate to recover its public standing having misjudged both the public's continuing support and affection for Bruno and its own cavalier attitude to mental illness, lead the next day's front page with the headline 'Sun's Fund For Bruno'. Overnight the *Sun* decided to 'help people with mental health problems like boxing hero Frank Bruno' (p. 1), and inside it carried an article by the chief executive of the mental health charity SANE. The *Sun* also led its editorial page 'The Sun Says', on the issue: 'Frank's fight: No one loves Frank Bruno more than The Sun. We've been by his side throughout his career, sharing his triumphs and helping shoulder his tragedies. To us, he's one of the family. Today, as Frank battles mental illness, we've launched a fund in his name to recognize the vital work done by the charity SANE. Depression is a dark cloud that hangs over many families. They will know from experience just what Frank and those who love him are going through. To Frank, we say: You've done the right thing in getting help. And you'll have millions of Sun readers in your corner as you fight your biggest fight of all. Get well soon, Big Man' (The *Sun*, 24 September, 2003, p. 8).

8   Bruno himself quotes from the article towards the end of his own autobiography.

9   Throughout the book Cashmore appears to assume a white speaking position (and audience) but rarely labels it as such. Thus he ends up discussing the expectations and constructs of Tyson that are produced by white racism but without naming it, hence black people, by default, become excluded from the category of the civilized, not just in the discourses Cashmore describes but within the terms of his own account. See, for example, when he argues: 'What we wanted was not a Tyson neutered, declawed, domesticated, or caged, but one whose very presence signaled danger. A Tyson so antithetical to the requirements of civilized society, so repugnant to cultivated tastes, so offensive to moral principles that there was no room for argument – he was outside the frontiers of normality. He was about as unlike us as it was possible to be. And he was black. And so were several million others' (2005: 251).

This raises the question as to who exactly the 'we' and 'us' are that is being invoked here.

10 Even before his final fight, Tyson had said in an interview with *USA Today:* 'My whole life has been a waste – I've been a failure ... I just want to escape. I'm really embarrassed with myself and my life. I want to be a missionary. I think I could do that while keeping my dignity without letting people know they chased me out of the country. I want to get this part of my life over as soon as possible. In this country, nothing good is going to come of me. I'm so stigmatized, there is no way I can elevate myself. They would give [the late] Jeffrey Dahmer a second chance before they gave me another one. If you saw a [police] lineup and saw Tyson and Dahmer and they asked, "Who killed and ate those people?" you would pick me and not Jeffrey' (Saraceno 2005).

11 Sport is an interesting cultural practice in this regard, as *not* winning, and therefore 'failing', is the common experience and emotional state that sport produces. Winning (finishing first) the league or cup, beating your opponent or your previous best time or score, is actually, and almost by definition, a rare occurrence. Most forms of sporting competition produce only one 'winner' and usually at least one – and more often scores of others – loser; even winners are only ever one game, set or match away from failure too. Instead, sport tends to produce a series of 'almost' moments, of fleeting glimpses of physical mastery, of nearly succeeding, of coming close to closing the gap between our idealized sporting abilities and our actual technical capabilities. The gap between the ideal and actual can never be closed but accepting that 'failure' does not necessarily mean that one is defined as a 'loser'. Learning to live with, accept and even embrace failure is a *constitutive* part of the sports experience, thus potentially offering a way to reject the notion of failure as an exceptional condition reserved only for those who are not real athletes/competitors. The artist and photographer Tracey Moffatt explores this liminal space of winning/losing, success/failure in the sporting context through her series of photographs titled *Fourth*, taken during the 2000 Sydney Olympics, in which she photographed Olympians who had just finished fourth, just outside of the medals. Her images are striking, in part because we are so used to seeing sports images of winners, the joyous and ecstatic moment of triumph and sporting supremacy, narratives, of course, strongly endorsed and promoted by sports governing bodies, the sports media, and above all by advertisers and marketers. Instead Moffatt focuses on the 'pain' of *not* winning, revealing a series of poignant and yet ultimately more 'human' expressions. Referring to those who place fourth at the Olympics Moffatt notes: 'It's sadder than coming last because when you come Fourth you have just missed out on a medal. You almost made it, but you just missed out. Fourth means that you are almost good. Not the worst (which has its own perverted glamour) but almost. Almost a star!' (quoted in Maggia 2006: 14; see also Halberstam 2007: 70–71).

12 On this point of reclaiming 'failure' as a positive space through which to rethink black masculinity, see the artist and cultural critic Isaac Julien when he notes: 'I think failure is something that should be celebrated. I don't want to be in a formation of black male identity where one has to hold oneself in a rigid way ... even against how we might feel about ourselves in terms of our pain, our scepticism, lack and self-doubt. All these things are as much a

part of black male identity as the things we might want to parade, like toughness and unity. We have to be willing to engage in a process of thinking through our failure as black men in this society. Black masculinity has always been a "failed masculinity" in relationship to white male colonialism. Black macho discourses of empowerment will never truly reach us where we live. There is something interesting we can learn from so-called failure, because our failure also contains our resistance. Failure to live "up" to oppressive masculinity is part of what it means to be queer ... Being black itself is seen as a failure in the white world. We want to remember that, and there is a way we can use that failure to critique white supremacy' (quoted in Belton 1995: 215).

# 4

# Sporting Multiculturalism: Nationalism, Belonging and Identity

What, then, are the major preoccupations that help to make up the attitude of the average Briton towards colored people? As has been said, a colored skin, especially when combined with Negroid features, is associated with alienness and with the lowest social status. Primitiveness, savagery, violence, sexuality, general lack of control, sloth, irresponsibility – all these are part of the image. On the more favorable side, Negroid peoples are often credited with athletic, artistic, and musical gifts, and with an appealing and childlike simplicity which is in no way incompatible with the remainder of the image. (Sheila Patterson)

The black diaspora culture currently being articulated in postcolonial Britain is concerned to struggle for different ways to be 'British' – ways to stay and be different, to be British *and something else* complexly related to Africa and the Americas, to shared histories of enslavement, racist subordination, cultural survival, hybridization, resistance, and political rebellion. (James Clifford)

There have been theoretical critiques of the 'dark' side of the Enlightenment project before, but it is 'the multicultural question' which has most effectively blown its contemporary cover. (Stuart Hall)

## Sporting Multiculturalism, Terrorism and the Olympics

For the first time in days the room inside the downtown Singapore convention center fell silent. At approximately 12:46pm on July 6, 2005, a 13-year-old local sailor walked slowly but purposefully towards Jacques Rogge, the President of the International Olympic Committee (IOC). The young woman carried a silk pillow that was embossed with five interlocking rings. Delicately balanced on top lay a large white envelope. The assembled media fixed their cameras on Rogge, as celebrities from the worlds of film, television, music and sport, as well as politicians from various countries, looked on anxiously. The atmosphere was tense and expectant. Rogge took the envelope and, somewhat clumsily, opened it. He paused and then announced in his French/Belgium-inflected English accent, 'The International Olympic Committee has the honor of announcing that the games of the thirtieth Olympiad in twenty twelve are awarded to the city of … London'.

An explosion of sound erupted in the room as cries of jubilation rang out. Cameras flashed. In front of the assembled television crews the English football player David Beckham turned to embrace London's then Mayor, Ken Livingstone, British government officials and politicians began to dance joyously, while groups of young children shrieked 'We won, we won!'. Simultaneously, 6750 miles away, thousands of people broke into cheering and singing as news of the announcement was relayed via huge screens set up in London's Trafalgar Square. Balloons were released and ticker-tape fell, seemingly, across the whole of London. The nation, at that moment, was in a state of sporting euphoria. The Olympics were coming to London. Media pundits declared that July 6, 2005 would be a day Londoners would never forget. At that very same moment, three young men from Leeds and another from Aylesbury, were making final preparations for their one-way journey to London the following day.

At around 8:50am on Thursday July 7, 2005, rush-hour commuters were packed into London's over-crowded underground transport system, known locally as 'the Tube'. Most were reading the early morning newspapers, many with 'special souvenir editions', proudly proclaiming the previous day's successful Olympics announcement. The headlines were unequivocal: 'One Sweet Word: London' stated the *Guardian*; 'Britain's Golden Day' announced the *Independent*. Londoners were enjoying their collective role in this local and national achievement.

Moments later, above ground, reports began to appear of a 'power surge' on the Tubes. Confusion arose as 24-hour television news channels began to show pictures of stations closing as police and other emergency services frantically arrived in ever-increasing numbers. Earlier reports of a power surge were questioned and news filtered through of a number of possible explosions. An hour after the initial incidents on the Tube, a bomb exploded on a bus in Tavistock Square, central London, killing thirteen people and injuring scores of others. It soon became clear that London had been subject to a wave of linked bombings. News of three separate explosions on the underground was eventually reported. In the end more than seven hundred people would be injured, many with serious life-changing disfigurements. Fifty-six people would die, including the four suspected bombers.

A number of urgent questions arise from the above juxtaposition. What, if anything, connects these two seemingly unrelated events, beyond their tragic and temporal association with the city of London? Further, when faced with the ethical issue of death itself, how can a cultural form as seemingly mundane as sport have a place within any serious discussion concerning politics, war and terrorism?

In a moment of historical cruelty that bordered on pathos, the news-stands of July 7, 2005 were filled with the previous day's images of smiling Londoners, joyful to the point of tears, celebrating what was, in the words of Ken Livingstone, 'one of the best days London has ever had'. Amongst the discarded morning papers full of headlines and photographs of London pride and joy, severed and bloodied human bodies lay dying. Whilst, at first glance, these two significant events seem only to be joined by the fate of circumstance, I want to suggest that a dominant theme does in fact connect the two. This theme speaks to a broader tension that has been central to political discourse in Britain, and indeed much of Europe and elsewhere (Modood and Werbner 1997), for nearly three decades, namely the question of multiculturalism.

The initial commentary as to why London had beaten the other cities (including Paris, Madrid, New York and Moscow) to host the 2012 Olympic summer games focused on the decision to include 30 'inner city' children from London's East End amongst the 100 representatives each city was allowed in the voting hall. Compared to the slick film produced for Paris by the renowned filmmaker Luc Besson, the London bid chose, instead, to focus on London's racial and ethnic diversity. It was the ordinary, everyday, lived multiculturalism of contemporary London, its cosmopolitan openness, that was seen to have swayed the IOC voting members. The immediate news coverage thus praised London's (and Britain's) successful multiculturalism and the role that sport in particular had played in producing both 'social cohesion' and 'community integration' whilst respecting cultural, religious and ethnic diversity. As the lead editorial in the *Independent*, titled 'A moment for Britain to glory in the Olympic spirit', put it:

> The final video presentation to IOC delegates yesterday made great play of the city's ethnic diversity. This was a masterstroke. London is a true world city, with inhabitants from every nation on Earth and citizens from a huge number of backgrounds. It is hard to think of a city more firmly in the tradition of the Olympic movement, which seeks to bring together all nations under the common banner of sporting excellence. (July 7, 2005: 36)

The *Guardian* newspaper praised the leadership of Sebastian Coe, the former Olympic middle-distance runner and chair of the London 2012 bid team, for his decision to invoke London's ethnic and racial diversity as a strategy to win over swaying IOC voters. In the *Guardian*'s front-page lead story Paul Kelso wrote, 'Sebastian Coe arrived to deliver his bid-clinching speech trailing behind him a secret weapon: 30 children from London's East End. Where rival bids filled their 100 allotted seats in the Raffles hotel auditorium with suits, London presented the International Olympic Committee with a grinning multiracial example of the city's potential' (Kelso 2005: 1). The *Guardian*'s Jackie Ashley summarized the general mood: 'if we have won the games partly because of our openness and diversity then we should celebrate that' (2005: 15).

However, in the days and weeks following the attacks of '7/7', as the events of July 7 would come to be known, a counter-argument concerning diversity and difference began to emerge as an apparent attempt to explain the atrocity. Once it became clear that the four bombers were in fact British and that these were so-called 'home-grown' terrorists, the public debate shifted towards examining the role of multiculturalism in 'fanning the flames' of terrorism. Many right-wing, as well as some liberal, commentators suggested that multiculturalism had 'gone too far' in promoting separate, segregated communities. Rather than assimilating into British values and mores, 'ethnic communities' had been allowed, if not actively encouraged, to celebrate their difference from the rest of 'mainstream society'.

According to such arguments, this process of multicultural tolerance had led to a breakdown in the normative order, a lack of respect on the part of 'ethnic minorities' towards the institutions of 'Britain', and the spread of extremism and radical Islamism among many. Rather than reading the bombings as a (profoundly misdirected) violent political act, as indeed the bombers' own video accounts would later confirm, the events were reduced to matters of religious identity and therefore of cultural difference. For some conservative pundits, London (and by extension Britain as a whole) was now Londonistan (Phillips 2006), a seething, amoral place where relativism and political correctness prevented honest discussion about the 'fifth column' infiltration of 'Islamofascists' into the very heart of the nation. Liberal tolerance was blamed for allowing certain ethnic groups to develop their own lifestyles and hence value-systems that had now 'produced' the terrorist acts. Thus, in *less than twenty-four hours*, 'multiculturalism' had shifted from a signifier that embodied all that was great and strong about Britain, to all that was wrong and weak with contemporary British society. Further, the embrace of multiculturalism was deemed to be so dangerous, that it could, if left unchecked, result in the end of British liberal democracy itself.

In the midst of these discussions sport was invoked, first, in the life story of one of the bombers and, secondly, as a potential remedy that might help guide the nation through the tumultuous shock of '7/7'. In the days following the attacks it emerged that one of the suicide bombers, Shazad Tanweer, was an avid cricketer, who had studied for a sport science degree. Born in Bradford, Tanweer had lived most of his unassuming twenty-two years in Leeds, working part-time at his father's chip shop. On the morning of July 7, 2005, Tanweer detonated his bomb close to Aldgate Underground Station, killing himself and seven others (Malik 2006). Journalists and political commentators seized on the supposed contradiction of the 'cricket-loving suicide bomber', with headlines such as 'A cricket-lover from a well-respected family' (Akbar 2005) and 'From student and cricket-lover to terror suspect' (Laville and Cobain 2005). When friends of Tanweer were interviewed, most expressed shock that he had committed the crime: 'I only played cricket in the park with him around 10 days ago. He is not interested in politics' (Laville and Cobain 2005: 1). The implicit and somewhat simplistic suggestion constructed in the media accounts seemed to be, how could someone who loved a sport as quintessentially English as cricket, and whose father owned a fish and chip shop, commit such a (non-British) heinous act?

Sport's supposed integrative power was forcefully asserted the weekend after the London bombings when Trevor Phillips, then Chair of the Commission for Racial Equality (CRE), argued in the *Observer* that the Olympics should act as a catalyst for social cohesion, not just for the city of London nor even the country but for the entire world too. Phillips suggested that the:

> unity in diversity that won us the Games and that saw us through last week's dreadful carnage will be at the heart of the 2012 Games. By the time London is finished, everyone on Earth should want to know how we created the diverse, integrated society we have. The 2012 Olympic flame will illuminate some wonderful sport. But it should also light the path ahead for the future of our common humanity. (2005: 5)

At the core of such arguments are a number of unexamined and often contradictory assumptions concerning the role and 'function' of sport within contemporary multicultural societies. As has been argued throughout this book, sport is often seen to be marginal to the everyday workings of power, relegated to the realm of voluntary leisure and therefore disconnected from formal politics. Yet, at the same time, it is accorded great powers by its boosters to produce both 'social cohesion' and 'community integration' in moments of national crisis. Sport is seen to be irrelevant to the concerns of world politics and international affairs, and yet somehow capable, in the eyes of some, of preventing young men from engaging in acts of political violence as a response to global events. What this brief discussion reveals is how contested the concept of 'multiculturalism' has become within contemporary political debates, the centrality of sport in shaping what it means to be British in the twenty-first century (and the various national identities subsumed under that sign), and the ever-shifting meanings attached to questions of race, sport and politics more generally.

This chapter does not seek to provide a systematic conceptualization of multiculturalism. Multiculturalism is arguably one of the most contested and debated terms both inside and outside of academia. At one level, the term highlights questions concerning the limits to liberalism itself, both as a political philosophy and its conceptual underpinning of western democratic states. Key here is the role and duty of the state in adjudicating the legitimacy of individual rights alongside group claims for cultural recognition from which follow a broader set of questions related to the nature of democracy, the scope of citizenship and the role of the law. Further, the 'multicultural question' can be understood as a challenge to the foundational tenets of liberal philosophy in terms of how *rights* are constituted and the related question as to who is allowed, and under what conditions, even to claim such rights. As Jürgen Habermas (1994: 107) puts it, 'Can a theory of rights that is so individualistically constructed deal adequately with struggles for recognition in which it is the articulation and assertion of collective identities that seems to be at stake?'

Such questions are not merely academic. State policies and even constitutions have been shaped by these ongoing discussions, as reflected in the very different approaches to how multiculturalism itself is recognized (or not) as an inherent good by various western liberal democratic states. Thus different conceptions of national identity and belonging have produced radically different attitudes to pressing political issues such as those related to assimilation/integration, diversity/solidarity and redistribution/recognition (for example, see Benhabib 2002; Gutmann 1994, 2003; Kenny 2004; Parekh 2006; Young 2000). For more critical theorists of multiculturalism, the term also draws attention to how the ideals of liberal humanism and the concepts of liberal political philosophy (and therefore of European modernity itself), such as 'democracy', 'citizenship', 'the state' and so on, far from being universal properties are in fact particular ideals born of white supremacy and European colonialism (Bannerji 2000; Goldberg 1994; Hall 2000). Or, as Barnor Hesse succinctly puts it, 'Modernity is racial' (2007: 643). In this context, multiculturalism is seen as a political intervention into and philosophical interrogation of the silences of western thought and practice, wherein the racial others and forms of racial imperialism that helped to shape the west – the constitutive outside – return to reveal the deeply racialized foundation of the west itself.

However, this chapter is less concerned with trying to develop (or challenge) a particular theory of multiculturalism than it is with trying to read *how* multiculturalism has been used within British political discourse over the past decade or so, and, relatedly, the role of sport *within* these debates. In this context we might suggest that 'multiculturalism' has become a surrogate way to discuss race, politics and identity. For some, the discussions around multiculturalism, which in Britain became part of mainstream political discourse in the 1980s, are a progressive riposte to conservative mono-cultural nationalisms that attempt to deny the externally constitutive elements of national cultures. Or, put another way, if monocultural and ethnic absolutist constructions of the nation work to symbolically (and in some cases legally) exclude blacks and others from the category of unequivocal citizenship then multicultural politics works to re-center questions of race and racism in order to produce a different theory of nationalism and national identity.

Here, national identity is understood as being shaped by multiple routes and influences and constructed through hybrid cultural forms that are themselves ever changing. In this sense, as some have argued, the notion of a multicultural society becomes tautological. If all national cultures are, by definition, formed out of and through differences (linguistic, regional, racial, ethnic and so on) then the multicultural is not a new condition *per se* but merely the inevitable process of national identity formation itself. The constitutive diversity of the nation is even more apparent for those countries that were most engaged in imperial projects, a point made by Edward Said when he notes that partly 'because of empire, all cultures are involved in one another; none is single and pure, all are hybrid, heterogeneous, extraordinarily differentiated, and unmonolithic' (1994: xxix).

For others, however, multiculturalism, far from being a progressive intervention designed to center the historical realities of colonialism in shaping present day forms of racism, has had the opposite effect. From this critical perspective, 'multiculturalism' became, during the 1980s in Britain especially, a way to 'manage' racism by reframing the question of racial inequality and discrimination as a question of 'culture', ethnicity and difference. It is claimed that the anti-racist politics of the 1980s and since, that might otherwise have focused on forms of *structural* inequality, became dissipated, focused instead on narrow questions of identity. 'Multiculturalism', notes A. Sivanandan, 'deflected the political concerns of the black community into the cultural concerns of different communities, the struggle against racism into the struggle for culture' (1990: 84), thus multiculturalism 'denies power relations by denying the hierarchical structure of society' (Sivanandan 1990: 115). This chapter engages these issues by examining the historical and contemporary role of sport in shaping wider public understandings of British and particularly English identity and the ongoing forms of resistance to these changes.

## Sporting Black Britons

Although, as was argued in Chapter 1, black people have been living in Britain since the third century with a sizeable if discontinuous black population existing from the sixteenth century through to the present, it is the post-Second World War period that marks the rapid growth of black British communities. The arrival of the ship *Empire Windrush* to the docks of Tilbury, London in June 1948 carrying 492 migrants (mainly Jamaican men) from the Caribbean, is seen as the symbolic moment for the profound transformation of British identity. This moment of 'inward' migration and settlement 'back' from the former colonies that starts in the late 1940s and continues throughout the 1950s and 1960s coincided with the decline of Britain as an imperial power that is itself often marked by the 1956 Suez crisis (Brown 2001; Judt 2005). The automatic connotations of 'Britain' with both 'empire' and 'whiteness' slowly begin to shift during this period. First from *without*, as Britain's waning global influence became evident with both the rise of the United States as the dominant western world power and as the anti-colonial revolutions of the Third World challenged British hegemony. 'The wind of change', as Harold Macmillan phrased it in a speech in Cape Town, South Africa, was blowing through the colonial world as black consciousness grew, a change that would dramatically alter Britain's previously hegemonic position over parts of Africa and elsewhere 'whether we like it or not' (Judt 2005: 278). And second, from *within* as 'colored' immigration, that many saw as merely a temporary economic measure to rebuild Britain's shattered post-war infrastructure, turned out to have a far greater impact beyond the realms of employment over time reshaping the cultural fabric of the nation itself.

These cultural changes and the 'crisis of identity' caused by the decline of empire and the uncertainty of Britain's place in a post-imperial world were also reflected in Britain's (and England's in particular) global standing within international sport. As the historian Tony Judt notes:

If the illusions of Empire died at Suez, the insular confidence of middle England had been under siege for some time. The disaster of 1956 merely accelerated its collapse. The symbolism of the English national cricket team's first defeat by a team from the West Indies (in 1950 and on the 'hallowed soil' of the home of the game at the Lord's cricket ground in London) was driven home three years later when England's soccer team was thrashed in 1953 at its national stadium – by a team from lowly Hungary and by the unprecedented margin of six goals to three. In the two international games that Englishmen had spread across the world, England itself was no longer supreme. (2005: 301)

Although Judt does not mention it, what was also significant about England's first Test series defeat to the West Indies was the fact that the West Indies were led to victory, in large part, by the batting of the 'three Ws' as they were known at the time, namely Clyde Walcott, Everton Weekes and Frank Worrell, and supported by the bowling of Sonny Ramadhin and Alf Valentine.[1] In other words, it was not just that England had suffered defeat 'at home' to the West Indies in the one sport so closely tied to Englishness and that formed a central part of the ideological component of colonialism, but that they were defeated by those very same black and brown colonial subjects. Sporting 'supremacy' could no longer be automatically coded as white.[2]

Football (as 'the national game') can perhaps be used then as a paradigmatic case study through which to chart the movement throughout the late nineteenth and twentieth century of black subjectivity in England (and Britain more generally). A situation where the lesser 'negro' breeds and primitives first became marginal 'colored' immigrants in the 1950s and 1960s, and then 'black' by the 1970s and 1980s, and finally and more complexly 'black British' by the 1990s, with the variants, soon after, of black English, Welsh, Scottish (and black Irish), towards what might now be tentatively called a black European identity. That is to say, the ways in which black diasporan peoples in Europe have begun to create and forge identities *as Europeans*.[3]

Black athletes have played professional football in England since the late nineteenth century, the Ghanaian-born Arthur Wharton credited with being the first black player to turn professional as early as 1889. Since then, black footballers have played intermittently for various teams in Britain throughout the early and mid-twentieth century (Vasili 2000). Viv Anderson's debut for the men's England national team on November 29, 1978 can be seen to mark a pivotal moment when the far-right chant of 'There Ain't No Black in the Union Jack' began to lose its populist hold.[4] By the 1980s black footballers had established themselves as central players within the professional game. In 1993 Paul Ince became the first black player to captain the men's England team and today an England team *without* black players is barely imaginable. Although women's football receives significantly less attention than the men's game, perhaps the most notable achievement in recent years has been the successful tenure since 1998 of Hope Powell as manager of the England women's team (Gilroy 2008).[5]

These demographic changes within football have had significant effects in reshaping the imagined national community. As Stuart Hall has noted:

> Take sport in Britain. Nothing is closer to the heart of the average Englishman – as opposed to the fields where classically blacks have been outstanding, such as cricket or boxing – than the heartland of soccer. There isn't an occasion when you can pick up a decent Sunday paper, with its photos of Saturday's matches, and not see black faces. Are blacks in the boardrooms of the clubs? Of course not. Are they relatively powerless in the institutions which organize the game? Of course. The question is whether they have any currency, any visibility in the culture of sport where the nation's myths and meanings are fabricated. The answer must be 'yes', and to say this is to note the significant degree to which the culture has turned in the past fifteen or so years. (1998: 43)

But this change in the culture of sport did not occur as easily as this narrative implies. The black presence in the 'national game' was resisted by the main footballing gatekeepers, be they the fans, coaches, managers, or sometimes other players themselves. While the black presence had grown in Britain since the 1940s, even by the early 1970s black players remained rare at the highest levels of the game. The exclusionary practices of English football had kept the national game (with the occasional exception) a largely all-white affair. This was not surprising given the occasionally hostile and often deeply prejudiced reaction that blacks faced at this time from their fellow white Britons.

Sheila Patterson's (1965) *Dark Strangers: A Study of West Indians in London*, first published in 1963 and then as an abridged paperback edition two years later, presents a vivid anthropological picture of white attitudes towards blacks and Asians during the 1950s and 1960s. In a section titled 'British ideas about coloured people', Patterson reports that the 'coloured migrant' and particularly 'the Negro' appear to be 'the supreme and ultimate stranger' (1965: 209). A range of negative attributes and stereotypes are generated by the mere facts of possessing a dark skin. The reproduction of 'nineteenth-century colonialist attitudes' (1965: 210) that are perpetuated within the educational system, help to keep alive such myths concerning the 'glorification of the Nordic "race" and "culture" and its condemnation of racial mixture on alleged "biological" grounds' (p. 210). Mass media images of blacks in television, film, comic books and the popular press help to circulate notions of black people as 'exotic, violent, and primitive' (1965: 211). The continuance of such preconceptions derives from the insecurity and crisis of identity affecting white Britons of all classes that has stemmed, in part, from 'the erosion of imperial power and national prestige' (p. 211). While some black women have recently benefited from the 'vogue for "Negro beauties"' (p. 211) such as Eartha Kitt and Shirley Bassey, this is largely because such light-skinned stars are not seen as having 'conspicuously Negroid features' (p. 211). In fact, it is probable, Patterson concludes, 'that the British tend to associate flattened noses and thick lips with pugilism, in which many Negroes have excelled, and that thereby the association of the Negro with primitive brutality is strengthened' (p. 211).

As with wider society, football itself was replete with stereotypical assumptions about black physicality. While blacks were acknowledged as having 'rhythm' and 'balance' they were also thought to lack both the cognitive capabilities to 'understand' the game and the stamina to survive the hard, aggressive nature of association football, and especially a sport that was played through winter where the black body, it was alleged, could not sufficiently perform. In December 1972 the English Football Association's official magazine *Football Association News* published an article entitled 'Where are Britain's colored stars?'. The article's opening paragraph stated, 'The most surprising thing about the often-discussed "Black Revolution" in football is that it has not happened. There are a few coloured players in English league football but they remain a few' (Brown 1972: 7). Ron Greenwood, then manager of West Ham United, explained that black footballers did in fact have some innate, non-cognitive qualities that were perhaps an advantage over white physical deficiency: 'I like to think this balance is something the young coloured boys possess, almost without thinking about it. It's almost inherent in them. It is quite amazing the way they can adjust their body to any situation which is demanded to control the ball. This is something that we, as a more solid, Nordic-type race, have not got' (p. 7). Similarly, Tony Waiters, the then recently appointed manager of the England youth team (and latterly the head coach of the Canadian national team and a prominent figure today within the National Soccer Coaches Association of America), added, 'They seem more supple than we are and have more mobility in the joints, perhaps because they come from a warm climate. They have a range of greater movement. They can be more skillful on the ball and they manipulate it as an end in itself, sometimes losing sight of the end product' (p. 7).

However, by the end of the 1970s 'the black revolution' was beginning to occur. Greenwood himself would eventually be appointed manager of England in 1977 and, perhaps sensing his innate 'balance', would give Viv Anderson his historic first England cap. In the 1977–78 season, Ron Atkinson, then manager of West Bromwich Albion, signed three leading black players, Cyrille Regis, Laurie Cunningham and Brendon Batson. The players were labeled by Atkinson the 'Three Degrees', after the all-female African American singing group that were popular at the time. A profile of the three players, published in the *Observer Sports Monthly* in 2003, noted that despite such 'breakthroughs' the reaction to black sporting success was often extreme:

> In truth, life for a black footballer in the mid-to-late Seventies was anything but glamorous. Cunningham, Batson and Regis may have been role models for young aspirational black footballers everywhere, but their prominence meant that they were subject to unrelenting abuse from the terraces – this, after all,

was when the National Front were openly recruiting outside grounds. 'We would regularly have 10 to 15,000 people racially abusing us at every game', recalls Regis. 'How could I fight back? Through my talent. And when you've won the game you can say: "That's my response".' (Green 2003: 64)

Later, when Regis was selected to play for England, he received a note that read, 'You'll get one of these through your knees if you step on our Wembley turf'. Inside was a bullet (Green 2003: 64; see also Back et al. 2001: 105–106). Such incidents revealed both the depths of English racism and the extent to which the national team was seen to embody an identity still rooted in a notion of imperial greatness and white supremacy that could only be damaged by the presence of black 'interlopers'.

Throughout the period from the early 1970s to the mid-1990s, questions of race, nationalism and belonging continued to powerfully collide within the arena of sport as black athletes increasingly gained recognition for their sporting achievements. The terrace chant of 'two world wars and one world cup', as Paul Gilroy (2001: xi) suggests, served to highlight 'the bewildering effects of England's post-colonial melancholia'. In 1995 *Wisden Cricket Monthly*, under the guise of trying to stimulate a 'national debate' on race, nationality and sport, printed an article by Robert Henderson, entitled 'Is it in the blood?' (1995: 9–10). The article alleged that black English cricketers playing for England against the West Indies, and South Asians playing against India and Pakistan, did not try as hard as their 'unequivocally English' counterparts. This was because black cricketers suffered from post/colonial revenge fantasies against 'the Empire', meaning that such players subconsciously wanted England to lose and thus played poorly.[6] Henderson grouped together both those cricketers who were born overseas but were now British citizens together with British-born South Asian and black players, suggesting that, in effect, all were 'foreigners' regardless as to what their passports might say:

> An Asian or a negro raised in England will, according to the liberal, feel exactly the same pride and identification with the place as a white man. The reality is somewhat different. It is an entirely natural thing to wish to retain one's racial/cultural identity. Moreover, the energetic public promotion of 'multiculturalism' in England has actively encouraged such expressions of independence. However, with such an attitude, and whatever his professional pride as a cricketer, it is difficult to believe that a foreign-born [*sic*] has any sense of wanting to play above himself simply because he is playing for England … If a player has such a lack of sentimental regard for the country which nurtured him, how much less reason have those without even one English parent or any of his educational advantages to feel deep, unquestioning commitment to England? Norman Tebbit's cricket test is as pertinent for players as it is for spectators. (1995: 10)

Lest anyone believe that the 'negroes' and the other perpetual foreigners could in fact become truly English, Henderson made clear that what really mattered, in the end, was biology itself. 'All the England players whom I would describe as foreigners', Henderson concluded, 'may well be trying at a conscious level, but is that desire to succeed *instinctive*, a matter of biology? There lies the heart of the matter' (1995: 10, emphasis in the original). Henderson subsequently argued that English national teams should ideally be all-white but if England had to field a few 'negroes' then team managers should be able to enforce racial quotas that would limit the number of blacks to no more than two or three players in any one team (Carrington 1998b: 118; see also Marqusee 2001). Thus black athletes playing in the national colors become for contemporary conservatives such as Henderson ethno-national interlopers, 'spoiling' the pristine veneer of the imagined and always lilywhite national body politic.

Such a position extended, as Henderson himself made explicit, the argument made by the Conservative right in Britain that sought to use sport as a way to dictate the conditions upon which black claims to citizenship could be made. In 1990 the then Conservative MP Norman Tebbit argued for what became known as the 'Tebbit test' wherein the 'loyalty' of British Asians and black Britons would be assessed according to who they cheered for in international cricket games. South Asians supporting India or Pakistan, for example, or blacks cheering for the West Indies, would be deemed an unpatriotic gesture, the significance of which extended beyond the sporting boundary to the issue of whether such people had the right to be British at all.

Yet despite this troubled past, and the culture of exclusion that was widely embedded within sport in general and football in particular, recent years have witnessed important transformations within 'the national game' (Back et al., 2001; Garland and Rowe 2001). An officially backed anti-racist campaign launched in the early 1990s coincided with a spectacular growth in the numbers of black and foreign-born players at the top clubs. The result of these shifts has meant that black players have come to embody both local (working-class) pride and the national spirit in a way almost unthinkable during the 1980s, with men's professional football one of the most cosmopolitan spaces in British public life.

Even the English national team, which for decades symbolized for many fans an 'all-white' form of xenophobic imperial nationalism, is now managed by a 'foreigner', the Italian Fabio Capello, due in large part to the paucity of English (male) managers with sufficient skill and qualifications to coach at the highest levels. Similarly, it is not uncommon to see the England men's team with as many black players as white, accompanied by the slow but gradual emergence of black England fans actively and proudly following the team at 'home and abroad' (Perryman 2006). These changes within the fabric of sporting and footballing cultures represent a significant and visible challenge to ethnic absolutist discourses of nationalism (Gilroy 1987), changes that have dramatically undermined the logic of common-sense racisms about black people's status as rightful citizens.

## The New Racial Times: There Ain't No Brown in the Union Jack

Largely absent from the above narrative of gradual inclusion and belonging in the 'national game' is the positioning of South Asian players, fans and communities, significant, not least, because in demographic terms they constitute a larger proportion of the British population than those of black African and black Caribbean descent.[7] Up until the mid 1990s South Asians were seen, in contrast to blacks, as a 'model minority'. South Asians were often defined, as a group, as hard working, traditional, family-orientated and religious. While South Asians may have had the *wrong* religion, being seen largely as Sikh, Hindu or Muslim, they at least had, so the argument went, a strong value system and a set of traditional beliefs that was helping to integrate Asians into 'mainstream' British society, in contrast to the inherently dysfunctional black families and their lawless black youth.

In the same year that *Wisden* published Henderson's article, Paul Johnson, a leading Conservative commentator and part-time spiritual advisor to Tony Blair, argued in *The Spectator* that Britain was facing an existential threat that could, if not confronted, result in the destruction of the country. Nations, Johnson argued, could 'be destroyed not just by invasion but by demographic penetration on a large scale' (1995: 20) and Britain was facing just such an enemy. The character of Britain had been fundamentally changed 'by infiltration and occupation by immigrants' (p. 20). Britain, Johnson suggested, was 'not a racist country and never has been' (p. 20) but racism did still exist as black anti-white racism, promoted by the 'race relations' industry and supported by the government. Black racism was now widespread within the United States where anti-white violence (he gives O.J. Simpson as an example) was preached by black leaders and activists.

In order to prevent this American tragedy reaching British shores and before the situation in Britain got any worse than it already was, Johnson proposed a plan that would allow for wealthy Hong Kong multi-millionaires (who were fearful of the impending 'hand over' of the territory from Britain to China), to 'buy' their British citizenship. The money received could then be used to fund a scheme for the repatriation of Britain's 'failed' black population. Johnson suggested that freehold land could be bought for this purpose, wherein the un-assimilatable blacks would be sent. Citing the ideas of the American sociologist Charles Murray, Johnson further argued that as 'the cultural gap between blacks and the other races of Western democracy is too great to make assimilation likely' (1995: 20) such a plan was necessary and urgent. Johnson concluded:

> Purchasing freehold land for resettlement of blacks will not be cheap, whether the site is in Africa, the Caribbean or alternative places such as Brazil. The capital investment would be considerable. On the other hand, the cost of underwriting the existing mess is not small either, especially now black racists have taken to burning down and looting their neighbourhoods whenever they feel like it. (p. 20)

By contrast, South Asians were excluded from Johnson's plan, presumably because their supposed reverence for tradition, religion, general passivity and conservative communal structures had made them model colonial subjects and therefore inherently suited to eventual assimilation.[8] In 2006, George W. Bush awarded Johnson the Presidential Medal of Freedom.

The intervening years since Johnson made that argument have seen a dramatic reversal of this narrative. It is now South Asian communities in general and South Asian (male) youth in particular who have become the new Asian folk devils (see Alexander 2000). Whereas in the 1970s, the dominant icon of public danger was that of the black male mugger (Hall et al. 1978), intertwined in the 1980s with that of the inner-city black rioter (Keith 1993; Rowe 1998), the 1990s witnessed a more ambivalent set of images and discourses.[9] This has largely been due to the impact of the brutal death, subsequent failed trials and finally the Macpherson Inquiry into the murder of the black teenager Stephen Lawrence (Cathcart 2000), which marked an important shift in racial discourse in Britain, especially in terms of how governmental bodies at both the national and local level have had to re-evaluate the extent to which their policies may be perpetuating forms of institutional racism (see Solomos 2003: 238–241).[10]

For the first time, the death of a black teenager and the incompetent failure of the police to prosecute his (seemingly known) killers was seen to be a *national* and not merely a *black community* tragedy. If the 1990s marks a moment of tentative inclusion for black communities in Britain, the decade when 'there ain't no black in the Union Jack' begins to lose its purchase and popular hold, then the same period signals the beginnings of a new racialized subject of exclusion: the Asian Muslim. A deliberate and powerful conflation of race, ethnicity and religion that becomes the new Other, against which British liberal democracy must stand. The urban disturbances that took place in the summer of 2001 in northern English towns and cities such as Oldham and Bradford and the rise of Islamophobia after the terrorist attacks that took place later that year in the United States provide the local and global context for the New Racial Times.

The effects of the bombings on July 7, 2005 and the subsequent terrorist attacks in Britain (attempted and actual) have served only to accelerate and deepen these racialized representations: the dreadlocked black youth engaged in pitched battles with the police is now displaced by the veiled and/or scarfed Muslim menace, made all the more sinister as this brown Other is regarded as an enemy within. The Asian subject that was previously understood to be docile, subservient, even weak, yet potentially assimilable, and, but for tone of skin and spice of food, almost one of 'us', is now seen to have 'turned'.

In this context, the 'gains' of the late 1990s seem perilously fragile and provisional. South Asians are now expected to 'prove' their loyalty to the rest of the nation, and, as I discuss below, even supposedly liberal commentators now openly debate whether or not Britain has had too much immigration and whether some minority groups and their lifestyles may not be, after all, incompatible with the British way of life. Support for far-right political parties such as the British National Party (BNP) has increased in many areas; the BNP has even achieved mainstream legitimacy by being allowed to appear on political debate shows such as the BBC's *Question Time*. The New Racial Times suddenly seem closer to the old racial politics of the 1960s.

### Where Did All the Multiculturalists Go?

The election of Tony Blair's Labour government in 1997 seemed to signal that a new politics of inclusion, diversity and opportunity had replaced the monocultural paternalism of the Conservative years. Suddenly talk of 'Tebbit tests' seemed outdated and reactionary. However, I want to suggest that such views, concerning the alleged inherent incompatibility of multi-culturalism with national unity and social progress, have now returned as mainstream positions. 'Multiculturalism' is increasingly cited as a major contributor to national destabilization, social unrest and even economic decline, promoting some commentators to talk of a widespread white back-lash against the very idea of multiculturalism (Hewitt 2005).

We might argue, then, that *state multiculturalism*, that is the formal poli-cies of government that seek to address and challenge racism as strategic goals, that define diversity as a good in and of itself, and that aim to foster a more open, expansive notion of nationhood and citizenship, had a remark-ably short shelf-life in Britain.[11] British state multiculturalism can be dated from, approximately, May 1997 when New Labour came to power to the autumn of 2000 with the publication of and reaction to the Parekh Report into the Future of Multi-ethnic Britain. John Solomos has argued that when 'New Labour came to power in May 1997 it was expected to uphold its electoral commitment to strengthen the 1976 Race Relations Act, and more generally to respond to demands from within its ranks to develop a more positive policy agenda on racism and multiculturalism … However, the policy debates since 1997 have highlighted the often contradictory and limited nature of New Labour's thinking on the subject' (2003: 89).

As noted earlier, the scale and size of the 1997 Tory defeat was read at the time as signaling the end of nearly two decades of conservative nation-alist populism. The warm beer accompanied by old maids cycling across villages searching for Holy Communion that John Major defined as the core cultural and civic traits of Britishness lost out to the bright new cosmo-politan world of a racially inclusive and forward-looking 'young Britain'. Norman Tebbit's claim during the Conservative party conference, shortly after their 1997 election defeat, that multiculturalism was a divisive force as 'one cannot uphold two sets of ethics or be loyal to two nations, any more than a man can have two masters' (Abrams 1997) was immediately labeled by his fellow Conservatives as an anachronistic statement that was out of place in the new party that their recently elected leader William

Hague wanted to create. Tebbit, and other Conservative monoculturalists, were now described as 'dinosaurs', out-of-date political figures from a bygone age. William Hague vowed he understood that just as Britain had changed so too would the Conservative party. The Conservatives would henceforth be welcoming to all, offer 'patriotism without prejudice' and would become a 'multiracial party'.

A decade on from this vision (and after a further two defeats in which the party repeatedly failed to reinvent itself), Hague's vision of a new Conservative party re-emerged in the 2007 conference speech of new leader David Cameron. Cameron name-checked William Hague as a positive motivating force for change within the party and attacked Labour for their overtly hyper-nationalist and subtly racist politicking. Condemning Prime Minister Gordon Brown's earlier call for 'British jobs for British workers!' as both unfeasible if not illegal under current European Union (EU) laws, Cameron (2008) said:

> Boy has this guy [Brown] got a plan. It's to appeal to that 4% of people in marginal seats. With a dog whistle on immigration there and a word about crime here, wrap yourself up in the flag and talk about Britishness enough times and maybe just maybe you can convince enough people that you are on their side. Well I say, God, we've got to be better than that.

As Cameron brought his speech to a close he implored the assembled delegates to change themselves and the nation by repeatedly using the refrain of 'we can get it if we really want it'. The speech ended in a strange postmodern political spectacle as the largely elderly and white audience gave Cameron the obligatory standing ovation and 'danced' between their seats as Jimmy Cliff's reggae classic 'You Can Get it if You Really Want' thundered out from the Bournemouth conference center PA system. The oppositional rhythms of the black Atlantic world were being reworked to provide an alternative soundtrack in the service of the British Conservative party's attempt at re-branding itself 'hip', relevant and modern.

But I want to argue that multiculturalism as an inherently positive signifier within political discourse had already been dead for years by the time of this latest implausible multicultural moment. Currently, multiculturalism can only be embraced within mainstream British political discourse if it is also linked to a denial or negation of racism. It is a belief in ethnic difference without mentioning inequality, racial diversity without discussing discrimination, in short an acceptance – 'tolerance' – of difference but one deliberately shorn of an historical account of racism and its contemporary register.

The Parekh Report on the Future of Multi-ethnic Britain, published in October 2000, marked an important moment in British history as regards a serious and sustained attempt to construct a forward-looking sense of Britishness that did not rely on the tropes of empire and imperial greatness.[12] The report's commissioners, chaired by Bhikhu Parekh, included a number of leading policy makers, academics and journalists, such as Yasmin

Alibhai-Brown, Stuart Hall and Trevor Phillips. The commission spent more than two years working on the report, engaging in visits across Britain, hosting research seminars on topics from the criminal justice system to education and social welfare, as well as commissioning specialist papers from leading academics such as Lola Young and Tariq Modood.

Acknowledging that Britain's move towards being a multiethnic and multicultural society had been decisive, the report also suggested that this change had not come about as a result of specific policies that were aimed at producing such a society but were the unintended consequences of a 'multicultural drift' (2000: 14).[13] Given this situation, it was necessary for the British government and other agencies to develop strategies for directly addressing racism while promoting a politics of inclusion that included diversity as a common good and goal. The report made a number of substantive policy recommendations in areas from policing, the arts, media and sport, employment and immigration, and confronted issues such as institutional racism and deaths in police custody.

The report also proffered the notion that in order to contest the idea of Britishness as a narrow, inward-looking and exclusionary identity, it should instead be re-imagined as a post-national 'community of communities'. The report suggested that:

> Britishness, as much as Englishness, has systematic, largely unspoken, racial connotations. Whiteness nowhere features as an explicit condition of being British, but it is widely understood that Englishness, and therefore by extension Britishness, is racially coded. 'There ain't no black in the Union Jack,' it has been said. Race is deeply entwined with political culture and with the idea of nation, and underpinned by a distinctly British kind of reticence – to take race and racism seriously, or even to talk about them at all, is bad form, something not done in polite company … Unless these deep-rooted antagonisms to racial and cultural difference can be defeated in practice, as well as symbolically written out of the national story, the idea of a multicultural post-nation remains an empty promise. (2000: 38–39)

The Parekh Report thus offered a thoughtful and serious opportunity to link discussions of race with those of nation, and to provide an alternative narrative of what Britishness both was and could be, one that reflected the modern-day realities of a post/colonial society with a series of specific, if modest, policy proposals. However, it was the assertion that Britishness had 'racial connotations' that was to cause the most discussion. On the day *before* the report's publication, and seemingly in an attempt to undermine its recommendations, the *Daily Telegraph* suggested that the then Home Secretary, Jack Straw, had endorsed what was considered to be a radical new conception of Britishness: 'Straw Wants to Rewrite Our History: "British" is a Racist Word, says Report' (October 10, 2000).[14]

Deliberately conflating 'racial connotations' with 'racist', the *Telegraph*'s reporting set the news agenda for how the Commissioners' report would be covered. Members of the Commission, including Parekh himself and Stuart

Hall, were lambasted as failed Marxists – 'sub Marxist gibberish' as the *Daily Telegraph* put it – from provincial universities, and the report was presented as an attack on Britain. At the launch of the Report, and no doubt to the bemusement of the commissioners, Jack Straw rejected the Commission's position on national identity stating, 'I don't accept the argument of those on the narrow nationalist right, nor on the part of the left that Britain, as a cohesive whole is dead ... I'm proud to be British and I'm proud of what I believe to be the best of British values'. The newspapers duly reported: '"Proud to be British" Straw raps race report' (*The Times*, October 12, 2000), 'Labour in retreat on race' (*Daily Mail*, October 12, 2000), 'Race report angers "proud Briton" Straw' (*Daily Express*, October 12, 2000). As Eugene McLaughlin and Sarah Neal noted, 'New Labour had successfully distanced itself publicly from the FMEB Commission and report. In so doing, the New Labour government also signaled its willingness to lay down the terms on which future debates about Britishness would take place' (2007: 920; see also Back et al. 2002; Pilkington 2003: 263–278).[15]

After the Macpherson report, 'institutional racism' might be seen to exist within 'institutions' in Britain but somehow not within the social structures of Britain itself. Disconnected from any serious discussion concerning racism 'multiculturalism' thus became an empty signifier. New Labour distanced itself from the modest but important proposals of the Parekh Report and in so doing negated any genuinely transformative form of official, state multiculturalism. The 'depressing and deeply symptomatic counterreaction' (Gilroy 2004: vii) highlighted just how powerful the white colonial frame remains in shaping the terms of the debate, what can be debated and how that debate takes place when it comes to the politics of race and nation.

### Race and the Politics of Solidarity

This is the political terrain from which writers such as David Goodhart, editor of *Prospect* magazine, have been able to present the so-called progressive dilemma, namely how to reconcile multiculturalism (diversity) and claims for equality (solidarity) encapsulated in the question, is Britain too diverse? Goodhart (2004, 2006) suggests that diversity itself undermines collective forms of solidarity, which is at the heart of the social democratic contract and the welfare state. 'Non-white' immigration is seen as a threat as indigenous communities begin to wonder why their taxes should be wasted on the differently colored and undeserving newcomers with whom they have little, if any, social or cultural connections. The answer, for neoliberal thinkers such as Goodhart, is to re-emphasize a so-called 'progressive nationalism' based on established 'British values' that newcomers have to learn if they are to be accepted, and relatedly, that the so-called indigenous can also feel proud of.

There are a number of problems with such arguments. The position implies an unchanging, stable and unanimist *Gemeinschaft* that supposedly existed in Britain up until the 1950s, when blacks and South Asians are first seen to arrive. This reconstruction of a largely homogeneous, settled people negates both the previous (pre-1948) waves of migration to Britain (Fryer 1984; Hesse 2000), as well as the internal class, regional, ethnic and linguistic cleavages that had to be violently suppressed in order to produce 'England', and 'Britain' as coherent, collective identities.

Such positions also conflate questions of (English) nationality and identity with those related to the (British) state and citizenship. Commentators such as Goodhart further assume that 'solidarity', understood as the necessary political category for progressive forms of social democratic politics, can only be forged from racial or ethnic sameness. In contrast, as many political theorists have noted, it is the recognition of shared social location and material interests, an ethical position of political identification and consciousness, that is the basis for any progressive politics and therefore has little to do with people's racial identities. As Juliet Hooker points out, it is:

> more useful to think about political solidarity as the product of structural conditions that require individuals who are strangers to one another to develop contingent solidarities, however momentarily, every day. The basis for such solidarity is not mutual identification, shared nationality, or some form of cultural or racial homogeneity. Rather, solidarity is seen as arising from the (geographical, social, political) spaces that individuals share as a result of which their actions have unavoidable consequences on the lives of others that also inhabit such locales. (2009: 170)

The precise sociological mechanisms for producing social solidarity are far more complex than Goodhart allows. Indeed, as Ray Pahl (2006) points out, it is 'the differences – or perhaps even the conflicts – that paradoxically produce solidarities and social glue'.

Such arguments recast all 'non-white' national subjects back into the category of the 'immigrant', thus allowing a series of binaries to be created from which the discussion, necessarily, turns to questions concerning integration, meaning assimilation, calls for the promotion of dominant British values, concerns about 'their' (in)compatibility – or otherwise – with 'our' way of life, and the political necessity, finally, to get 'tough' on immigration. Thus, seen through the perspective of the white colonial frame, white people, regardless of their actual ancestry, become 'indigenous Britons' while the rest, irrespective of their complex and mixed genealogies become, in the words of Goodhart, 'settled minorities' (2004, 2006).

Quite how long is required to make the move from 'settled' to 'indigenous' is never spelled out, though lurking behind such distinctions is the implicit criterion that only whites can ever be unequivocally English/British, no matter what black people's passports might say. For some, more critical theorists, such arguments return the political debate over race, identity and nationalism back to the 1960s. Paul Gilroy, for instance, argues that:

> *Prospect* has spearheaded the adaptation and updating of well-worn themes drawn from the Powell lexicon. Immigration is always an invasion, and the inevitably following race war is a culturally-based conflict born from a fundamental, pre-political incompatibility. The only vague novelty here lay in the folding of these ancient motifs into a nominally 'left' discourse. (2005: 41–42)

Developing a historical account, Goodhart also states that it is a 'fallacy' to argue that colonialism was necessarily bad for the colonized and it cannot be blamed, as he alleges some do, for all of today's ills. He notes too that all civilizations have engaged in slavery and conquest at some point, and that the errors of the past (if indeed they were errors) should not be evaluated by today's moral standards – 'we should be careful not to judge the past by the standards of the present' (2006). Such an argument can be seen as an attempt to draw an absolute break between the colonial past and the contemporary present in which the very 'idea of Europe' and of Britishness in particular is 'cleansed' of its racial entanglements. But as has been argued throughout this book, discourses of race and racial difference were central to the forging of European identities and therefore of whiteness itself.

Michael Hardt and Antonio Negri (2000: 128) point out that only through opposition to the colonized subject does 'the metropolitan subject really become itself … The gilded monuments not only of European cities but also of modern European thought itself are founded on the intimate dialectal struggle with its Others'. As argued earlier, the foundational categories of Enlightenment thought, those of liberalism, secularism, universalism, liberty and so on, not only came into being in the context of colonialism, but were themselves produced as a way to create the very notion of European identity, an identity that had to be demarcated from its abject other, the 'non-European' black African, in order to produce itself – the white mythologies central to the creation of a 'racialized modernity' and of 'the west' (Hesse 2007).

Goodhart has a limited theory of racism, as to produce a more complex account would problematize his central arguments and force him to consider the *continuance* of colonial forms of racism into the present. Similarly, as Neal Ascherson (2006) notes, there is little understanding of how difference and hybridity can produce new forms of solidarity rather than simply weakening the old. More salient than the veracity and intention of the assertions themselves, however, is the fact that Goodhart's arguments have received extensive and positive coverage within the British media, including the liberal media. Goodhart's analysis, that intellectually speaking is closer to the conservative nationalism of Robert Henderson and Paul Johnson than it is to the progressive multiculturalism of Bikhu Parekh and Stuart Hall, is an indication of the continuing crisis of national identity in Britain and the continual failure of leading commentators, pundits and politicians to seriously address contemporary racial discourse and practices.[16] Such arguments seem to chime with an emerging political consensus reflecting the desire for a reassertion and promotion of stronger British values as a way to shore up the fragility of a fractured and traumatized national body politic and a return to the politics of assimilation.

## New England: Multicultural Sporting Futures

If Stuart Hall is right about the centrality of football in narrating the myths and meanings of the nation, then the lack of South Asian professional football players becomes a public marker that is seen to confirm *their* inherent difference from the rest of 'mainstream' Britain. Black supporters and players can be issued with what Les Back et al. (2001) call 'passports to inclusion' into contemporary footballing cultures, although, of course, such passports can be revoked and downgraded from citizenship to merely permanent residency at a moment's notice. Dan Burdsey has suggested that, historically, South Asian athletes have rarely entered into British national sporting folklore: 'The sight of a British Asian sportsperson representing Britain or one of its constituent nations remains a disturbingly infrequent sight' (2007b: 611).

Yet beyond the world of football different performances of Englishness can be found. The rise to public attention and even hero worship among England's sporting publics of Mudhsuden Singh Panesar and Lewis Carl Hamilton is worth considering for the 'fleeting, prefigurative glimpses of a different nation' (Gilroy 2001: xvii) that they offer. Since his international Test debut against India in March 2006, where his first and symbolic Test wicket was that of Sachin Tendulkhar, 'Monty' Panesar has captured the imagination of cricketing fans like few South Asian players before him. He is often referred to in journalistic profiles as a 'cult figure' and is widely seen as the best England spin bowler for a generation or more. One hundred and ten years after K.S. Ranjitsinhji was given the same award, Panesar was selected as one of the five Wisden Cricketers of the Year in 2007. His exuberant celebrations at the fall of a wicket, together with his proudly worn beard and *patka*, has lead to him being dubbed, among other nicknames, the 'Sikh of Tweak'.

Similarly, Lewis Hamilton has re-written the record books in Formula One motor racing. Finishing second in the driver's championship by a single point, while consistently out-driving his two-time world champion teammate Fernando Alonso, was an unimaginable outcome at the beginning of his first season, where the initial talk from motor racing experts was of the odd podium finish at best and a year spent gaining experience. His impact is such that he is credited with saving Formula One, at least in Britain, after the retirement of Michael Schumacher and the fear that the sport would fade from public view and with it much needed sponsorship money.[17] The *Guardian*'s Richard Williams (2007) noted that, 'Single-handedly he has restored public interest in a sport that had sunk up to the axles in its own cynicism'. Young, bright and good-looking, he also represented a brilliantly successful attempt by an outsider to breach the walls of an exclusive club.

Some have compared his place in motor racing history as equal not just to the likes of James Hunt, Nigel Mansell and Damon Hill but potentially to Jackie Stewart, Jim Clark and Graham Hill. Profiles and commentators have marveled at Hamilton's steadfast concentration and focus and his willingness not merely to learn but to excel. As Damon Hill enthused, 'He's come into F1 and dealt with everything that has been thrown at him with no problem at all. He seems to be completely at home. It's as if F1 is simply the next stage in his career, a logical progression – but he's acting like there's another stage beyond F1. I've never seen anything like it' (Hamilton 2007). Hamilton ended his rookie year as a national sporting figure by being voted runner-up in the 2007 BBC Sports Personality of the Year, and being awarded both *GQ* magazine's Sportsman of the Year and *F1 Racing* magazine's Man of the Year. The following year Hamilton became the youngest ever Formula One champion, further establishing himself as one of Britain's leading sports stars.

What is striking about both men is that they do not speak to the traditional ways in which British Asian and black athletes have classically been framed. They come from the sprawling suburbs – Panesar from Luton, Hamilton from Stevenage – and not the inner cities so beloved of the tabloid 'rags-to-riches', out-of-the-ghetto sporting narratives. Both are softly spoken. Panesar, a Loughborough University graduate, sometimes exhibits awkwardness at journalists' predictable questions. Hamilton, a model of understatement and professional respect for his rivals, is variously described as 'likable and humble'. Both eschew the type of 'in-your-face' masculine bravado often associated with boxers and track athletes. They seem unlikely to be compared to a 'Mike Tyson' or a 'Jack Johnson'. Theirs is not the 'immigrant' story of the likes of the football player John Barnes or the sprinter Linford Christie, both of whom came to England early in their lives and made it their home, yet who struggled to reconcile what Du Bois referred to as the war between being black and being a New World Citizen. For Panesar and Hamilton their Englishness is simply an unremarkable, uncontestable given. So although they are 'mould breaking' in as much as Panesar is the first Sikh cricketer to have played for England and Hamilton the first black Formula One driver to have won the world title, they are also establishing new paradigms for what it means to be English. There is, to put it simply, no script at this historical conjuncture for understanding how we are to read the political and symbolic significance of a black English Formula One driver or a devout Sikh leading England's spin bowling attack.

Of course, both athletes, despite their current high public standing, are still framed in problematic ways. The constant discussions about Panesar's physicality and the fake beards and imitation head scarves now worn at cricket grounds have an uneasy resonance that plays on (and sometimes ignores) the line between on the one hand jovial hero worship and sporting admiration and on the other the darker side of white mimicry of the racialized Other in which markers of religious and cultural difference are reduced to crude caricatures in the service of white laughter. An interview in *The Sunday Times* included the following: 'Take me as you find me, he [Panesar] seems to say — unruly beard, big goggly eyes, unsynchronised limbs and all. And the public has done just that. Fans love nothing more than the sportsman who blends wholehearted effort with a dash of clumsiness. He's Eddie the Eagle, Eric the Eel and court-jester-made-good all rolled into one' (Wilde 2006). Such reporting tends to reduce an accomplished, dedicated and thoughtful international cricketer to a cartoon-like comedic object of ridicule whose apparent purpose is to entertain 'ol' massa' in the field.

Similarly, part of the fascination with 'young Lewis' derives from the sheer novelty of a *black man* in Formula One. Despite the efforts of his racing team McLaren to 'play down' the 'race stuff' earlier in his career by discouraging journalists from asking Hamilton questions about his color, 'race' remains a constitutive part of the many narratives about Hamilton. Profiles of the driver often talk in metonymic terms about him being a 'breath of fresh air', 'irresistibly different' and 'new and exciting'. 'Race' is both ever present and absent in the media framing of Hamilton. As the *Guardian* journalist Gary Younge (2007) notes, one response underneath a YouTube posting of Hamilton's driving exploits 'suggested his driving proficiency came from "all that practice he's had nicking cars". At other times the references are more oblique. He has been compared to Tiger Woods, Theo Walcott and Amir Khan – but rarely Nigel Mansell, James Hunt or David Beckham'.

Both Hamilton and Panesar have been heralded as the new faces of multicultural England. The *Wisden* Cricketer of the Year profile described Panesar as 'an instant multicultural icon, a figure proclaiming a success for racial integration in fraught 21st-century Britain' (John 2007). The *Sunday Times* similarly noted that the 'public warmth' for Panesar could be explained in part as 'his presence ... makes the England cricket team more multicultural. People want their team to look like this' (Wilde 2006). In this moment Panesar becomes the anti-Shazad Tanweer, reassuring the British public of the redemptive, integrative function that sport – and cricket especially – is supposed to have in making the 'natives' into Englishmen, even if they still refuse to drink the warm beer after the match.

Though cautious in their public pronouncements, and in Panesar's case often conservative in outlook, both athletes motion towards the type of convivial multiculture that Gilroy (2005) suggests has become a part of the unexceptional everyday experience of Britain's major cities – as opposed to the formal, political and policy debates over official, state multiculturalism. As Panesar himself has said, 'If me playing for England does something to show that our society is multicultural, then that's good. I think it does show how Britain is a multicultural society, that there aren't any differences and we are all one as a country. That's good for Britain and good for the people of this country' (Wilde 2006).

Hamilton too, in the few times he has been allowed to speak more freely, has talked of his role models being his father, Nelson Mandela and Martin Luther King, and his musical tastes ranging from Bob Marley and Marvin Gaye to Nas. He has appeared on MTV Base and hung out with Pharell Williams when he competed at Indianapolis. Thus unlike the former boxer Frank Bruno, Hamilton does not need to hide his blackness. He did not wait until he had won the world championship before coming out of the 'racial closest'. For Hamilton there is no closet. As he puts it, 'Being black is not a negative. It's a positive, if anything, because I'm different. In the future it can open doors to different cultures and that is what motor sport is trying to do anyway. It will show that not only white people can do it, but also black people, Indians, Japanese and Chinese. *It will be good to mean something*' (Jacques 2007, emphasis added).

Hamilton's national standing as perhaps *the* icon of multicultural Englishness was enhanced when he won the Formula One championship two days before the US Presidential election. Predictably, the British press made much of this connection. The *Daily Mirror* wondered if it was a 'good omen' that 'a young, charismatic black man has shown resilience, skill and determination to win against the odds. Now roll on Barack Obama' (*Daily Mirror*, November 3, 2008, p. 10), while Aida Edemariam's (2008) *Guardian* article pondered whether the week would be the greatest ever in black history. Even the *Sun* extolled the significance of the 'first black world motor racing champion' in its leader, praising the young driver who had earlier in the season had to deal with racist Spanish fans donning black face and mocking his family. Yet, the *Sun* noted, Hamilton had shown great humility throughout his ordeals and was a true role model and national hero: 'It's hard to believe he's done all this at 23. He has years yet to achieve so much more. Lewis Hamilton is a true superstar on the world stage. We're proud he's ours.' Our Frank had become Our Lewis.

## Corporate Sporting Multiculturalism

This is a type of multiculturalism that is clearly marketable. It appears that light-skinned suburban black rather than inner-city ebony, and conservative Sikh rather than outspoken radical Muslim is a profitable form of corporate multiculturalism. Panesar's then agent David Ligertwood told the *Sunday Times*:

> He's a lot more in demand now. He's been popular all summer [2006], but that has turned into commercial interest ... There's an X-factor with Monty. He's not just another player. He stands out as a character. Everybody can see he's a good bloke and a fun guy, but a serious cricketer, and they warm to that. He also embraces his Asian background. People may have been looking at guys in the street with beards and feeling negative about them. Monty makes them feel good. (Wilde 2006)

Likewise, Hamilton's earnings have increased from his purported first year salary of £250,000 to what is now expected to be an earnings capability in the tens of millions *per year* with media speculation that his final career earnings could reach $1 billion. Rakhee Vithlani, head of multicultural communications at Weber Shandwick PR, told the *Observer*:

> Hamilton's ethnic background gives him a 'value add' in terms of marketability. In the US, the African-American market accounts for $561bn … boosted by stars such as Tiger Woods and the Williams sisters, but over here brands are only just beginning to catch on to the spending power of our ethnic communities … Black icons are seen as trendsetters in terms of market value. Stars like Lewis Hamilton are worth their weight in gold. (Kessel 2007: 5)

In a glossy advertisement in the 2007 special issue of *Esquire* magazine's 'The Big Black Book: The style manual for successful men', Hamilton is photographed gazing out of the window of a Bombardier Learjet dressed immaculately in a tailored suit, the sunlight gently caressing his motionless frame. His poised, confident and beautifully young face does not look out-of-place in this private jet. It is the new face of the twenty-first century black athlete, able to sell private jets to the world's corporate elite. The advertisement reads: 'THE RACE IS ON: Live it fast. Rocket your entourage to the ultimate destination at speeds exceeding 460 knots. Live it large. Treat yourself and seven guests to voluminous cabin comfort, feeling right at home, away from home. Live it high. Climb to 43,000 feet in less than 25 minutes. Soar above the crowd at 51,000 feet. Live it in style. Touch down on the runway, creating anticipation before your next race. Live it like three-time grand prix winner Lewis Hamilton, and become a living legend.'

This raises the question as to what exactly that 'something' is, that Hamilton claims his presence brings. In his autobiography Hamilton makes great play of the importance of his father's and therefore his own Grenadian background, even calling it at one point his 'real home' (2008: 19). He is clearly proud of his mixed heritage and Caribbean roots and defines his Britishness in very open ways. It appears that Hamilton would not likely pass the Tebbit test. Yet, when it comes to discussing racism (or anything much beyond his sport) he says merely that 'race' is not an issue for him and that he wishes people would behave better and be more polite to one another (2008: 21–22). He hints at 'bad experiences' he has had in the past but does not expand on what these were. Indeed his largely uncontroversial autobiography, full of the predictable motor racing incidents and stories from his short senior career, is remarkable for how *apolitical* he comes across. Sounding more like the early Bruno, Hamilton relays meeting the Conservative leader for the first time: 'Before I met David Cameron I was not sure what I would make of him. Normally, I don't particularly like politics but he was a really nice guy and I was incredibly impressed. He was a very interesting and genuine person and, as I found out, a great family man' (2008: 272).

It is true that both Panesar and Hamilton have expanded the range of meanings associated with Englishness. At a time of renewed electoral success for far-right groups committed to the curtailing if not the outright denial of democratic and civil rights to 'non-white' British subjects, in the context of rising anti-Muslim rhetoric and the deeply imbedded institutional forms of anti-black white racism, and the widespread attack on 'multiculturalism' from across the mainstream political spectrum, such re-imaginings of national identity should not be dismissed lightly. Yet there is a danger that 'stars' such as Hamilton simply help to produce a postmodern spectacle of black radicalism that is divorced from actual politics; a spectacle that can invoke the cool symbolism and chic imagery of progressive black politics associated with the *image* of Muhammad Ali, Tommie Smith and John Carlos, Nelson Mandela, Martin Luther King, Jr, Bob Marley, Angela Davis and so on, but without engaging the political *realities* that such figures fought against. Merely signifying results, in the end, in the abdication of anti-racist praxis, sporting or otherwise. A politics of style and style of politics that corporate sporting multiculturalism can easily accommodate, and that ultimately renders the 'radical' black athlete both complicit and compromised.

This is a situation in which the contemporary black athlete is granted public visibility and personal economic wealth, but under tenuous conditions of corporate patronage that can be revoked at a moment's notice for any transgression beyond the confines of a permissible blackness predicated upon narrowly defined bourgeois norms and acceptable modes of behavior. Public and even private violations of these norms and dominant scripts results, once again, as Du Bois had earlier noted about white reactions to Jack Johnson's actions, in the thrill of national and increasingly international disgust at the 'errant' behavior of deviant black athletes who are duly disciplined with excessive fines, lengthy suspensions, and sometimes even imprisonment, and the resulting loss of sponsorship deals and endorsements. As Tiger Woods, an athlete that Hamilton is often compared to, would discover in late 2009 following a series of allegations concerning his apparent marital infidelity, even those black athletes considered 'clean-cut', 'wholesome' and 'respectable', that is to say those defined in opposition to the debased forms of sporting negritude, can quickly and easily be reduced to the category of abject blackness.

On the front cover of *Vanity Fair*'s February 2010 edition, Tiger Woods is shown naked from his waist up, beads of sweat running down his darkened body, the Nike-sponsored corporate smile now replaced with a brooding intense scowl. The soft-focused, carefully airbrushed images that normally adorn photographic spreads of the rich and famous in magazines such as *Vanity Fair* are now replaced by the fetishized display of Woods' black skin stretched over his muscular form. Woods is depicted as both threatening (angry, powerful) and sexually desirable (ripped muscles, glistening in his own sweat). The Nike cap so iconically associated with the branding of Woods over the past decade is gone, replaced instead with a black skull cap. On the front cover and in the series of accompanying photographs, taken by Annie Leibovitz, Woods looks more like a convict working out inside a barren prison gym. Woods stares directly into the camera, pulling curls with each muscled arm, veins bulging on his biceps. Woods' first name, which of course lends itself to a range of bestial similes, is imprinted across his chest, inviting the reader to gaze at the 'real', darker Woods contained inside: 'TIGER: Raw, never-before-seen photos!'.[18] The image of the 'post-racial' Tiger Woods – 'non-threatening and non-contro-versial' as Buzz Bissinger's (2010) accompanying article puts it – is now replaced with this 'darker' representation, a more sinister side of Woods that had always been, or so we were told, lurking inside him. The signifier 'Tiger' and Woods himself now associated with O.J. Simpson (Bissinger 2010: 83) and Barry Bonds (p. 145), 'escort dates' (p. 83), 'porn stars and nightclub waitresses' (p. 83) with 'lips almost as thick as their very full breasts' (p. 83), and a 'sex addict who could not get enough' (p. 145) thus letting down his fans and friends and most importantly defiling his 'beauti-ful blonde wife' (p. 86). Even the world's most celebrated and highest paid black athlete, for so long the epitome of corporate sporting multicultural-ism, could not, in the end, escape the specter of Jack Johnson.

## St George and the London Olympics

Identity, Stuart Hall (1991: 21) suggests, is 'a structured representation that only achieves its positive through the narrow eye of the negative. It has to go through the eye of the needle of the other before it can reconstruct itself'. As regards to what we might label as English ethnicity, the racial Other has now become a part of the self. There is no outside racial Other to Englishness any more. The center itself has been reconfigured from within. Multiculturalism read as the 'return of the repressed' (Hesse 2000: 228) erases once and for all any notion of a retreat back into the myths of 'free born Englishmen'. That historical moment has passed. Though often disavowed by the recent populist books on 'the English question', it is precisely this 'new' hybridity of Englishness that has *always* been its defining characteristic. Hall's early 1990s observations have proved prescient, when he suggested that:

> [it] was only by dint of excluding or absorbing all the differences that consti-tuted Englishness, the multitude of different regions, peoples, classes, genders that composed the people gathered together in the Act of the Union, that Englishness could stand together for everybody in the British isles. It was always negotiated against difference … And that is something which we are only now beginning to see the true nature of, when we are beginning to come to the end of it. (1991: 22)

The growth in broader-based support for the men's England national team reflects the positive post-Euro 1996 changes in football fan culture, which accelerated after the 2002 World Cup (Perryman 2002). Put simply, the

England national football team looks different and partially more representative of multicultural England than it has ever done. A team of star players such as Rio Ferdinand, Ashley Cole and Theo Walcott is profoundly different to what existed before, reflecting a more comfortable, convivial form of multiculture. This has allowed a degree of South Asian and black identification with the national team that simply did not exist even a decade ago.

The sociological question to be addressed in this context concerns who is allowed to represent the nation and under what conditions of inclusion/exclusion. This causes us to think more critically about both the possibilities for, *and limitations of*, using sport and particular athletes as cultural reference points for identity formation. Due to the resolutely priapic fabric of Britain's professional sporting cultures, for example, such national icons remain overwhelming male, despite the best efforts over the years of individual athletes such as Paula Radcliffe, Denise Lewis and Kelly Holmes. All the while Britain fails to produce outstanding sportswomen outside of track and field, and while women's team sports remain marginal (if they exist at all) to the mass media, national sporting icons will likely remain a largely male affair. This should caution against overly optimistic claims concerning the progressive possibilities of the politics of sporting representation when only men's teams and male athletes are deemed worthy of truly symbolizing the nation.

A critical and global analysis of the role of popular culture, and sport in particular, in helping communities to live, work and play with and through difference, in an age still marked by the historical scars of Empire and racial exclusion, is a necessary and urgent task. However such an analysis needs to avoid over-inflating the importance of sport as well as particular (usually male) athletes as if they are simply 'role models' for an entire nation. But we similarly and simultaneously need to understand and map the continued importance that sporting spectacles play in giving shape to national identities, especially when national sovereignty and subjectivity itself are increasingly fraught with racially charged fissures and forms of exclusion.

London's 2012 summer Olympic and Paralympic games offer an opportunity to make real sport's often-claimed but rarely realized capacity (Ross 2009: 77–101) for social, economic and cultural regeneration – both aesthetically in terms of the physical landscape and environment of East London and the surrounding areas but also more widely, in terms of London's, England's and Britain's, co-existing communities, an opportunity to address the deep-rooted antagonisms of race, nation and empire that so mark the post/colonial, multicultural present. In the aftermath of the attacks on '7/7' Trevor Phillips argued that sports in general, and the Olympics in particular, had always been intermeshed with real world politics and the global concerns of the day. Phillips noted how, in 1936, Adolf Hitler had 'cowed the Olympic movement into letting the Games be used as a platform for its dreams of Aryan supremacy. In 1968, in Mexico City, African Americans held their black-gloved fists aloft to announce the arrival of black power. And in 1980 the world divided over the Moscow

Games, with a partial Western boycott marking the final stage in the titanic struggle that we called the Cold War' (2005: 4). The 2012 London Games, Phillips suggested, also stood at an equally momentous moment:

> London's victory in the race for the 2012 Olympics carries an equally historic message. At the start of the 21st century, the great issue of our times is this: can the peoples of a multi-ethnic and multi-faith world share the planet in peace? Can we cross the lines of difference and share a moment in which the talents and the endeavour of the young become more important than their colour or their ethnicities? And can people of diverse traditions ever learn to share the same dreams and ambitions? (2005: 4)

It is easy to be dismissive of such hyperbolic rhetoric. Phillips' words were as much intended to reassure the nation, and the IOC, that the decision to award London the Olympic games was the correct one, than anything else. That said, it would be equally misjudged to simply relegate the importance of the Games to the marginalia of public discussion about politics, identity and belonging. To paraphrase the Parekh Report, the Olympics provide an important public space within which to re-imagine the national story, as one where the idea of a multicultural post-national narrative becomes both real and desirable, a story that rather than disavowing Britain's imperial past would acknowledge its painful complexity in shaping the present. Englishness, adrift for so long in the multicultural seas, could then finally come home, along the Thames and into the Olympic Village, alongside the other 'home nations' that make up that curious, hybrid sporting nation called 'Great Britain and Northern Ireland'. The 2012 Games might just signal the revival of a truly multicultural nation finally at ease with itself, a nation able to honestly confront the past in order to produce a more progressive and egalitarian, twenty-first century society.

## Notes

1  We should remember, of course, that even in the 1950s the West Indies was always captained by a white player, blacks deemed unable and incapable of exhibiting the leadership skills necessary to manage the team. Thus white control over the team and the symbolic importance of white colonial 'mastery' over the West Indies in general was maintained, until Frank Worrell was eventually appointed as the first black captain of the national team in 1960 (for an account of this struggle see James 1963/1994; see also Whitaker 2000).
2  We should also add that the West Indies squared the four match series by beating England at Lords by a resounding 326 runs on June 29, 1950. By chance, this was also the very same day that the England football team lost 1–0 to the USA at the 1950 World Cup finals, thus ensuring their first-round exit. If anything symbolized the shift of global power within the west, from Britain to the United States, it was this startling result. In fact, it has been suggested that the implausible notion that the USA could defeat England at football meant that 'many newspapers around the world reported the result as a victory by England of

11–1 or 10–0, believing that a typographical error had occurred in the transmission "US 1–0 England"' (Wheelock 2002).

3   This is an identity that is at once both complexly related to the wider African diaspora and at the same time distinctly European too. This identity has afforded many black Europeans a way to articulate *multiple* identifications that resist easy national assimilation by staking a claim to belong to the nation while at the same time challenging dominant forms of racially exclusive European nationalism. Hence this 'new' subjectivity can positively claim identification as, for example, a 'Londoner' or 'Berliner' *and* 'a European', thus negating the nation-state altogether. See Barnor Hesse (2010).

4   It is worth pointing out that while Viv Anderson's debut for England is widely and rightly seen as an important moment in challenging the all-white symbolism of the 'national game', other national sports teams had long ago broken the 'color bar' as regards black players. Notably James Preston ('the dusky Plymouth man' as the *Sportsman* referred to him) made his debut for the England rugby team in 1907 (Green 1998: 164), and the Welsh rugby league player Clive Sullivan in 1972 became the first black Briton to captain a national side when he was appointed to captain the Great Britain rugby league team (Spracklen 2001).

5   Paul Gilroy notes: 'The well-named Hope stands for more than the belated prospect of being recognized as being both black and English. Unlike the under-performing men's team, which, as we all know, plays for money rather than honour, her underfunded England footballers are all amateurs. That means that somehow, in spite of their frustrations, they play for their evolving country essentially out of love' (2008: 195–196).

6   The publication of the article caused controversy, but only after the journalist Mike Marqusee, anti-racist activists and black and South Asian cricket players complained (see Hawkey 1995; Steen 1995). Inadvertently revealing the profound depths of racism within the culture of the English cricket establishment, and by extension within *Wisden Cricket Monthly* itself, then editor David Frith's editorial response the following month stated, 'Robert Henderson's article "Is It In the Blood?" (*WCM* July) did not place a question-mark beside foreign-born England cricketers. It was already there. Reservations have rumbled around the cricket grounds and in the sports columns of the newspapers for several years' (*Wisden Cricket Monthly*, August, 1995, p. 5).

7   Significant too is that recent discussions concerning the limits of multiculturalism have occurred during a period when the term 'Black' as a political signifier, that previously could include both South Asian *and* black African/Caribbean cultural identities in the forging of anti-racist collectivist politics, has largely collapsed.

8   At the time Johnson appeared as a guest on the Channel Four late-night debate show *Devil's Advocate*, hosted by the long-time anti-racist campaigner Darcus Howe. When Howe pointed out that a number of recent and well-reported urban disturbances had involved South Asian rather than black youth and that this fact alone undermined his argument that black people were uniquely rebellious and should be deported, Johnson simply denied that any such violent acts had occurred.

9   Ambivalent in the sense that racist discourses certainly continued throughout the 1990s and into the present, the fears over so-called Jamaican 'yardies' and gun-toting/knife-wielding black men being the latest manifestation. Yet more

complex and 'positive' frames of reference for blackness emerged in which the black presence was not simply seen as alien and/or threatening. Thus I am trying to indicate the contradictory and in some ways ambivalent nature of the present racial configuration.

10   In April 1993 a black teenager called Stephen Lawrence was stabbed to death by a group of white male youths. It appeared the murderers were known to the police (within 24 hours members of the public had given the same names to the police as regards the potential killers) but a mixture of police incompetence, potential corruption and racism on the part of the investigating officers meant that no one was ever convicted in a criminal court for Lawrence's murder. (It took the police two weeks before any arrests were made, at which point most of the evidence needed for a criminal prosecution had disappeared.) The Lawrence family brought an unsuccessful private prosecution against the suspected killers in 1996. Shortly after New Labour came to power in 1997 a special public inquiry was established to look into the events of the murder and subsequent police investigation, chaired by Sir William Macpherson of Cluny. The report, published in early 1999, became known as the 'Macpherson Report'. It concluded that the Metropolitan Police force was institutionally racist and that officers had engaged in forms of 'unwitting' racist behavior in their investigation. The report defined institutional racism as: 'The collective failure of an organization to provide an appropriate and professional service to people because of their colour, culture or ethnic origin. It can be seen or detected in processes, attitudes and behaviour which can amount to discrimination through unwitting prejudice, ignorance, thoughtlessness and racist stereotyping which disadvantage minority ethnic people' (Cathcart 2000: 409).

11   I am referring here to national political discourse. It could be argued with some justification that throughout the 1980s (see, for example, the various policies enacted by the Greater London Council) and into the 1990s there was an active local authority politics of multiculturalism within many metropolitan areas and that continues to some degree today. This is true. My argument here concerns how *central* government has explicitly used multiculturalism both as a conceptual frame to develop progressive social policies and as an ideal through which to give positive meaning to a *new* notion of what it means to be British. In this limited sense I am suggesting that, contrary to most accounts of the term, state multiculturalism actually had a very short shelf-life within British political discourse.

12   The 'Parekh Report: The Report of the Commission on the Future of Multi-Ethnic Britain' was commissioned by the Runnymede Trust (an independent think-tank) in 1998 and chaired by the political theorist Bikhu Parekh. The Runnymede Trust asked the commission to analyze the present state of Britain as a multi-ethnic country, to suggest ways in which racial discrimination and disadvantage can be countered, and to make social policy recommendations that would show how Britain could become a vibrant multicultural society 'at ease with its rich diversity' (Parekh 2000).

13   This part of the report is clearly influenced, if not directly drafted, by Stuart Hall (see Hall 2000).

14   All newspaper headlines taken from McLaughlin and Neal (2007) unless otherwise stated.

15   The following week Stuart Hall attempted to correct the record. Writing in *The Observer*, Hall argued: 'Not one of the 100-plus recommendations in the

Runnymede Trust's report on *The Future of Multi-Ethnic Britain* attracted media comment last week. Instead, the report was swamped by a tide of criticism. It was said to have argued that 'to be British is racist' and that therefore the term 'Britain' should be 'consigned to the dustbin of history'. It would indeed be presumptuous to propose writing Britain out of history and, in fact, the report did no such thing. We did say that, historically, the idea of Britishness carried 'largely unspoken racial connotations' – meaning that, in common understanding, the nation is usually imagined as white. Given the history of these islands, this seemed to us an incontrovertible statement of fact. Perhaps unwisely, the report expected journalists to understand the distinction between 'racial' (as in a 'racial group') and 'racist' (as in 'a racist group')' ('A Question of Identity', *The Observer*, October 15, 2000, p. 27; see also Samir Shah, 'Get Your Facts Right First, Please', in *The Guardian* October 20, 2000, p. 24).

16   As the journalist Gary Younge (2004) noted, 'Mr Goodhart pretends to be a liberal intellectual daring enough to tackle what he calls 'the progressive dilemma' of balancing solidarity and diversity. Whatever we think of his arguments, we should take him at his word and test his thesis against the standards he has set himself. If he is liberal we should reasonably assume that he is anti-racist. If he is an intellectual we can presume his thesis will stand up to basic scrutiny. On the first count he fails miserably. Throughout his essay he wilfully confuses issues of race and immigration as though they were inevitably linked and inherently interchangeable. What starts as a thesis about managing migration to preserve the welfare state – the fact that the NHS and many other public services owe their existence to mass migration earns an entire parenthesis towards the end – develops into a diatribe about the flaws of ethnic diversity'.

17   In December 2009 Schumacher returned to Formula One motor racing after signing a three-year contract with Mercedes.

18   In thinking about the sexualization and 'blackening' of Tiger Woods as well as the manner in which Leibovitz in particular becomes fascinated with depicting Woods in this way, Kobena Mercer's account of the ways in which white colonial fantasies are replayed through contemporary and pornographic forms of scopic mastery is worth revisiting. Mercer notes that the 'glossy, shining, fetishized surface of black skin thus serves and services a white male desire to look and to enjoy the fantasy of mastery precisely through the scopic intensity that the pictures solicit' (1994: 176), and again when he notes that the 'shining surface of black skin serves several functions in its representations: it suggests the physical exertion of powerful bodies, as black boxers always glisten like bronze in the illuminated square of the boxing ring; or, in pornography, it suggests intense sexual activity "just before" the photograph was taken, a metonymic stimulus to arouse spectatorial participation in the imagined *mise-en-scène*' (Mercer 1994: 183–184).

# Conclusion: Race, Sport and the Post/colonial

The capitalist notion of sports is fundamentally different from that which should exist in an underdeveloped country. The African politician should not be concerned with producing sportsmen, but conscious individuals who also practice sports. If sports are not incorporated into the life of the nation, i.e., in the building of the nation, if we produce national sportsmen instead of conscious individuals, then sports will quickly be ruined by professionalism and commercialism. (Frantz Fanon)

## Twenty First Century Golden Ghettos

A century after Jack Johnson defeated 'The Great White Hope' Jim Jeffries in 1910 in what was then dubbed 'The Fight of the Century', the world of sport looks dramatically different. Sporting contests today are rarely seen as explicitly embodying racial meanings in which victory for one side is seen as a racial defeat for the other. Few claimed, for example, that Kevin McBride's 2005 victory over Mike Tyson demonstrated the inherent racial supremacy of white Irishmen over African Americans, as would have been the case at the beginning of the twentieth century. In fact for many, sports signal perhaps more than any other cultural arena or social institution, not just the promise but the actualization of a post-racial settlement, where race no longer matters and where racism has all but disappeared. Sport is seen as a cultural barometer for measuring the deeper, structural changes within western societies concerning the changing meanings of race and the declining significance of racism.

In sports such as tennis and golf, previously understood as the final bastions of white privilege and segregation, the success of Serena and Venus Williams and Tiger Woods has helped to both redefine the boundaries of black sporting achievement and served to reshape those sports most associated with the old forms of racial exclusion. Similarly, beyond the familiar areas of black athleticism the African American speed skater Shani Davis and motor cross racer James Stewart have expanded the possibilities for black success into sporting spaces previously considered all-white. Europe's football teams at both the domestic 'club' level, as well as many national teams, have been transformed by the emergence of leading black players, helping to dramatically reconfigure local, regional and national identities in the process. In the year that marked the sixtieth anniversary since Jackie Robinson challenged professional baseball's segregationist policies, both teams competing for Super Bowl XLI – the one sporting event in the United States that comes closest to being a national sporting occasion – were led for the first time by African American head coaches, namely Tony Dungy of the Indianapolis Colts and Lovie Smith of the Chicago Bears. The following year, in 2008, Paul Ince became the first black Briton to manage a Premier League football team, seemingly reflecting the greater opportunities for the black athlete to not just play at the highest levels across a range of sports, but to manage and coach as well. With South Africa hosting the 2010 World Cup finals in football, the first major international sporting event to be held on the African continent, the transition from the old colonial sporting structures to the twenty-first century post/colonial world is seen to be complete: Arthur de Gobineau's 'Caffres' not just playing and competing against the former white colonial masters, but organizing and running the world's most watched sports mega event.

In *White-Washing Race: The Myth of a Color-blind Society*, Michael Brown and his collaborators point out that the closing decades of the twentieth century witnessed profound demographic changes in the racial typography of the United States, such that the old binary divisions that forced all discussions around race into a Manichean black/white discourse are today irrevocably complicated. Brown et al. (2003) go on to observe that many old political alliances have been replaced by new multiracial coalitions. As interracial marriages increase, they note, 'the very meaning of race has been tangled in ways that were once inconceivable. And with the development of black cultural and athletic icons, blackness has been transformed from a badge of oppression into an image that is desired and emulated' (2003: x). Given the opportunities now available to blacks (and others historically excluded from full participation in sport) to compete in professional sports, some have argued that 'compared to the situation in the 1920s – the so-called "Golden Age of Sports" – the importance of race has diminished' (Guttmann 1978: 33). According to such arguments, sport, from the playing fields to the terraces and stadiums, has largely cleansed itself of the racial prejudice and discrimination that marked its birth. The 'aggression, brutality, and sadism' (2005: 197), as Theodor Adorno noted in the opening epigraph to this book, that could be found in 'those who regularly shout from the sidelines' (p. 197) is seen to have disappeared with the integration of professional sports and the waning of overt forms of white supremacist racism.

Lincoln Allison, for example, suggests that white fans chanting the names of black footballers and cricket players is confirmation that the previously racist elements of white English sporting culture have been transformed due to the hero-worship of black athletes. Allison argues that racism, or what he prefers to call 'racialism', was indeed a factor within western societies from around 1850 until 1945 (what he calls the century of racialism) after which racism, based on notions of biological difference and supremacy, largely disappeared as an organizing principle and social force within the west.

According to Allison, some minor forms of racism still exist, but largely because 'politically correct' academics have defined the term so broadly as to encompass forms of 'cultural racism' which should not be considered racism proper. Allison goes on to suggest that those who continue to see racism 'everywhere' are the modern day equivalents of those who once claimed to find witchcraft in people, that is to say, an accusation that could never be disputed because the 'crime' did not exist in the first place. In fact, Allison argues, anti-racists have become the mirror image of nineteenth century racial scientists as both claim to be able to see racial differences where none actually exist: 'It is a neat historical irony that pluralistic, multi-racial, 'politically correct' society naturally creates broadening definitions of race and racism (so that it becomes difficult, if not impossible, to establish one's innocence of the crime, as it once was of witchcraft) because this is so closely parallel to the insistence of white racial scientists in the century of racialism that there must be some significant physical differences between races' (1998: 149).

Defending what he calls a 'common sense and common optimism about the effect of sport on race relations' (p. 149), Allison gives an example of what he calls the 'good side of sport'. For Allison, the positive impact of West Indian cricketers playing in England, such as Clive Lloyd, largely helped to dissipated any latent racism as white fans came to embrace the sporting skills and technical merits of black athletes. Reflecting on his own admiration for Lloyd, and those of his fellow white Lancashire supporters, Allison notes that such identifications made 'racialism' untenable; 'if there was anything which black people lacked, or which distinguished them from us as we wished to be, it could not possibly be anything which mattered. That some Lancashire fans called Lloyd "Supercoon" was overtly "racist", but their attitudes, in my experience, were deeply respectful' (1998: 143). To the misinformed 'politically correct' outsider, white fans during the 1970s calling one of the West Indies and cricket's greatest ever players a 'Supercoon' may appear to be a grotesque and belittling example of contemporary racism but, Allison assures us, it was in fact a sign of deep affection and inter-racial respect. Thus for Allison, and other conservatives who subscribe to the view that sport has an inherently positive effect in eradicating racism through sporting contact, sports themselves have both challenged racism within wider society and become meritocratic arenas enabling social mobility and inter-racial harmony. The belief that sports are 'one of the most meritocratic, color blind institutions' (Brown et al., 2003: 48) in modern societies remains a widely held view, both within sports themselves and in society as a whole.

Similarly, Loïc Wacquant argues that sport, and the space of the boxing gym in particular, does indeed produce a de-racializing effect. Although he would clearly not share Allison's conservative idealism about the disappearance of racism within wider society, Wacquant nevertheless maintains that as far as the sporting encounter itself is concerned, these moments, at least within the domain of boxing, become in effect non-racial (if not quite post-racial). The dramatic meeting between 'black' and 'white' boxers is one between man and man, fighter and fighter, in which technique, ability and the craft of boxing usurp any racial ideologies that may lay outside the ring: 'the boxing club is the fulcrum of a web of corporeal disciplines, forms of sociability, and moral vectors that tend to depress and deflect ethnoracial vision and division as they impress and enforce commitment to the craft and its rules' (2005: 452). While conceding that racial discourse once structured boxing encounters, Wacquant suggests that this is no longer the case:

> While in past eras an interracial fight took on special significance – this type of bout was called 'a natural' and drew special attention and emotions, from the days of 'Papa' Jack Johnson into the 1980s ... today's run-of-the-mill professional boxers are largely indifferent as to whether they face a white, black, or Latino opponent. African-American fighters in particular attribute little if any significance to the ethnicity of their opponent and they do not consider themselves the representatives of their community when they step into the squared circle. (2005: 452)

Quite why boxing suddenly stopped being a site for the production of racialized meanings in the 1990s is unclear, but Wacquant suggests that the very physicality of sports enables it, under particular circumstances, to transcend the everyday realities of racism, rendering racial difference within the ring redundant and without meaning.

And yet, if we look a little closer, we see that the rush to embrace sports as the future harbinger and contemporary instantiation of a post-racial, meritocratic world where the racial signification of sports is relegated to the history books of the early twentieth century, looks somewhat premature. It remains the case that while black athletes have achieved success on the sports field within a number of diverse sports, permanent access to coaching positions and the executive boardrooms remains, as Stuart Hall noted earlier, limited to an exceptional few. Most American professional sports structures, outside of the playing arena, remain overwhelmingly white and male with the situation worse still within the semi-professional ranks of college sports where the sports-industrial complex generates extraordinary levels of profit from largely wage-free black sporting labor (St Louis 2009). If opportunities for senior level coaching positions within American sports remain restricted for black coaches then the situation within Britain (and throughout Europe in general) is even worse. Britain's sports structures, from senior coaching positions, to the membership of governing bodies, to the mainstream media outlets (including broadcast and print media) remain, with notable exceptions such as Hope Powell and Herman Ouseley, largely all-white affairs with precious little acknowledgment that a problem even exists. Paul Ince, heralded as a breakthrough appointment at the time, was subsequently sacked after only six months as manager of Blackburn Rovers. The political commentator Martin Jacques (and one of the few white voices within the British media to offer any sustained critique of the ingrained nature of white privilege within British sport) used the dismissal of Ince as a way to highlight the prevalence of British sport's institutional racism and the continuing silence of sport's key gatekeepers on this issue:

> The power structures of the game accord with those of other major British institutions: the preponderance of white people and the chronic under-representation of ethnic minorities. The reason the situation is so shocking in football is that this is a game which – from the Premiership to the amateur leagues – palpably involves a huge number of black players. The natural progression is from player to manager, and yet this route is blocked for black players. And the cause of this is nothing to do with potential or ability, but a belief that black players may perform well on the pitch but are not suitable to lead and manage. These are stereotypes that are manifest throughout society, as evidenced by the paucity of black people in positions of authority. This is why there is little adverse comment about the state of football: in a white-dominated society this remains the norm and, consequently, it is barely noticed and rarely commented on in football. There should be zero tolerance of the outrageous double standards which prevail in football: that black players are acceptable but black managers are not, that the virtual absence of black presenters or pundits from the studios, or of black representatives from the corridors of the FA, is somehow fine. A concerted effort by leading figures in football, the media, MPs and football fans could shift attitudes and help to make soccer a model for other sports, and even for society more widely. (Jacques 2009)

Overt forms of racism have not disappeared from sports cultures, as the experience of black footballers playing in Europe in recent years has shown. The outbreak of violent forms of anti-black racism has forced football's governing bodies at the European and international levels to issue proclamations condemning racism white highlighting the threat that racism poses to the very fabric of the game, though often backed up by ineffective measures to discipline those national and club teams guilty of the worst excesses (Kassimeris 2009). The very fact that monkey chants and racial abuse have returned to football stadiums in the heart of Europe, from Italy to Serbia and from Spain to Croatia, indicates that the forms of scientific racism that promoted the idea of white supremacy and popular European folklores concerning black degeneracy remain deeply and complexly embedded within contemporary sporting cultures.

Given the continued sexualization of the black sporting body (Carrington 2001/2002) and the ways in which sport itself has increasingly been co-opted in the service of reinforcing dominant racial ideologies concerning both 'natural' black athleticism and black intellectual inferiority, some critical theorists have concluded that whatever emancipatory potential sport may once have had, such progressive forms of cultural politics are no longer possible. John Hoberman (1997), for example, argues that far from producing a de-racializing effect and a space for effective anti-racist politics, contemporary hyper-commercialized sports cultures simply intensify and amplify our racial preoccupations. Rather than the idea of race as a social 'fact' diminishing, sport keeps alive the myth of race and further consolidates its presence within the popular imagination. Sport, in other words, serves a largely ideological function in reproducing dominant ideologies convincing whites (as well as some blacks) that black people really are creatures of the body and not of the mind. Hoberman further suggests that black intellectuals, desperate to find some positive value in a cultural activity that blacks have historically achieved success in, mistakenly over-valorize sport's potential as a source of social empowerment and cultural creativity: 'Black critiques of sports tend to lack coherence, because they cannot reconcile a deep attachment to athleticism and its charismatic black hero with the inevitable exploitation of black athletes by white image-makers and the white financial interests they serve' (1997: 85). Black people complete the cycle of their own destruction by leading otherwise productive and potentially academically gifted children into sports and away from more beneficial forms of educational attainment and social mobility. This 'addiction to athleticism' (p. 85) results in well-meaning but misguided black parents pushing their children into sports thus helping to foster a broader anti-intellectual culture within black communities, or what Hoberman terms a 'social pathology' (p. 85). Sport, in short, as the subtitle to Hoberman's (1997) book *Darwin's Athletes* succinctly puts it, damages black America and helps to preserve the myth of race. Long after the scientific claims of black degeneracy have been discredited, racial Darwinism is reproduced via the high media profile given to the image of the 'muscular Negro' and by the very presence and actions of black athletes. Hoberman pessimistically concludes that this 'Darwinian drama' (1997: 209) has been kept alive by the celebration of black athleticism and by black boxers in particular: 'What the public career of Mike Tyson has cost black Americans is incalculable in the literal sense of the term, but it is reasonable to assume that his well-publicized brutalities in and out of the ring have helped to preserve pseudo-evolutionary fantasies about black ferocity that are still of commercial value to fight promoters and their business partners in the media' (p. 209).

While Hoberman's diagnosis of the 'dark side' of black involvement with sport is undoubtedly true, at least in terms of how sport tends to solidify popular notions of racial alterity, the argument ends up replacing one exaggerated and naïve paradigm, namely that sport erases racism and racial discourse through inter-racial contact, with its conceptual opposite, namely that sport can *only* reproduce dominant racial ideologies and relatedly that black subjects who engage in sport are, in effect, racial cultural dupes (Hartmann 2002). Hoberman's provocative account is partial and in the end a distortion of the totality of both the black experience in sport and the ideological effects of that engagement.[1] The intellectual task of understanding the relationship between sport, race and politics is in fact much more difficult and complex than these rather hyperbolic interventions would suggest. We need to avoid adopting theoretically naïve and empirically suspect positions, however widely held they may be, that suggest that the significance of race has diminished merely because formal segregation no longer exists and white fans now sing the names of black players. The sociological and historical evidence supports the thesis that ideas about race have *changed and shifted* over the past century, and continue to do so, but this is not to say that racism itself, and the racialized cultural structures and ways of seeing the world, has disappeared. Such arguments rely upon a static definition of racism that is so limited and narrow that only overt forms of white supremacy that lead to intentional acts of genocide, violence or public persecution get to 'count' as racism. There is little sense within such accounts of the protean nature of racism – a scavenger ideology as Fredrikson (2002) puts it – nor of the ways in which contemporary racial discourses become embedded within social structures, economic relations and cultural representations and practices, such that 'race' can survive as an idea and racism can reproduce itself metonymically without recourse to the old (and publically discredited) nineteenth century racial schemas.

Similarly, and as Fanon so expertly demonstrated, the ability to consume the Other while practicing racism, to hold stereotypical beliefs about blacks while claiming to not see race, to idolize black representations while not being able to treat actual black people as equal human beings, has long been recognized as a central component of how racism is reproduced in putatively 'non-racial' spaces. Given the argument developed earlier, namely that sport can be defined as a liminal space that is structured by desire, it should not be surprising to find that even within so-called advanced western post-industrial nations, the sports field is often the space where we are most likely to find forms of fanatical hyper-identification and even idolized devotion towards black athletic bodies *and* some of the most violent expressions of anti-black racism, sometimes occurring within the *same* sporting locations and directed towards the *very same* athletes. It becomes all the more necessary, then, to track the changing meanings of race in order to understand how racist effects can be produced without the need for 'racist intent'. To understand, as a number of critical theorists have shown, how racism becomes all the more powerful precisely because it has been able to survive attempts to easily label it as such (Bonilla-Silva 2010; Feagin 2010; Goldberg 2009; Roediger 2008; Winant 2004). In this context, when the Age of Obama has accelerated popular claims that racism is no longer a determinant of life chances within the United States and the west more generally, it is vital that race scholars pay more attention to sports than they have tended to do up until now as sport remains a critical site for the reproduction (and rearticulation) of forms of racial knowledge and commonsense and an important location in the contested and ongoing struggles over ideology, politics and identity.

## Can the Black Athlete Speak?

*Race, Sport and Politics* started with a broad definition of racial formation as a sociohistorical process through which racial categories were created, inhabited, transformed and destroyed. The argument presented suggested that sports should be understood as a racial project through which the very category of race has been inhabited and (at times) transformed. It was argued that as a result of struggles both within and beyond its borders, sport itself has given new and specific meanings to blackness and whiteness. It was in the context of European colonialism that the black athlete was born, not as an object but as an idea. The complex relationships between race and sexual desire, race and gender construction, and race and nationalism have been traced using sport – and the lives and sporting careers of particular black athletes – to show how the idea of 'the black athlete' served to rearticulate these relationships. These various moments have undoubtedly altered the cultural meanings of race, occasionally providing an important space for black political practices that have offered powerful narratives of freedom and redemption from white racism.

But can we imagine sport as *destroying* racial categories altogether? Are we forever locked into a cycle of transformation and reformulation? A dialectic of race and sport that forever remakes itself but which can never be overcome? It might be worth returning here to our earlier discussion on the contradictory and paradoxical elements of sport as a form of structured freedom, a form of play delimited by constraints, but that nevertheless has within its ludic structure the potential for forms of creativity and expression that locate it as an important site for human expression. Richard Gruneau captures well this dynamic of sport's appeal and utopian promise that helps us to avoid the debilitating and rather unproductive debate that posits the notion that sport *either* brings the world together in some ludic jamboree thus dissolving our racial differences, or that sport *can only* serve to heighten and magnify racial tensions and differences. Instead Gruneau notes the need to emphasize:

> that the meanings, metaphoric qualities, and regulatory structures which define sports as social possibilities are all indissolubly connected to the making and the remaking of particular ways of living and to historical struggles over the monopolistic capacity to define the kind of life that people ought to live in a political community. These struggles – and their impact on the enabling and constraining features of play, games, and sports as structures *through which* and, sometimes, *against which* humans act – can only be understood in the broader context of the conflicts of interest and unequally distributed social resources that exist in any form of social organization. (1983/1999: 102)

Fanon's observation many years ago that what the anti-colonial struggle required was not the need to produce more athletes but rather to develop *conscious individuals* who also practiced sports, seems to be as relevant today as it was during the 1950s when, as C.L.R. James (1963/1994) has shown, black athletes engaged the anti-colonial politics of the day *alongside* their commitment to sport, and as Harry Edwards (1969) has shown, black athletes of the 1960s saw their struggles in and around sport *as part of* the wider Civil Rights struggles. The question remains as to whether or not today's black athletes (and others committed to the present and future of sports) are able to develop a critical consciousness sufficient to the challenges of the twenty-first century, and if they are, whether the current corporatization of sporting cultures will allow for the types of oppositional voices that once dared to challenge dominant structures within the sporting black Atlantic world to be heard.

Black athletes have re-made sports, but not under conditions and rules of their own choosing. The extent to which sport as a racial project can once again be used for progressive purposes will rest, in large part, on the ability of those invested in sports cultures to hold on to, develop and articulate a critical consciousness that goes beyond the sports boundary. If that can be done, and if the black athlete can once again find the means to speak, then the 'useless' play of sport may turn out to be an important space for the realization of black dreams of freedom in the long struggle to be accorded the right to occupy the status of the human.

## Note

1    This is leaving aside, of course, Hoberman's problematic generalizations about black intellectual life and his own pathologizing of black communities which ends up reproducing a conservative narrative of how black people are themselves to blame for their own conditions, thus negating the structural determinants of both poverty and white racism. On the question as to whether or not cultural arenas, like sport, should be understood as sites of political engagement and the consequences of that, see Richard Iton's more sophisticated reading, when he notes: 'Hyperactivity on the cultural front usually occurs as a response to some sort of marginalization from the processes of decision-making or exercising control over one's own circumstances; what might appear to be an overinvestment in the cultural realm is rarely a freely chosen strategy. American blacks are not "different" in this respect because they have chosen to be but because of the exclusionary and often violent practices that have historically defined black citizenship and public sphere participation as problematic and because of the recognition that the cultural realm is always in play and already politically significant terrain. In other words, not engaging the cultural realm, whether defensively or assertively, would be, to some degree, to concede defeat in an important – and relatively accessible – arena' (2008: 17).

# References

Abdel-Shehid, G. (2005) *Who Da Man? Black Masculinities and Sporting Cultures*. Toronto: Canadian Scholars' Press Inc.

Abrams, F. (1997) 'Tory Conference: Anger as Tebbit Questions Loyalties of "two-nation"', *The Independent*, October 8; http://www.independent.co.uk/news/tory-conference-anger-as-tebbit-questions-loyalties-of-twonation-immigrants-1234581.html. (Accessed 7 December 2009)

Adorno, T. (2005) *Critical Models: Interventions and Catchwords*. New York: Columbia University Press.

Akbar, A. (2005) 'A Cricket-lover From a Well-respected Family', *The Independent*, July 13, p. 4.

Alexander, C. (2000) '(Dis)Entangling the "Asian Gang": Ethnicity, Identity, Masculinity', in B. Hesse (ed.), *Un/settled Multiculturalisms: Diasporas, Entanglements, Transruptions*. London: Zed Books.

Alexander, E. (1996) '"We're Gonna Deconstruct Your Life!": The Making and Un-making of the Black Bourgeois Patriarch in *Ricochet*', in M. Blount and G. Cunningham (eds), *Representing Black Men*. London: Routledge.

Allison, L. (1998) 'Biology, Ideology and Sport', in L. Allison (ed.), *Taking Sport Seriously*. Aachen: Meyer and Meyer.

Althusser, L. (2005) *For Marx*. London: Verso.

Amaechi, J. (2008) *Man in the Middle*. New York: ESPN Books.

Amenta, E. (2007a) *Professor Baseball: Searching for Redemption and the Perfect Lineup on the Softball Diamonds of Central Park*. Chicago, IL: University of Chicago Press.

Amenta, E. (2007b) 'Softball and the Social Scientist', *Contexts*, 6 (2): 40–45.

Amenta, E. (2007c) 'Saved by Baseball', *The Chronicle of Higher Education*, Careers Section C, C1–C4.

Andersson, M. (2007) 'The Relevance of the Black Atlantic in Contemporary Sport: Racial Imaginaries in Norway', *International Review for the Sociology of Sport*, 42 (10): 65–68.

Andrews, D. (ed.) (2001) *Michael Jordan Inc.: Corporate Sport, Media Culture and Late Modern America*. Albany, NY: State University of New York Press.

Andrews, D. (2007) 'Response to Bairner's "Back to Basics: Class, Social Theory, and Sport"', *Sociology of Sport Journal*, 24 (1): 37–45.

Andrews, D. (2009) 'Sport, Culture and Late Capitalism', in B. Carrington and I. McDonald (eds), *Marxism, Cultural Studies and Sport*. London: Routledge.

Armstrong, G. and Giulianotti, R. (eds) (2004) *Football in Africa: Conflict, Conciliation, and Community*. Houndmills: Palgrave Macmillan.

Ascherson, N. (2006) 'Replies to David Goodhart', *Prospect*, June, http://www.prospectmagazine.co.uk/2006/06/repliestodavidgoodhart/. (Accessed 7 December 2009)

Ashley, J. (2005) 'The World in One City', *The Guardian*, July 7, p. 15.

Back, L., Crabbe, T. and Solomos, J. (2001) *The Changing Face of Football: Racism, Identity and Multiculture in the English Game*. Oxford: Berg.

Back, L., Keith, M., Khan, A., Shukra, K. and Solomos, J. (2002) 'New Labour's White Heart: Politics, Multiculturalism and the Return of Assimilation', *The Political Quarterly*, 73 (4): 445–454.

Bairner, A. (2001) *Sport, Nationalism, and Globalization: European and North American Perspectives*. Albany, NY: State University of New York Press.

Bairner, A. (2007a) 'Back to Basics: Class, Social Theory, and Sport', *Sociology of Sport Journal*, 24 (1): 20–36.

Bairner, A. (2007b) 'Rebuttal', *Sociology of Sport Journal*, 24 (1): 46–48.

Bairner, A. (2009) 'Re-appropriating Gramsci: Marxism, Hegemony and Sport', in B. Carrington and I. McDonald (eds), *Marxism, Cultural Studies and Sport*. London: Routledge.

Bale, J. (2008) 'From the Anthropology Days to the Anthropological Olympics', in S. Brownell (ed.), *The 1904 Anthropology Days and Olympic Games: Sport, Race, and American Imperialism*. Lincoln, NB: University of Nebraska Press.

Bale, J. and Cronin, M. (eds) (2003) *Sport and Postcolonialism*. Oxford: Berg.

Bannerji, H. (2000) *The Dark Side of the Nation: Essays on Multiculturalism, Nationalism and Gender*. Toronto: Canadian Scholars Press.

Bass, A. (2002) *Not the Triumph but the Struggle: The 1968 Olympics and the Making of the Black Athlete*. Minneapolis: University of Minnesota Press.

Bass, A. (2005) (ed.) *In the Game: Race, Identity, and Sports in the Twentieth Century*. Basingstoke: Palgrave.

Becker, H.S. (2008) *Art Worlds*, 2nd edn. Berkeley, CA: University of California Press.

Belton, D. (1995) 'Where We Live: A Conversation with Essex Hemphill and Isaac Julien', in D. Belton (ed.), *Speak My Name: Black Men on Masculinity and the American Dream*. Boston: Beacon Press.

Benhabib, S. (2002) *The Claims of Culture: Equality and Diversity in the Global Era*. Princeton, NJ: Princeton University Press.

Bérubé, M. (2009) 'Afterword: High-definition Sports Capitalism', in B. Carrington and I. McDonald (eds), *Marxism, Cultural Studies and Sport*. London: Routledge.

Bissinger, B. (2010) 'Tiger in the Rough', *Vanity Fair*, February, No. 594, pp. 80–145.

Blackburn, R. (1997) *The Making of New World Slavery: From the Baroque to the Modern, 1492–1800*. London: Verso.

Blaut, J.M. (1993) *The Colonizer's Model of the World: Geographical Diffusionism and Eurocentric History*. New York: The Guilford Press.

Bonilla-Silva, E. (2010) *Racism Without Racists: Color-blind Racism and the Persistence of Racial Inequality in the United States* (3rd edn). New York: Rowan & Littlefield.

Booth, D. (1998) *The Race Game: Sport and Politics in South Africa*. London: Routledge.

Bourdieu, P. (1978) 'Sport and Social Class', *Social Science Information*, 17 (6): 819–840.

Bourdieu, P. (1988) 'Program for a Sociology of Sport', *Sociology of Sport Journal*, 5 (2): 153–161.

Bourdieu, P. and Wacquant, L. (1992) *An Invitation to Reflexive Sociology*. Chicago, IL: University of Chicago Press.

Boyd, T. (2003) *Young, Black, Rich and Famous: The Rise of the NBA, the Hip Hop Invasion and the Transformation of American Culture*. London: Doubleday.

Brah, A. (1996) *Cartographies of Diaspora: Contesting Identities*. London: Routledge.

Brennan, T. (1997) *At Home in the World: Cosmopolitanism Now*. Cambridge, MA: Harvard University Press.

Brooks, S. (2009) *Black Men Can't Shoot*. Chicago, IL: University of Chicago Press.

Brown, B. (1972) 'Where Are Britain's Coloured Stars'?, *Football Association News*, December 1, pp. 7–8.

Brown, D. (2001) '1956: Suez and the End of Empire', *The Guardian*, March 14; http://www.guardian.co.uk/politics/2001/mar/14/past.education1. (Accessed 7 October 2009)

Brown, M., Carnoy, M., Currie, E., Duster, T., Oppenheimer, D., Shultz, M. and Wellman, D. (2003) *White-Washing Race: The Myth of a Color-blind Society*. Berkeley, CA: University of California Press.

Brownell, S. (ed.) (2008) *The 1904 Anthropology Days and Olympic Games: Sport, Race, and American Imperialism*. Lincoln, NB: University of Nebraska Press.

Bruno, F. (1992) *Eye of the Tiger: My Life, Frank Bruno*. London: Weidenfeld & Nicolson.

Bruno, F. (1997) *Frank Bruno: From Zero to Hero*. London: Andre Deutsch.

Bruno, F. (2005) *Frank: Fighting Back*. London: Yellow Jersey Press.

Bryant, J.M. (2008) 'A New Sociology for a New History? Further Critical Thoughts on the Eurasian Similarity and Great Divergence Theses', *Canadian Journal of Sociology*, 33 (1): 147–164.

Burdsey, D. (2006) '"If I ever play football Dad, can I play for England or India?": British Asians, Sport and Diasporic National Identities', *Sociology*, 40 (1): 11–28.

Burdsey, D. (2007a) *British Asians and Football: Culture, Identity, Exclusion*. New York: Routledge.

Burdsey, D. (2007b) 'Role with the Punches: The Construction and Representation of Amir Khan as a Role Model for Multiethnic Britain', *Sociological Review*, 55 (3): 611–631.

Cahn, S. (2004) '"Cinderellas" of Sport: Black Women in Track and Field', in P. Miller and D. Wiggins (eds), *Sport and the Color Line: Black Athletes and Race Relations in Twentieth-Century America*. London: Routledge.

Cameron, D. (2008) 'Call that election. We will fight. Britain will win', Conservative Party Conference Speech 2007; www.conservatives.com/News/Speeches/2007/10/David_Cameron. (Accessed 7 December 2009)

Carby, H. (1998) *Race Men: The WEB Du Bois Lectures*. London: Harvard University Press.

Carrington, B. (1998a) 'Sport, Masculinity and Black Cultural Resistance', *Journal of Sport and Social Issues*, 22 (3): 275–298.

Carrington, B. (1998b) 'Football's Coming Home, But Whose Home? And Do We Want It? Nation, Football and the Politics of Exclusion', in Adam Brown (ed.), *Fanatics! Power, Identity and Fandom in Football*. London: Routledge.

Carrington, B. (1999) 'Cricket, Culture and Identity: An Exploration of the Role of Sport in the Construction of Black Masculinities', in S. Roseneil and J. Seymour (eds), *Practising Identities: Power and Resistance*. Basingstoke: Palgrave.

Carrington, B. (2000) 'Double Consciousness and the Black British Athlete', in K. Owusu (ed.), *Black British Culture and Society: A Text-Reader*. London: Routledge.

Carrington, B. (2001/2002) 'Fear of a Black Athlete: Masculinity, Politics and the Body', *new formations*, Special Issue: 'The Rendez-vous of Conquest': Rethinking Race and Nation, 45 (Winter): 91–110.

Carrington, B. (2007) 'Merely Identity: Cultural Identity and the Politics of Sport', *Sociology of Sport Journal*, 24 (1): 49–66.

Carrington, B. (2010) 'Improbable Grounds: The Emergence of the Black British Intellectual', *South Atlantic Quarterly*, 109 (2): 369–389.

Carrington, B. and McDonald, I. (2009) 'Marxism, Cultural Studies and Sport: Mapping the Field', in B. Carrington and I. McDonald (eds), *Marxism, Cultural Studies and Sport*. London: Routledge.

Cashmore, E. (2005) *Tyson: Nurture of the Beast*. Cambridge: Polity Press.

Cathcart, B. (2000) *The Case of Stephen Lawrence*. Harmondsworth: Penguin Books.

CCCS (1982) *The Empire Strikes Back: Race and Racism in 70s Britain*. London: Routledge.

Clarke, J. and Critcher, C. (1985) *The Devil Makes Work*. Houndsmill: Macmillan.

Clarke, K. and Thomas, D. (eds) (2006) *Globalization and Race: Transformations in the Cultural Production of Blackness*. Durham, NC: Duke University Press.

Cleaver, H. (2009) 'Foreword: Sports?', in B. Carrington and I. McDonald (eds), *Marxism, Cultural Studies and Sport*. London: Routledge.

Clifford, J. (1994) 'Diasporas', *Cultural Anthropology*, 9 (3): 302–338.

Coakley, J. (1998) *Sport in Society: Issues and Controversies* (8th edn). London: McGraw–Hill.

Coakley, J. and Dunning, E. (eds) (2000) *Handbook of Sport Studies*. London: Sage.

Cohen, R. (2008) *Global Diasporas: An Introduction* (2nd edn). London: Routledge.

Collins, P.H. (2004) *Black Sexual Politics: African Americans, Gender and the New Racism*. London: Routledge.

Connell, R.W. (1983) *Which Way Is Up?* London: Allen and Unwin.

Connell, R.W. (1987) *Gender and Power*. Cambridge: Polity Press.

Connell. R.W. (1999) 'Foreword to the 1999 Edition', in R. Gruneau, *Class, Sports and Social Development*. Champaign, IL: Human Kinetics.

Connell, R.W. (2005) *Masculinities* (2nd edn). Cambridge: Polity Press.

Court, J. (2007) 'Inside Intel Is There a "Slave-Ship" Agenda?', *Huffington Post*, August 10; http://www.huffingtonpost.com/jamie-court/inside-intel-is-there-a-s_b_60011.html. (Accessed 7 December 2009)

Critcher, C. (1986) 'Radical Theories of Sport: The State of Play', *Sociology of Sport Journal*, 3 (4): 333–343.

Cummings, D.L. (1995) 'Black Steel', *The Source*, September, pp. 80–102.

Darby, P. (2002) *Africa, Football, and FIFA: Politics, Colonialism, and Resistance*. London: Taylor and Francis.

Dent, T. (ed.) (1992) *Black Popular Culture*. Seattle, WA: Bay Press.

Douglass, F. (1845/2003) *Narrative of the Life of Frederick Douglass, an American Slave*. New York: Barnes and Noble Classics.

Du Bois, W.E.B. (1914) 'Editorial: The Prize Fighter', *The Crisis: A Record of the Darker Races*, 8 (4): 181.

Dufoix, S. (2008) *Diasporas*. Berkeley, CA: University of California Press.

Dunning, E. (2005) 'Figurational/Process-Sociological Notes on Loïc Wacquant's *Body and Soul*', *Qualitative Sociology*, 28 (2): 171–177.

Dyreson, M. (2008a) 'Prolegomena to Jesse Owens: American Ideas about Race and Olympic Races from the 1890s to the 1920s', *International Journal of the History of Sport*, 25 (2): 224–246.

Dyreson, M. (2008b) 'American Ideas about Race and Olympic Races in the Era of Jesse Owens: Shattering Myths of Reinforcing Racism?', *The International Journal of the History of Sport*, 25 (2): 247–267.

Dyson, M. (1993) 'Be Like Mike?: Michael Jordan and the Pedagogy of Desire', *Cultural Studies*, 7 (1): 64–72.

Early, G. (ed.) (1998) *I'm a Little Special: A Muhammad Ali Reader*. London: Yellow Jersey Press.

Edemariam, A. (2008) 'A Great Week in Black History?', *The Guardian G2*, November 4, p. 5.

Edwards, B. (2001) 'The Uses of Diaspora', *Social Text*, 19 (1): 45–73.

Edwards, B. (2003) *The Practice of Diaspora: Literature, Translation and the Rise of Black Internationalism*. Cambridge, MA: Harvard University Press.

Edwards, H. (1969) *The Revolt of the Black Athlete*. New York: The Free Press.

Ellison, R. (1952) *Invisible Man*. New York: Penguin Books.

Elvin, M. (2008) 'Defining the *Eplicanda* in the "West and the Rest" Debate: Bryant's Critique and Its Critics', *Canadian Journal of Sociology*, 33 (1): 168–185.

Entine, J. (2000) *Taboo: Why Black Athletes Dominate Sports and Why We're Afraid to Talk About It*. New York: Public Affairs.

Eze, E. (2001) *Achieving Our Humanity: The Idea of the Postracial Future*. London: Routledge.

Fanon, F. (1952/2008) *Black Skin, White Masks*. New York: Grove Press.

Fanon, F. (1963/2004) *The Wretched of the Earth*. New York: Grove Press.

Farred, G. (1996) (ed.) *Rethinking C.L.R. James*. Oxford: Blackwell.

Farred, G. (2000) 'Cool as the Other Side of the Pillow: How ESPN's Sports Center Has Changed Television Sports Talk', *Journal of Sport and Social Issues*, 24 (2): 96–117.

Farred, G. (2003) *What's My Name? Black Vernacular Intellectuals*. London: University of Minnesota Press.

Fausto-Sterling, A. (2000) 'Gender, Race, and Nation: The Comparative Anatomy of "Hottentot" Women in Europe, 1815–1817', in L. Schiebinger (ed.), *Feminism and the Body*. Oxford: Oxford University Press.

Feagin, J. (2006) *Systemic Racism: A Theory of Oppression*. London: Routledge.

Feagin, J. (2010) *The White Racial Frame: Centuries of Racial Framing and Counter-Framing*. New York: Routledge.

Firmin, A. (1885/2002) *The Equality of the Human Races*. Urbana, IL: University of Illinois Press.

Fredrikson, G. (2002) *Racism: A Short History*. Princeton, NJ: Princeton University Press.

Frith, D. (2005) 'Editorial', *Wisden Cricket Monthly*, August, p. 5.

Frith, S. (2007) 'Why Music Matters', *Critical Quarterly*, 50 (1–2): 165–179.

Fryer, P. (1984) *Staying Power: The History of Black People in Britain*. London: Pluto Press.

Gains, L. (no date) *The Impossible Dream: An Autobiography by Larry Gains*. London: Leisure Publications.

Garland, J. and Rowe, M. (2001) *Racism and Antiracism in Football*. Basingstoke: Palgrave.

Gilman, S. (1985) *Difference and Pathology: Stereotypes of Sexuality, Race, and Madness*. London: Cornell University Press.

Gilroy P. (1987) *There Ain't No Black in the Union Jack: The Cultural Politics of Race and Nation*. London: Routledge.

Gilroy, P. (1992) 'Cultural Studies and Ethnic Absolutism', in L. Grossberg, C. Nelson and P.A. Treichler (eds), *Cultural Studies*. London: Routledge.

Gilroy, P. (1993a) *The Black Atlantic: Modernity and Double Consciousness*. London: Verso.

Gilroy, P. (1993b) *Small Acts: Thoughts on the Politics of Black Cultures*. London: Serpents Tail.

Gilroy, P. (1994a) 'Diaspora', *Paragraph*, 17 (3): 207–212.

Gilroy, P. (1994b) 'After the Love Has Gone: Bio-politics and Etho-poetics in the Black Public Sphere', *Third Text*, 28/29: 25–45.

Gilroy, P. (1996) 'Route Work: The Black Atlantic and the Politics of Exile', in I. Chambers and L. Curti (eds), *The Post-colonial Question: Common Skies, Divided Horizons*. London: Routledge.

Gilroy, P. (2000) *Between Camps: Nations, Cultures and the Allure of Race*. London: Allen Lane.

Gilroy, P. (2001) 'Foreword', in B. Carrington and I. McDonald (eds), *'Race', Sport and British Society*. London: Routledge.

Gilroy, P. (2004) *After Empire: Melancholia or Convivial Culture?* London: Routledge.

Gilroy, P. (2005) 'Melancholia or Conviviality: The Politics of Belonging in Britain', *Soundings*, 29 (Spring): 35–46.

Gilroy, P. (2008) 'The Great Escape: From Enoch Powell to Hope Powell and Beyond', in M. Perryman (ed.), *Imagined Nation: England after Britain*. London: Lawrence & Wishart.

Giulianotti, R. (2005) *Sport: A Critical Sociology*. Cambridge: Polity Press.

Giulianotti, R. and Robertson, R. (eds) (2007) *Globalization and Sport*. Oxford: Blackwell.

Glenn, D. (2003) 'Searching for Respect: Richard Sennett's Latest Work Examines the Costs of Meritocracy', *The Chronicle of Higher Education*, Section: Research & Publishing, 49 (18): A12.

Gobineau, A. de (1856) *The Moral and Intellectual Diversity of Races with Particular Reference to Their Respective Influence in the Civil and Political History of Mankind*. Philadelphia, PA: J.B. Lippincott & Co.

Goldberg, D. (ed.) (1994) *Multiculturalism: A Critical Reader*. Oxford: Blackwell.

Goldberg, D. (2002) *The Racial State*. Oxford: Blackwell.

Goldberg, D. (2009) *The Threat of Race: Reflections on Racial Neoliberalism*. Malden, MA: Wiley–Blackwell.

Goldstone, J. (2008) 'Capitalist Origins, the Advent of Modernity, and Coherent Explanation: A Response to Joseph M. Bryant', *Canadian Journal of Sociology*, 33 (1): 119–132.

Goodhart, D. (2004) 'Too Diverse?', *Prospect*, February; http://www.prospectmaga-zine.co.uk/2004/02/toodiverse/. (Accessed 7 December 2009)

Goodhart, D. (2006) 'National Anxieties', *Prospect*, June; http://www.prospect magazine.co.uk/2006/06/nationalanxieties/. (Accessed 7 December 2009)

Gould, S.J. (1996) *The Mismeasure of Man* (2nd edn). London: Penguin.

Graves, J. (2005) *The Race Myth: Why We Pretend Race Exists in America*. New York: Plume.

Green, C. (2003) 'Leaders of the New School', *Observer Sports Monthly*, 43 (September): 64–65.

Green, J. (1998) *Black Edwardians: Black People in Britain, 1901–1914*. London: Frank Cass.

Gruneau, R. (1983/1999) *Class, Sports and Social Development*. Champaign, IL: Human Kinetics.

Gutmann, A. (ed.) (1994) *Multiculturalism: Examining the Politics of Recognition*. Princeton, NJ: Princeton University Press.

Guttmann, A. (1978) *From Ritual to Record: The Nature of Modern Sports*. New York: Columbia University Press.

Guttmann, A. (1994) *Games and Empires: Modern Sports and Cultural Imperialism*. New York: Columbia University Press.

Guttmann, A. (1996) *The Erotic in Sports*. New York: Columbia University Press.

Guttmann, A. (2003) *Identity in Democracy*. Princeton, NJ: Princeton University Press.

Guttmann, A. (2004) *Sports: The First Five Millennia*. Amherst, MA: University of Massachusetts Press.

Habermas, J. (1994) 'Struggles for Recognition in the Democratic Constitutional State', in A. Guttmann (ed.), *Multiculturalism: Examining the Politics of Recognition*. Princeton, NJ: Princeton University Press.

Halberstam, J. (2007) 'Notes on Failure', in K. Benesch and U. Haselstein (eds), *The Power and Politics of the Aesthetic in American Culture*. Heidelberg: Universitatsverlag.

Hall, S. (1988) *The Hard Road to Renewal: Thatcherism and the Crisis of the Left*. London: Verso.

Hall, S. (1991) 'The Local and the Global: Globalization and Ethnicity', in A.D. King (ed.), *Culture, Globalization and the World-System*. Basingstoke: Macmillan.

Hall, S. (1996) 'When Was "The Post-colonial"? Thinking at the Limit', in I. Chambers and L. Curti (eds), *The Post-colonial Question: Commons Skies, Divided Horizons*. London: Routledge.

Hall, S. (1998) 'Aspiration and Attitude … Reflections on Black Britain in the Nineties', *new formations*, 33 (Spring): 38–46.

Hall, S. (2000) 'Conclusion: The Multi-Cultural Question', in B. Hesse (ed.), *Un/settled Multiculturalisms: Diasporas, Entanglements, Transruptions*. London: Zed Books.

Hall, S., Critcher, C., Jefferson, T., Clarke, J. and Roberts, B. (1978) *Policing the Crisis: Mugging, the State and Law and Order*. Houndmills: Palgrave.

Hamilton, L. (2008) *Lewis Hamilton: My Story*. London: HarperSport.

Hamilton, M. (2007) 'The Only Way Is Up', *Observer*, October 7; http://www.guardian.co.uk/sport/2007/oct/07/motorsports.lewishamilton2. (Accessed 7 December 2009)

Harding, S. (2008) *Sciences from Below: Feminisms, Postcolonialities, and Modernities*. Durham, NC: Duke University Press.

Hardt, M. and Negri, A. (2000) *Empire*. London: Harvard University Press.

Hargreaves, J.A. (ed.) (1982) *Sport, Culture and Ideology*. London: Routledge.

Hargreaves, J.E. (1986) *Sport, Power and Culture*. Cambridge: Polity Press.

Harris, R. (2009) 'Black British, Brown British and British Cultural Studies', *Cultural Studies*, 23 (4): 483–512.

Hartman, S. (1997) *Scenes of Subjection: Terror, Slavery, and Self-making in Nineteenth-century America*. New York: Oxford University Press.

Hartmann, D. (2002) 'Sport as Contested Terrain', in D. Goldberg and J. Solomos (eds), *A Companion to Racial and Ethnic Studies*. Malden, MA: Blackwell.

Hartmann, D. (2003) *Race, Culture and the Revolt of the Black Athlete: The 1968 Olympic Protests and Their Aftermath*. Chicago, IL: University of Chicago Press.

Harwood, A. (2003) 'Exclusive: My Tears for Bruno', *Daily Mirror*, October 4, pp. 4–5.

Hawhee, D. (2004) *Bodily Arts: Rhetoric and Athletics in Ancient Greece*. Austin, TX: University of Texas Press.

Hawkey, I. (1995) 'Pride and Prejudice', *The Sunday Times* Sport, July 9, p. 11.

Hearn, J. (2004) 'From Hegemonic Masculinity to the Hegemony of Men', *Feminist Theory*, 5 (1): 49–72.

Hegel, G.W.F. (1830/1975) *Lectures on the Philosophy of World History*. Cambridge: Cambridge University Press.

Henderson, R. (1995) 'Is It In the Blood?', *Wisden Cricket Monthly*, July, pp. 9–10.

Henry, I. (2001) *The Politics of Leisure Policy* (2nd edn). Houndmills: Palgrave Macmillan.

Hesse, B. (1999) 'Reviewing the Western Spectacle: Reflexive Globalization Through the black diaspora', in A. Brah, M. Hickman and Mac An Ghail (eds), *Global Futures*. London: Macmillan.

Hesse, B. (ed.) (2000) *Un/settled Multiculturalisms: Diasporas, Entanglements, Transruptions*. London: Zed Books.

Hesse, B. (2007) 'Racialized Modernities: An Analytics of White Mythologies', *Ethnic and Racial Studies*, 30 (4): 643–663.

Hesse, B. (2010) 'Afterword: Black Europe's Undecidability', in D. Clarke-Hine, T. Keaton and S. Small (eds), *Black Europe and the African Diaspora*. Urbana, IL: University of Illinois Press.

Hewitt, R. (2005) *White Backlash and the Politics of Multiculturalism*. Cambridge: Cambridge University Press.

Hoberman, J. (1997) *Darwin's Athletes: How Sport Has Damaged Black America and Preserved the Myth of Race*. Boston, MA: Mairner Books.

Hoberman, J. (2004) 'African Athletic Aptitude and the Social Sciences', *Equine and Comparative Exercise Physiology*, 1 (4): 281–284.

Hong, F. (2006) *Sport, Nationalism and Orientalism: The Asian Games*. London: Routledge.

Hooker, J. (2009) *Race and the Politics of Solidarity*. Oxford: Oxford University Press.

hooks, b. (1994) 'Feminism Inside: Toward a Black Body Politic', in T. Golden (ed.), *Black Male: Representations of Masculinity in Contemporary American Art*. New York: Whitney Museum of American Art.

hooks, b. (2004) *We Real Cool: Black Men and Masculinity*. London: Routledge.

Horne, D. and Jary, D. (2004) 'Anthony Giddens: Structuration Theory, and Sport and Leisure', in R. Giulianotti (ed.), *Sport and Modern Social Theorists*. Houndmills: Palgrave Macmillan.

Hubbard, T. (2008) 'Contemporary Sport Sociology and Ancient Greek Athletics', *Leisure Studies*, 27 (4): 379–394.

Iber, J. and Regalado, S. (eds) (2007) *Mexican Americans and Sports: A Reader in the Athletics and Barrio Life*. College Station, TX: Texas A&M University Press.

Ikard, D. (2007) *Breaking the Silence: Toward a Black Male Feminist Criticism*. Baton Rouge, LA: Louisiana State University Press.

Ingham, A. and Donnelly, P. (1997) 'A Sociology of North American Sociology of Sport: Disunity in Unity, 1965 to 1996', *Sociology of Sport Journal*, 14 (4): 362–418.

Iton, R. (2008) *In Search of the Black Fantastic: Politics and Popular Culture in the Post-Civil Rights Era*. New York: Oxford University Press.

Jacques, M. (2007) 'A New Hero for Our Times', *Guardian*, October 22; http://www.guardian.co.uk/commentisfree/2007/oct/22/comment.race. (Accessed 7 December 2009)

Jacques, M. (2009) 'A Total White Out', *The New Statesman*, June 18; http://www.newstatesman.com/sport/2009/06/black-players-football-white. (Accessed 7 December 2009)

James, C.L.R. (1963/1994) *Beyond a Boundary*. London: Serpent's Tail.

Jefferson, T. (1787/1982) *Notes on the State of Virginia*. London: W.W. Norton & Company.

John, E. (2007) 'Wisden Cricketer of the Year 2007: Monty Panesar', *Wisden Cricketer's Almanack*; http://www.cricinfo.com/wisdenalmanack/content/story/287064.html. (Accessed 7 December 2009)

Johnson, J. (1927/1992) *In and Out of the Ring*. New York: Citadel Press.

Johnson, J.W. (1933) *Along This Way: The Autobiography of James Weldon Johnson*. New York: The Viking Press.

Johnson, K. (2006) 'The Legacy of Jim Crow: The Enduring Taboo of Black–White Romance', *Texas Law Review*, 84: 739–766.

Johnson, P. (1995) 'The Logical End of Black Racism is a Return to Africa', *The Spectator*, December 30, p. 20.

Judt, T. (2005) *Postwar: A History of Europe Since 1945*. London: Penguin Books.

Kanneh, K. (1998) *African Identities: Race, Nation and Culture in Ethnography, Pan-Africanism and Black Literatures*. London: Routledge.

Kassimeris, C. (ed.) (2009) *Anti-Racism in European Football: Fair Play for All*. Plymouth: Lexington Books.

Keith, M. (1993) *Race, Riots and Policing: Lore and Disorder in a Multi-racist Society*. London: UCL Press.

Kelley, R. (1996) 'The World the Diaspora Made: C.L.R. James and the Politics of History', in G. Farred (ed.) *Rethinking C.L.R. James*. Oxford: Blackwell.

Kelley, R. (2000) 'A Poetics of Anti-colonialism', in A. Césaire, *Discourse on Colonialism*. New York: Monthly Review Press.

Kelley, R. and Lewis, E. (eds) (2000) *To Make Our World Anew: A History of African Americans*. Oxford: Oxford University Press.

Kelso, P. (2005) 'One Sweet Word: London', *The Guardian*, July 7, p. 1.

Kenny, M. (2004) *The Politics of Identity*. Cambridge: Polity Press.

Kessel, A. (2007) 'Race Driver', *The Observer*, July 1, p. 5.

Kimmel, M. (2006) *Manhood in America: A Cultural History* (2nd edn). New York: Oxford University Press.

Kimmel, M. (2008) *Guyland: The Perilous World Where Boys Become Men*. New York: HarperCollins.

King, C. (2004) *Offside Racism: Playing the White Man*. Oxford: Berg.

King, Jr, M. (1963/2000) *Why We Can't Wait*. New York: Signet Classic.

King, R. (2008) *Native Americans and Sport in North America: Other People's Games*. New York: Routledge.

Kusz, K. (2007) *Revolt of the White Athlete: Race, Media and the Emergence of Extreme Athletes in America*. New York: Peter Lang.

Landesman, C. (1998) 'Half Man, Half Logo', *The Independent* Wednesday Review, June 24, p. 1.

Langlois, R. (2008) 'The Closing of the Sociological Mind?', *Canadian Journal of Sociology*, 33 (1): 133–146.

Lapchick, R. (2009) 'Lilian Thuram's Off-the-Pitch Courage', at ESPN On-line, February 26; http://sports.espn.go.com/espn/blackhistory2009/columns/story?columnist=lapchick_richard&id=3934455. (Accessed 7 December 2009)

Laville, S. and Cobain, I. (2005) 'From Student and Cricket-Lover to Terror Suspect', *The Guardian*, July 13, p. 1.

Lazarus, N. (1999) *Nationalism and Cultural Practice in the Postcolonial World*. Cambridge: Cambridge University Press.

Lemert, C. (2003) *Muhammad Ali: Trickster in the Culture of Irony*. Cambridge: Polity Press.

Linebaugh, P. and Rediker, M. (1990) 'The Many-Headed Hydra: Sailors, Slaves, and the Atlantic Working Class in the Eighteenth Century', *Journal of Historical Sociology*, 3 (3): 225–252.

Linebaugh, P. and Rediker, M. (2000) *The Many-Headed Hydra: The Hidden History of the Revolutionary Atlantic*. London: Verso.

Lynch, B. (1914) *The Complete Boxer*. New York: Fredrick A. Stokes.

MacAloon, J. (1988) 'A Prefatory Note on Pierre Bourdieu's "Program for a Sociology of Sport"', *Sociology of Sport Journal*, 5 (2): 150–152.

MacDonald, D. (2007) 'Apologies from Intel for Sprinter Ad', Intel Web Site; http://www.intel.com/news/sprintad.htm?iid=homepage+news_sprintad. (Accessed 7 December 2009)

Macey, D. (2000) *Frantz Fanon: A Life*. London: Granta Books.

Mackey, E. (2002) *The House of Difference: Cultural Politics and National Identity in Canada*. Toronto: University of Toronto Press.

Maggia, F. (2006) 'Between Dreams and Reality', in Maggia, F. (ed.), *Tracey Moffatt: Between Dreams and Reality*. Milano: Skira.

Maguire, J. (1999) *Global Sport: Identities, Societies, Civilizations*. Cambridge: Polity Press.

Maguire, J. (2005) *Power and Global Sport: Zones of Prestige, Emulation and Resistance*. London: Routledge.

Malik, S. (2006) 'The Suicide Bomber in His Own Words', *New Statesman*, July 3, pp. 26–29.

Mangan, J.A. (1998) *The Games Ethnic and Imperialism: Aspects of the Diffusion of an Ideal* (2nd edn). London: Frank Cass.

Mangan, J.A. (2008) '"Duty unto Death" – the Sacrifical Warrior: English Middle Class Masculinity and Militarism in the Age of the New Imperialism', *International Journal of the History of Sport*, 25 (9): 1080–1105.

Marqusee, M. (2001) 'In Search of the Unequivocal Englishman: The Conundrum of Race and Nation in English Cricket', in B. Carrington and I. McDonald (eds), *'Race', Sport and British Society*. London: Routledge.

Marqusee, M. (2005) *Redemption Song: Muhammad Ali and the Spirit of the Sixties* (2nd edn). London: Verso.

Massey, D. (1994) *Space, Place and Gender*. Cambridge: Polity Press.

May, R. (2008) *Living through the Hoop: High School Basketball, Race, and the American Dream*. New York: New York University Press.

McClintock, A. (1995) *Imperial Leather: Race, Gender and Sexuality in the Colonial Contest*. London: Routledge.

McLaughlin, E. and Neal, S. (2007) 'Who Can Speak to Race and Nation? Intellectuals, Public Policy Formation and the *Future of Multi-ethnic Britain* Commission', *Cultural Studies*, 21(6): 910–930.

McKittrick, K. (2006) *Demonic Grounds: Black Women and the Cartographies of Struggle*. Minneapolis, MN: University of Minnesota Press.

McNeil, D. (2009) 'Lennox Lewis and Black Atlantic Politics: The Hard Sell', *Journal of Sport and Social Issues*, 33 (1): 25–38.

Mercer, K. (1994) *Welcome to the Jungle: New Positions in Black Cultural Studies*. London: Routledge.

Messner, M. (1992) *Power at Play: Sports and the Problem of Masculinity*. Boston, MA: Beacon.

Messner, M. (2007) *Out of Play: Critical Essays on Gender and Sport*. New York: State University of New York Press.

Miller, K. (2008) 'Working Musicians: Exploring the Rhetorical Ties between Musical Labour and Leisure', *Leisure Studies*, 27 (4): 427–441.

Miller, P. (1998) 'The Anatomy of Scientific Racism: Racialist Responses to Black Athletic Achievement', *Journal of Sport History*, 25 (Spring): 119–151.

Miller, P. and Wiggins, D. (eds) (2004) *Sport and the Color Line: Black Athletes and Race Relations in Twentieth-Century America*. London: Routledge.

Miller, T. (1997) '"… The Oblivion of the Sociology of Sport"', *Journal of Sport and Social Issues*, 21 (2): 115–119.

Miller, T. (2001) *Sportsex*. Philadelphia, PA: Temple University Press.

Miller, T., Lawrence, G., McKay, J. and Rowe, D. (2001) *Globalization and Sport: Playing the World*. London: Sage.

Mills, J. (ed.) (2005) *Subaltern Sports: Politics and Sport in South Asia*. London: Anthem Press.

Modood, T. and Werbner, P. (eds) (1997) *The Politics of Multiculturalism in the New Europe: Racism, Identity and Community*. London: Zed Press.

Montagu, A. (1997) *Man's Most Dangerous Myth: The Fallacy of Race* (6th edn). London: Altamira Press.

Morgan, D. (1999) 'Jack Johnson: Reluctant Hero of the Black Community', *Akron Law Review*, 32 (3): 529–556.

Morgan, W. (1988) 'Adorno on Sport: The Case of the Fractured Dialectic', *Theory and Society*, 17 (6): 813–838.

Morgan, W. (1994) *Leftist Theories of Sport: A Critique and Reconstruction*. Urbana, IL: University of Illinois Press.

Muñoz, J. (1999) *Disidentifications: Queers of Color and the Performance of Politics*. Minneapolis, MN: University of Minnesota Press.

Murray, A. and Callahan, J. (2000) (eds) *Trading Twelves: The Selected Letters of Ralph Ellison and Albert Murray*. New York: The Modern Library.

Mutua, A. (ed.) (2006) *Progressive Black Masculinities*. New York: Routledge.

Neal, M. (2005) *New Black Man*. New York: Routledge.

Nobles, M. (2000) *Shades of Citizenship: Race and the Census in Modern Politics*. Stanford, CA: Stanford University Press.

Okpewho, I., Davies, C. and Mazrui, A. (eds) (2001) *The African Diaspora: African Origins and New World Identities*. Bloomington, IN: Indiana University Press.

Omi, M. and Winant, H. (1994) *Racial Formation in the United States: From the 1960s to the 1990s* (2nd edn). London: Routledge.

Pahl, R. (2006) 'Hidden Solidarities', *Prospect*, September, http://www.prospect magazine.co.uk/2006/09/hiddensolidarities/. (Accessed 7 December 2009)

Parekh, B. (2000) *The Parekh Report: The Future of Multi-ethnic Britain*. London: Profile Books.

Parekh, B. (2006) *Rethinking Multiculturalism: Cultural Diversity and Political Theory* (2nd edn). Basingstoke: Palgrave Macmillan.

Patterson, O. (1998) *Rituals of Blood: Consequences of Slavery in Two American Centuries*. New York: Basic Books.

Patterson, S. (1965) *Dark Strangers: A Study of West Indians in London*. London: Penguin Books.

Phillips, M. (2006) *Londonistan: How Britain Is Creating a Terror State Within*. London: Gibson Square Books.

Phillips, T. (2005) 'Let's Show the World its Future', *The Observer: Olympics 2012*, July 10, pp. 4–5.

Perryman, M. (2002) *Going Oriental: Football after the World Cup 2002*. London: Mainstream Publishing,

Perryman, M. (2006) *Ingerland: Travels with a Football Nation*. London: Simon and Schuster.

Piascik, A. (2009) *Gridiron Gauntlet: The Story of the Men who Integrated Pro Football in their Own Words*. New York: Taylor Trade Publishing.

Pieterse, J. (1995) 'Globalization as Hybridization', in M. Featherstone, S. Lash and R. Robertson (eds), *Global Modernities*. London: Sage.

Pilkington, A. (2003) *Racial Discrimination and Ethnic Diversity in Britain*. Houndmills: Palgrave Macmillan.

Pronger, B. (2000) 'Homosexuality and Sport: Who's Winning?', in J. McKay, M. Messner, and D. Sabo (eds), *Masculinities, Gender Relations, and Sport*. London: Sage.

Regester, C. (2004) 'From the Gridiron and the Boxing Ring to the Cinema Screen: The African-American Athlete in pre-1950 Cinema', in J. Mangan and A. Ritchie (eds), *Ethnicity, Sport, Identity: Struggles for Status*. London: Routledge.

Rhoden, W. (2006) *Forty Million Dollar Slaves: The Rise, Fall, and Redemption of the Black Athlete*. New York: Three Rivers Press.

Richards, J. (2007) 'Intel Apologises for "Racist" Computer Ad', *The Times*, August 7; http://technology.timesonline.co.uk/tol/news/tech_and_web/article2192554.ece. (Accessed 7 December 2009)

Roberts, R. (1983) *Papa Jack: Jack Johnson and the Era of White Hopes*. London: The Free Press.

Roediger, D. (2005) *Working Toward Whiteness: How America's Immigrants Became White*. New York: Basic Books.

Roediger, D. (2008) *How Race Survived US History: From Settlement and Slavery to the Obama Phenomenon*. London: Verso.

Ross, A. (2009) *Nice Work If You Can Feel It: Life and Labor in Precarious Times*. New York: New York University Press.

Rowe, D. (2004) 'Antonio Gramsci: Sport, Hegemony and the National Popular', in R. Giulianotti (ed.), *Sport and Modern Social Theorists*. Basingstoke: Palgrave Macmillan.

Rowe, D., McKay, J. and Lawrence, G. (1997) 'Out of the Shadows: The Critical Sociology of Sport in Australia, 1986 to 1996', *Sociology of Sport Journal*, 14 (4): 340–361.

Rowe, M. (1998) *The Racialisation of Disorder in Twentieth Century Britain*. Aldershot: Ashgate.

Runstedtler, T. (2005) 'In Sports the Best Man Wins: How Joe Louis whupped Jim Crow', in A. Bass (ed.), *In the Game: Race, Identity, and Sports in the Twentieth Century*. Basingstoke: Palgrave.

Runstedtler, T. (2009) 'Visible Men: African American boxers, the new negro and the global color line', *Radical History Review*, 103 (Winter): 59–81.

Said, E. (1978/2003) *Orientalism*. New York: Penguin Books.

Said, E. (1994) *Culture and Imperialism*. London: Vintage.

Sammons, J. (1988) *Beyond the Ring: The Role of Boxing in American Society*. Chicago, IL: University of Illinois Press.

San Juan, E. Jr (1999) *Beyond Postcolonial Theory*. Houndmills: Macmillan.

Sammons, J.T. (1994) '"Race" and sport: A critical, historical exmanination', *Journal of Sport History*, 21(3): 203–278.

Saraceno, J. (2005) 'Tyson: "My whole life has been a waste"', *USA Today*, June 2; http://www.usatoday.com/sports/boxing/2005-06-02-tyson-saraceno_x.htm. (Accessed 7 December 2009)

Scott, J. (1985) *Weapons of the Weak: Everyday Forms of Peasant Resistance*. New Haven, CT: Yale University Press.

Scott, J. (1990) *Domination and the Arts of Resistance: Hidden Transcripts*. New Haven, CT: Yale University Press.

Sennett, R. (2008) *The Craftsman*. New Haven, CT: Yale University Press.

Shropshire, K. (1996) *In Black and White: Race and Sports in America*. London: New York University Press.

Silverman, K. (1996) *The Threshold of the Visible World*. London: Routledge.

Sivanandan, A. (1990) *Communities of Resistance: Writings on Black Struggles for Socialism*. London: Verso.

Smart, B. (2005) *The Sport Star: Modern Sport and the Cultural Economy of Sporting Celebrity*. London: Sage.

Solomos, J. (2003) *Race and Racism in Britain* (3rd edn). Houndmills: Palgrave Macmillan.

Sorek, T. (2007) *Arab Soccer in a Jewish State: The Integrative Enclave*. Cambridge: Cambridge University Press.

Spickard, P. (2007) *Almost All Aliens: Immigration, Race, and Colonialism in American History and Identity*. London: Routledge.

Spracklen, K. (2001) '"Black Pearl, Black Diamonds" Exploring Racial Identities in Rugby League', in B. Carrington and I. McDonald (eds), *'Race', Sport and British Society*. London: Routledge.

Spracklen, K. (2008) 'The Holy Blood and the Holy Grail: Myths of Scientific Racism and the Pursuit of Excellence in Sport', *Leisure Studies*, 27 (2): 221–227.

St Louis, B. (2007) *Rethinking Race, Politics, and Poetics: C.L.R. James' Critique of Modernity*. New York: Routledge.

St Louis, B. (2009) 'Post-Marxism, Black Marxism and the Politics of Sport', in B. Carrington and I. McDonald (eds), *Marxism, Cultural Studies and Sport*. London: Routledge.

Steen, R. (1995) 'Pride and Prejudice', *The Sunday Times* Sport, July 9, p. 11.

Steinberg, S. (2007) *Race Relations: A Critique*. Stanford, CA: Stanford University Press.

Streible, D. (2008) *Fight Pictures: A History of Boxing and Early Cinema*. Berkeley, CA: University of California Press.

Thobani, S. (2007) *Exalted Subjects: Studies in the Making of Race and Nation in Canada*. Toronto: University of Toronto Press.

Thomas, E. (2004) *More Than an Athlete*. Atlanta, CA: Moore Black Press.

Toback, J. (2009) *Tyson*. Sony Pictures, USA. 90 mins.

Tomlinson, A. (2004) 'Pierre Bourdieu and the Sociological Study of Sport: Habitus, Capital and Field', in R. Giulianotti (ed.), *Sport and Modern Social Theorists*. Houndmills: Palgrave Macmillan.

Tonkin, B. (2008) 'Richard Sennett: Back to the Bench', *The Independent*, 8 February; http://www.independent.co.uk/arts-entertainment/books/features/richard-sennett-back-to-the-bench-779345.html. (Accessed 7 December 2009)

Urry, J. (2003) *Global Complexity*. Cambridge: Polity Press.

Vargas, J. (2008) *Never Meant to Survive: Genocide and Utopias in Black Diaspora Communities*. New York: Rowman & Littlefield.

Vasili, P. (1996) 'Walter Daniel Tull, 1888–1918: Soldier, Footballer, Black', *Race and Class*, 38 (2): 51–70.

Vasili, P. (1998) *The First Black Footballer – Arthur Wharton, 1865–1930: An Absence of Memory*. London: Frank Cass.

Vasili, P. (2000) *Colouring Over the White Line: The History of Black Footballers in Britain*. Edinburgh: Mainstream Publishing.

Vergès F. (1996) 'Chains of Madness, Chains of Colonialism: Fanon and Freedom', in A. Read (ed.), *The Fact of Blackness: Frantz Fanon and Visual Representation*. London: ICA.

Wacquant, L. (2004) *Body and Soul: Notebooks of an Apprentice Boxer*. Oxford: Oxford University Press.

Wacquant, L. (2005) 'Carnal Connections: On Embodiment, Apprenticeship, and Membership', *Qualitative Sociology*, 28 (4): 445–474.

Wagg, S. (ed.) (2005) *Cricket and National Identity in the Postcolonial Age: Following On*. London: Routledge.

Walcott, R. (2003) *Black Like Who? Writing Black Canada* (2nd edn). Toronto: Insomniac Press.

Ward, G. (2004) *Unforgivable Blackness: The Rise and Fall of Jack Johnson*. New York: Alfred A. Knopf.

Washington, R. and Karen, D. (2001) 'Sport and Society', *Annual Review of Sociology*, 27: 187–212.

Whannel, G. (2009) 'Between Culture and Economy: Understanding the Politics of Media Sport', in B. Carrington and I. McDonald (eds), *Marxism, Cultural Studies and Sport*. London: Routledge.

Wheelock, S. (2002) 'States of Euphoria', BBC Sport; http://news.bbc.co.uk/sport3/worldcup2002/hi/team_pages/usa/newsid_1964000/1964700.stm. (Accessed 7 December 2009)

Whitaker, M. (2000) 'Worrell's Tortured Path to West Indies' Top Job', *The Independent*, August 24; http://www.independent.co.uk/sport/cricket/worrells-tortured-path-to-west-indies-top-job-695843.html. (Accessed 7 December 2009)

White, A. (2008) *Ain't I a Feminist? African American Men Speak Out on Fatherhood, Friendship, Forgiveness, and Freedom*. Albany, NY: State University of New York Press.

Wiggins, D. (1989) '"Great Speed But Little Stamina": The Historical Debate over Black Athletic Superiority', *Journal of Sport History* 16 (2): 158–185.

Wiggins, D. (1997) *Glory Bound: Black Athletes in a White America*. New York: Syracuse University Press.

Wiggins, D. and Miller, P. (eds) (2003) *The Unlevel Playing Field: A Documentary History of the African American Experience in Sport*. Urbana, IL: University of Illinois Press.

Wilde, S. (2006) 'The Big Interview: Monty Panesar', *The Sunday Times*, August 6; http://www.timesonline.co.uk/tol/sport/article601153.ece. (Accessed 7 December 2009)

Williams, E. (1944/1994) *Capitalism and Slavery*. Chapel Hill, NC: University of North Carolina Press.

Williams, R. (2007) 'Novice Pays the Price for Youth but will be One for the Ages', *The Guardian*, 22 October, http://www.guardian.co.uk/sport/2007/oct/22/motorsports.comment. (Accessed 28 January 2010)

Winant, H. (2004) *The New Politics of Race: Globalism, Difference, Justice*. Minneapolis, MN: University of Minnesota Press.

Witherspoon, K. (2008) *Before the Eyes of the World: Mexico and the 1968 Olympic Games*. DeKalb, IL: Northern Illinois University Press.

Wolff, A. (2009) 'The NFL's Jackie Robinson', *Sports Illustrated*, 12 October, pp. 60–71.

Woodward, K. (2007) *Boxing, Masculinity and Identity: The 'I' of the Tiger*. London: Routledge.

Yep, K. (2009) *Outside the Paint: When Basketball Ruled at the Chinese Playground*. Philadelphia, PA: Temple University Press.

Young, I. (2000) *Inclusion and Democracy*. Oxford: Oxford University Press.

Young, L. (1996) *Fear of the Dark: 'Race', Gender and Sexuality in the Cinema*. London: Routledge.

Young, R. (1995) *Colonial Desire: Hybridity in Theory, Culture and Race*. London: Routledge.

Young, R. (2001) *Postcolonialism: An Historical Introduction*. Oxford: Blackwell.

Younge, G. (2004) 'Bitter White Whine', *Guardian*, February 26, http://www.guardian.co.uk/politics/2004/Feb/26/immigrationandpublicservices. (Accessed 7 December 2009)

Younge, G. (2007) 'Made in Stevenage', *Guardian*, June 16; http://www.guardian.co.uk/uk/2007/jun/16/formulaone.sport. (Accessed 7 December 2009)

Zirin, D. (2007) *Welcome to the Terrordome: The Pain, Politics, and Promise of Sports*. Chicago, IL: Haymarket Books.

Žižek, S. (2009) *Violence: Six Sideways Reflections*. London: Profile Books.

# Index

NOTE: Page numbers in *italic type* refer to illustrations, page numbers followed by 'n' refer to footnotes.

# Research Methods
# Books from SAGE

Read sample chapters online now!

DISCOVERING STATISTICS USING SPSS THIRD EDITION

ANDY FIELD

THIRD EDITION
RESEARCH DESIGN
Qualitative, Quantitative, and Mixed Methods Approaches

JOHN W. CRESWELL

Robert K. Yin
Case Study Research
Design and Methods
Fourth Edition

APPLIED SOCIAL RESEARCH METHODS SERIES

Second Edition
QUALITATIVE INQUIRY & RESEARCH DESIGN
Choosing Among Five Approaches

John W. Creswell

Doing a Literature Review
Chris Hart

STATISTICS for People Who (Think They) HATE STATISTICS

NEIL J. SALKIND

SECOND EDITION
INTERVIEWS
Learning the Craft of Qualitative Research Interviewing

Steinar Kvale
Svend Brinkmann

THE QUALITATIVE RESEARCHER'S COMPANION

A. MICHAEL HUBERMAN
MATTHEW B. MILES

Basics of QUALITATIVE RESEARCH 3e

Juliet Corbin
Anselm Strauss

www.sagepub.co.uk

$SAGE

# Research Methods
# Books from SAGE

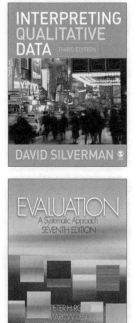

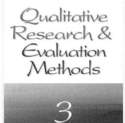

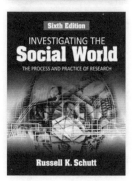

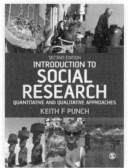

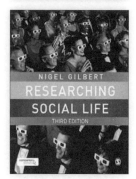

**www.sagepub.co.uk**

**SAGE**

# The Qualitative Research Kit

Edited by Uwe Flick

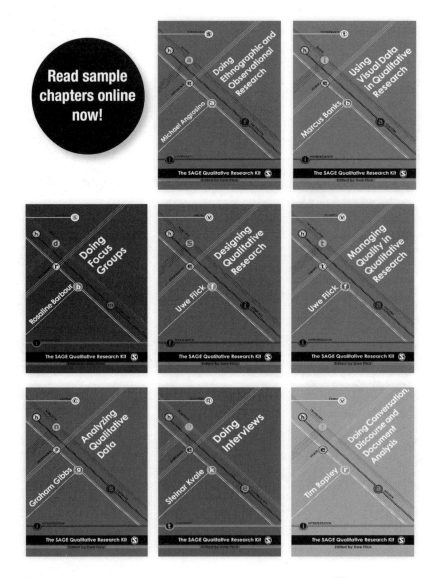

Read sample chapters online now!

Doing Ethnographic and Observational Research — Michael Angrosino — The SAGE Qualitative Research Kit — Edited by Uwe Flick

Using Visual Data in Qualitative Research — Marcus Banks — The SAGE Qualitative Research Kit — Edited by Uwe Flick

Doing Focus Groups — Rosaline Barbour — The SAGE Qualitative Research Kit

Designing Qualitative Research — Uwe Flick — The SAGE Qualitative Research Kit — Edited by Uwe Flick

Managing Quality in Qualitative Research — Uwe Flick — The SAGE Qualitative Research Kit — Edited by Uwe Flick

Analyzing Qualitative Data — Graham Gibbs — The SAGE Qualitative Research Kit — Edited by Uwe Flick

Doing Interviews — Steinar Kvale — The SAGE Qualitative Research Kit — Edited by Uwe Flick

Doing Conversation, Discourse and Document Analysis — Tim Rapley — The SAGE Qualitative Research Kit — Edited by Uwe Flick

www.sagepub.co.uk

SAGE